THE BIG BOOK of TOOLS
for RTI at Work™

WILLIAM M. **FERRITER**
MIKE **MATTOS**
ROB J. **MEYER**

Solution Tree | Press

Copyright © 2025 by Solution Tree Press

Materials appearing here are copyrighted. With one exception, all rights are reserved. Readers may reproduce only those pages marked "Reproducible." Otherwise, no part of this book may be reproduced or transmitted in any form or by any means (electronic, photocopying, recording, or otherwise) without prior written permission of the publisher.

555 North Morton Street
Bloomington, IN 47404
800.733.6786 (toll free) / 812.336.7700
FAX: 812.336.7790

email: info@SolutionTree.com
SolutionTree.com

Visit **go.SolutionTree.com/RTIatWork/BBTRTI** to download the free reproducibles in this book. To access the exclusive online reproducibles in this book, enter the unique access code found on the inside front cover. Readers with ebooks, please email orders@solutiontree.com to receive access.

Printed in the United States of America

Library of Congress Cataloging-in-Publication Data

Names: Ferriter, William M., author. | Mattos, Mike (Mike William) author. | Meyer, Rob J., author.
Title: The big book of tools for RTI at work / William M. Ferriter, Mike Mattos, Rob J. Meyer.
Other titles: Big book of tools for response to intervention at work
Description: Bloomington, IN : Solution Tree Press, [2024] | Four chapters in The big book of tools for RTI at work mirror the organization of school intervention efforts, as detailed in the second edition of Taking action: A handbook for RTI at work. | Includes bibliographical references and index.
Identifiers: LCCN 2024007526 (print) | LCCN 2024007527 (ebook) | ISBN 9781958590355 (paperback) | ISBN 9781958590362 (ebook)
Subjects: LCSH: Response to intervention (Learning disabled children)--United States. | Learning disabled children--Education--United States. | Individualized instruction--United States.
Classification: LCC LC4705 .F47 2024 (print) | LCC LC4705 (ebook) | DDC 371.9--dc23/eng/20240609
LC record available at https://lccn.loc.gov/2024007526
LC ebook record available at https://lccn.loc.gov/2024007527

Solution Tree
Jeffrey C. Jones, CEO
Edmund M. Ackerman, President

Solution Tree Press
President and Publisher: Douglas M. Rife
Associate Publishers: Todd Brakke and Kendra Slayton
Editorial Director: Laurel Hecker
Art Director: Rian Anderson
Copy Chief: Jessi Finn
Senior Production Editor: Miranda Addonizio
Copy Editor: Jessica Starr
Proofreader: Anne Marie Watkins
Text and Cover Designer: Abigail Bowen
Acquisitions Editors: Carol Collins and Hilary Goff
Content Development Specialist: Amy Rubenstein
Associate Editors: Sarah Ludwig and Elijah Oates
Editorial Assistant: Anne Marie Watkins

I dedicate this book to my daughter Reece, who challenges me to be a better father, teacher, and learner every single day. I love you, kid—and am so grateful for the joy that you bring me.
—WILLIAM M. FERRITER

I dedicate this book to a true gentleman, a gifted scholar, and the man who walked my bride down the aisle . . . Mr. Thomas Coyne.
—MIKE MATTOS

I dedicate this book to my wife, Maeve. Thank you for supporting this work. I further dedicate this book to my son, Seamus. You make me a better person.
—ROB J. MEYER

Acknowledgments

Creating this book has been an expedition not just of the mind but of the heart—a journey that, while ours in its conception, has been shaped, supported, and enriched by a remarkable constellation of individuals. To them, we owe a debt of gratitude and appreciation.

First and foremost, we extend our heartfelt thanks to our editor—Miranda Addonizio—and the format, design, and copyediting team at Solution Tree Press that has worked tirelessly on this text. Your keen insights, unwavering patience, and meticulous attention to detail have not only refined our work but have also fostered our growth as writers. Your ability to see the diamond in the rough and to guide us in polishing it to perfection has been nothing short of transformative.

We are also profoundly thankful to Douglas Rife, Jeff Jones, Ed Ackerman, and Shannon Ritz—Solution Tree's publisher, chief executive officer, chief operating officer, and vice president of professional development, respectively—for believing in the vision of this text and for providing the platform to spread its word. Your expertise and enthusiasm have been pivotal in advancing our work, and your constant support has been a beacon of encouragement throughout our careers as writers, presenters, and professional development providers.

We must also acknowledge our thought partners—colleagues, mentors, and friends—who have engaged us in countless conversations, debates, and reflections. Your intellectual generosity, critical questioning, and shared excitement have enriched this work and deepened our own understanding and passion for the topics that we explore together.

Special thanks are due to the schools, districts, and communities who have shared their experiences and wisdom with us. Your stories are the bedrock of this project, and we are honored to have been entrusted with them. Your efforts to implement the RTI at Work process have been a guiding light, ensuring that the ideas we share remain authentic and impactful.

And finally, to the readers who embark on this journey with us, thank you for your curiosity, engagement, and commitment to the students you serve. We sincerely hope that this book resonates with you, inspires thought, and sparks conversation.

This book is a testament to our efforts and to the collective support, wisdom, and encouragement of everyone we have learned alongside—those mentioned and unmentioned. To all of you, we offer our deepest gratitude.

Rob J. Meyer:

I would like to thank coauthors Bill and Mike for the opportunity to collaborate in creating this resource. I must also thank all the Solution Tree authors and associates whom I have had the opportunity to learn from. Not only has your work had an impact on me, but it is also a positive force that serves students across the world.

Solution Tree Press would like to thank the following reviewers:

John D. Ewald
Education Consultant
Frederick, Maryland

Amber Gareri
Instructional Specialist, Innovation and Development
Pasadena ISD
Pasadena, Texas

Kristin Gellinck-Frye
Director Special Programs
Westside USD
Quartz Hill, California

Benjamin J. Kitslaar
Principal
West Side Elementary School
Elkhorn, Wisconsin

Lindsey Matkin
Principal
Kinard Middle School
Fort Collins, Colorado

Molly A. Riddle
Assistant Professor of Elementary Mathematics Education
Indiana University Southeast School of Education
New Albany, Indiana

Visit go.SolutionTree.com/RTIatWork/BBTRTI to download the free reproducibles in this book. To access the exclusive online reproducibles in this book, enter the unique access code found on the inside front cover. Readers with ebooks, please email orders@solutiontree.com to receive access.

Table of Contents

Reproducible pages are in italics.

About the Authors xiii

Introduction 1
   The Purpose and Structure of This Book 2
   How to Use This Book 5

1 Grasping the Bigger Picture 11
   The RTI at Work Process 12
   The PLC Foundation 15
   Conclusion 18

2 Tools for Establishing a Culture of Collective Responsibility 19
   Resources Designed to Establish a Culture of Collective Responsibility 20
   Conclusion 31

Resources Designed to Establish a Culture of Collective Responsibility

Tool: Building Your Guiding Coalition 34
Tool: Ten Considerations for the Guiding Coalition 36
Tool: Analysis and Action Planning Template for Guiding Coalitions 38
Tool: Using Faculty Survey Data to Target the Work of Guiding Coalitions ... 45
Tool: Analyzing Faculty Survey on the Work of Guiding Coalitions 46
Tool: Planning a Cycle of Inquiry for Guiding Coalitions 49
Sample: Planning a Cycle of Inquiry for Guiding Coalitions 50
Tool: Using AI Tools to Support Collaborative Team Development 51
Survey: Rating Our Readiness for RTI 52
Tool: Reflecting on Our Faculty's Readiness for RTI 53
Tool: Evaluating Our Mission Statement 54
Tool: Developing Collective Commitments 56
Tool: Site-Based Teams Aligned to the RTI at Work Process 58
Tool: Teams Needed in RTI at Work—A Principal's Reflection 60
Tool: Forming Teacher Teams 62
Survey: Midyear Collaborative Team Check-In 64
Tool: Team Collaboration Time—Planning Guide and Schedule 67

Tool: Have We Created Time for Teacher Collaborative Teams? 68
Tool Overview: Developing Team Norms 70
Tool: Commit to Team Norms 71
Tool: Developing Specific Actions to Address the Needs of Our Peers 73
Sample: Developing Specific Actions to Address the Needs of Our Peers 74
Tool: Addressing the Three Common Reasons for Resistance to Change 76
Tool: Rating Your Readiness for Our New Initiative 78

3 Tools for Building Tier 1 of Your Intervention Pyramid 79

Section 1: Resources Designed to Support Tier 1
  Teacher Team Essential Actions 80
Section 2: Resources Designed to Support Tier 1
  Schoolwide Essential Actions 90
Conclusion 96

Resources Designed to Support Tier 1 Teacher Team Essential Actions

Tool: Using REAL to Identify Essential Standards 99
Tool: Essential Standards Chart 100
Tool: Essential Standards Unit Plan 101
Sample: Mathematics Essential Standards Unit Plan 102
Tool: Using AI Tools to Deconstruct an Essential Standard 104
Tool: Using AI Tools to Develop a Proficiency Scale 105
*Tool: Examining Your Work With the Team Teaching-Assessing-
  Learning Cycle* 106
Tool: Common Formative Assessment Pretest 108
Answer Key: Common Formative Assessment Pretest 109
Tool: Assessment Design Checklist 111
Tool: Building a Common Formative Assessment 114
Tool: Performance Tracking Table 115
Sample: Performance Tracking Table—Elementary School Mathematics 116
Sample: Performance Tracking Table—Middle School Science 118
Tool: Reflecting on the Role Grades Can Play as Feedback 119
Sample: Assessment Wrapper for Primary Students 121
Tool: Practice Test Tracking Template for Secondary Students 124
Sample: Practice Test Tracking Template for Secondary Students 125
Tool: Teaching Primary Learners About Short-Term Goal Setting 126
*Tool Overview: Creating Next-Step Checklists to Involve Students in
  the Intervention Process* 127
Student Tool: Next-Step Checklist 128
Sample: Next-Step Checklist—Sixth-Grade Matter Unit 129
Tool: Team Protocol for Analyzing Assessment Results 130
Tool: Looking at End-of-Unit Assessment Data 132
Tool: Targeting Tier 2 Interventions 135
Sample: Targeting Tier 2 Interventions 137

Tool: Essential Standards Student Tracking Chart *138*
Tool: Reflecting on Our Cycle of Instruction *139*

Resources Designed to Support Tier 1 Schoolwide Essential Actions

Tool: Ensuring Access to Essential Grade-Level Curriculum *141*
Tool: Developing a Master Schedule for Three Tiers of Instruction *142*
Template: Developing a Master Schedule for Three Tiers of Instruction *145*
Tool: Eliciting Feedback on Our Master Schedule *146*
Tool: Reflecting on Your Master Schedule *147*
Checklists: Establishing Common Expectations, Targeting Instruction, and Reinforcing Positive Behaviors *148*
Tool: Reflecting on the Recipe for a Successful Learner *151*
Tool: Reviewing the Skills Necessary to Succeed in the Modern Workplace .. *153*
Checklist: Concentrating Instruction on Social and Academic Behaviors *155*
Student Tool: What Do Successful People Do Differently? *157*
Tool: Assessment Purpose Map *159*
Tool: Assessment Stoplight Analysis *161*
Tool: Assessment Reflection by Type *162*
Tool: Grading Reflection and Planning *164*
Tool: Standards-Based Mindset Reflection and Planning *165*
Tool: Grading Practices Implementation *166*
Tool: Preventions to Proactively Support Student Success *168*
Tool Overview: Creating a Predictable-Is-Preventable Plan *169*
Tool: Creating a Predictable-Is-Preventable Plan *170*
Sample: Predictable-Is-Preventable Plan for Multilingual Students *172*

4 Tools for Building Tier 2 of Your Intervention Pyramid 175

Section 1: Resources Designed to Support Tier 2 Teacher Team Essential Actions 176
Section 2: Resources Designed to Support Tier 2 Schoolwide Essential Actions 182
Conclusion 188

Resources Designed to Support Tier 2 Teacher Team Essential Actions

Tool: Building Shared Knowledge About Tier 2 Interventions and Extensions *190*
Answer Key: Building Shared Knowledge About Tier 2 Interventions and Extensions *192*
Tool: Team-Based Intervention Plan for Struggling Learners *194*
Tool: Targeting Tier 2 Interventions for an Individual Student *195*
Checklist: Differentiation Strategies *197*
Tool: Tier 2 AI Prompts for Classroom Teachers *199*
Tool: Prerequisite Planning Document *201*
Tool Overview: Preparing a Prerequisite Pretest *203*

Tool: Preparing a Prerequisite Pretest...................204
Tool: Analyzing Prerequisite Pretest Results...............206
Tool: Supplemental Intervention Practice Reflection Template...............208
Tool: Rating the Effectiveness of Interventions on Your Learning Team......210
Tool: Individual Student Intervention Report...................211
Tool: Building Your Learning Team's Knowledge About Extensions.........213
Tool: Weekly Extension Planning Template...................214
Tool Overview: Creating a Tiered Task Card to Extend Student Learning....215
Student Tool: Creating a Tiered Task Card to Extend Student Learning......216
Sample: Tiered Task Card—Middle Grades Science: Fossils...............217
Sample: Tiered Task Card—Middle Grades Mathematics: Slope............218
Tool: Using AI Chatbots to Develop Extension Tasks...................219

Resources Designed to Support Tier 2 Schoolwide Essential Actions

Tool: Questions to Consider When Creating a Schedule for Supplemental Interventions...................221
Tool: Evaluating Your Plan for Providing Supplemental Interventions........224
Tool: Staff Survey on the Efficacy of a Supplemental Intervention Period....226
Tool: Developing Schoolwide Criteria for Identifying Students in Need of Tier 2 Behavioral Support...................228
Protocol: Developing Schoolwide Criteria for Identifying Students in Need of Tier 2 Behavioral Support...................230
Tool Overview: Evaluating Your Systematic Response to Student Interventions...................232
Tool: Evaluating Your Systematic Response to Student Interventions........233
Tool: Staff Recommendation Form for Students Needing Behavioral Support....236
Tool: Reviewing Your Plan for Providing Supplemental Interventions for Students Struggling With Social Behaviors, Academic Behaviors, and Health and Home Challenges...................238
Tool: Planning Interventions for Students With Attendance Issues.........243
Student Tool: Student Survey on Missing or Late Work...................246
Student Tool: Learning Profile Survey—Secondary...................248
Student Tool: Learning Profile Survey—Primary...................250
Tool: RTI at Work Pro-Solve Intervention Targeting Process—Tier 1 and Tier 2...252
Tool: Defining Lead Responsibilities for Academic and Behavioral Interventions...................253

5 Tools for Building Tier 3 of Your Intervention Pyramid 255

Section 1: Resources Designed to Support Tier 3 Schoolwide Essential Actions...................257
Section 2: Resources Designed to Support Tier 3 Intervention Team Essential Actions...................263
Conclusion...................267

Resources Designed to Support Tier 3 Schoolwide Essential Actions

Tool: Identifying Our Interventionists 269
Tool: End-of-Meeting Reflection for Intervention Teams 271
Tool: Intervention Team Implementation Continuum 273
Tool: Communicating the Purpose of the Intervention Team 276
Tool: Universal Screening Planning Guide 277
Protocol: Universal Screening Planning Guide 279
Tool: Universal Screening Tracking Template 280
Tool: Universal Screening Review Protocol 282
Sample: Universal Screening Review Protocol 284
Tool: Surveying Teachers About Universal Screening 286
Tool: Scenarios to Calibrate Tier 3 Decisions 287
Sample: Responses to Scenarios to Calibrate Tier 3 Decisions 290
Tool: Planning for and Prioritizing Tier 3 Interventions 291
Tool: Teacher Referral Form 296
Sample: Teacher Referral Form—Academics 297
Sample: Teacher Referral Form—Social Behaviors 298
Tool: Teacher Referral Processing Protocol 299
Tool: Action Plan to Support a Referred Student 301
Sample: Action Plan to Support a Referred Student 303
Tool Overview: Intervention Evaluation and Alignment Chart 305
Tool: Intervention Evaluation and Alignment Chart 306
Protocol: Intervention Evaluation and Alignment Chart 307
Tool: Guiding Coalition Review of Tier 3 Interventions 308

Resources Designed to Support Tier 3 Intervention Team Essential Actions

Tool: Intervention Planning Tool for Site Interventionists 312
Tool: Reviewing the Intervention Team Meeting Cycle 313
Tool: Intervention Team Meeting Dashboard 316
Tool: Teacher and Interventionist Communication Template 318
Tool: Teacher Report on Student Progress 320
Tool: Considerations to Increase Intervention Effectiveness 321
Tool: Communicating Intervention Plans to Parents 324
Tool: Intervention Team Reflection Before a Special Education Referral 325

Epilogue 327

References and Resources 329

Index 335

About the Authors

William M. Ferriter, MS, uses his twenty-nine years of experience as a full-time classroom teacher to create content for educators on topics ranging from establishing professional learning communities (PLCs) and effective systems of intervention to integrating meaningful differentiation, extension, and student-involved assessment opportunities into classroom instruction. Bill brings readers practical experience gained through extensive work with his own professional learning teams and the students in his classrooms.

Educators appreciate the practicality of his writing, knowing that the content shared was developed and implemented by a career classroom teacher. Every book he writes is designed to give participants a clear understanding of the *whys* behind the introduced ideas and tangible examples of how to turn those ideas into classroom and collaborative practices that work.

Bill is also a coauthor of several Solution Tree titles, including *Building a Professional Learning Community at Work®: A Guide to the First Year*; *Making Teamwork Meaningful: Leading Progress-Driven Collaboration in a PLC at Work*; *Creating a Culture of Feedback*; and *You Can Learn! Building Student Ownership, Motivation, and Efficacy With the PLC at Work Process*. Finally, he is the author of *The Big Book of Tools for Collaborative Teams in a PLC at Work*.

Bill earned a bachelor of science degree and master of science degree in elementary education from the State University of New York at Geneseo.

To learn more about Bill's work, visit www.buildingconfidentlearners.com. You can also follow Bill @williamferriter on LinkedIn.

 **Mike Mattos** is an internationally recognized author, presenter, practitioner, and consultant. In 2024, he was recognized by the Global Gurus organization as one of the thirty most influential educational thought leaders in the world. Mike co-created the RTI at Work™ approach to systematic interventions and is a thought leader in professional learning communities and the PLC at Work process. He is honored to advance the work of his mentors, Richard DuFour, Robert Eaker, and Becky DuFour.

Mike is extremely proud of the twenty-three years he served on site as a history and mathematics teacher and administrator. He is a former principal of Marjorie Veeh Elementary School and Pioneer Middle School in California. At both schools, Mike helped create model professional learning communities, improving learning for all students. In 2004, Marjorie Veeh, an elementary school with a large population of youth at risk, won the California Distinguished School and National Title I Achieving School awards. A National Blue Ribbon School, Pioneer is among only thirteen schools in the United States that the GE Foundation selected as a Best-Practice Partner and is one of eight schools that Richard DuFour chose to feature in the video series *The Power of Professional Learning Communities at Work: Bringing the Big Ideas to Life*. For his leadership, Mike was named the Orange County Middle School Administrator of the Year by the Association of California School Administrators.

Mike has coauthored many best-selling books focused on multitiered systems of supports (MTSS) and PLCs, including *Learning by Doing: A Handbook for Professional Learning Communities at Work*; *Concise Answers to Frequently Asked Questions About Professional Learning Communities at Work*; *Simplifying Response to Intervention: Four Essential Guiding Principles*; *Pyramid Response to Intervention: RTI, Professional Learning Communities, and How to Respond When Kids Don't Learn*; *Uniting Academic and Behavior Interventions: Solving the Skill or Will Dilemma*; *It's About Time: Planning Interventions and Extensions in Secondary School*; *It's About Time: Planning Interventions and Extensions in Elementary School*; *Best Practices at Tier 1: Daily Differentiation for Effective Instruction, Secondary*; *Best Practices at Tier 1: Daily Differentiation for Effective Instruction, Elementary*; and *The Collaborative Administrator: Working Together as a Professional Learning Community*. He has also published numerous professional articles.

To learn more about Mike's work, visit AllThingsPLC (www.allthingsplc.info) and www.mikemattos.info, or follow him @mikemattos65 on X, formerly known as Twitter.

About the Authors

 **Rob J. Meyer, EdD,** is an experienced educator currently serving as the director of teaching and learning at Beaver Dam Unified School District in Wisconsin. With more than eighteen years in education, he previously served as a social studies teacher, a secondary school assistant principal, and a primary school principal. Rob successfully uses the PLC at Work process to improve outcomes for the students he serves. By focusing on a districtwide effort to implement research-based systems of continuous improvement, he helped improve data across sites, which led to a Model PLC at Work school designation in his district.

As someone who believes in the power of collaboration, Rob is a past president of the Wisconsin ASCD. Additionally, he has presented at several conferences on educational leadership and mentored instructional leaders.

Rob received a bachelor's degree in broadfield social studies with a minor in history, as well as teaching credentials, from the University of Wisconsin–Stevens Point. He earned a master's degree in educational leadership from Cardinal Stritch University in Milwaukee, Wisconsin. Rob also earned a superintendent credential and doctorate in education at Edgewood College in Madison, Wisconsin, where he teaches doctoral courses in curriculum and instruction.

To book William M. Ferriter, Mike Mattos, or Rob J. Meyer for professional development, contact pd@solutiontree.com.

Introduction

Make sure that you always have the right tools for the job. It's no use trying to eat a steak with a teaspoon.
—Anthony Hincks

You might not give much thought to tools. You pick up the tool; you use it. But before we dive into this book of tools, its purpose, and how to use it, coauthor Mike Mattos recalls an experience that drove home the importance of choosing the right tool at the right time:

> *Like my coauthors, my living conditions during my early adult years consisted exclusively of rented spaces. From college dorm rooms to apartments, my lodgings were part of larger complexes that were owned and maintained by others. One benefit of being a tenant was when repairs were needed, the only tool required to fix the problem was my phone. The heater stopped working in my dorm room; I called the resident assistant to get it repaired. There was a broken sprinkler by my apartment front door that was shooting up water like Old Faithful; I called my landlord and maintenance took care of it.*
>
> *But after my first year of teaching, my wife and I were most fortunate to purchase our first home—a little California bungalow that was built in 1904. The primary reason why we were able to afford the quaint little place was that our realtor said it was a "fixer." Within days of moving in, we realized that calling it a fixer was an understatement—it was more like a "fix-est," as it needed the most help.*
>
> *On our third morning as new homeowners, we woke up to a puddle of water on our lone bathroom floor. Quickly checking under the sink, I noticed a slow leak coming from the drain pipe. With no landlord to call—and a checking account balance that could hardly cover the cost of a plumber—I set to work on this pressing home repair. Upon closer inspection, I determined the leak was coming from a connection between two pipes, with the wet remains of an old rubber seal below on the floor. Fixing the leak would require loosening the large metal pipe nut and replacing the worn-out rubber seal.*

I first tried to loosen the nut with my hands, but it did not budge, so I reached for my tool bag. Now, when I say tool bag, I am being technically correct— it was a canvas bag and there were multiple tools inside. To be exact, it contained four tools—a hammer, two screwdrivers, and a tape measure. As the screwdrivers and tape measure were useless to help loosen the large pipe nut, I reached for the hammer. Abraham H. Maslow's (1966) famous quote quickly became a reality to me: "If the only tool you have is a hammer, it is tempting to treat everything as if it were a nail" (p. 16). I tried to strategically hit the pipe nut to loosen it. After about thirty minutes, all I had to show for my efforts were a bent pipe, a bloody knuckle on my index finger, and repeated practice at not using the Lord's name in vain.

Taking my wife's advice, I defeatedly drove off to the local hardware store. I explained my situation to the sales associate in the plumbing area, and she responded with a chuckle, "It sounds like you diagnosed the leak correctly. You are just using the wrong tool for the job." She then handed me a standard-sized pipe wrench and a new rubber seal. Once I got back home, it took less than ten seconds to loosen the pipe nut and just a few more minutes to successfully repair the leak.

Looking back on that day, I was very fortunate that the plumbing problem was minor, and the repair didn't require a deep level of plumbing experience. You could fill my garage with every specialized tool known in the plumbing world, but it would not make me a professional plumber. A tool can only be as effective as the hands that are guiding it. But I did learn a valuable lesson that day: having the right tool for the task can make all the difference.

The Purpose and Structure of This Book

The purpose of *The Big Book of Tools for RTI at Work*™ is to provide educators with the right tools to create a highly effective multitiered system of supports (MTSS)—an essential outcome for any school or district that is truly dedicated to ensuring high levels of learning for every student. Specifically, this resource is a collection of tools designed to explicitly support the work of the three critical teams in the RTI at Work process. Whether you are a member of a collaborative team identifying grade-level essential standards, a school guiding coalition assessing the effectiveness of your Tier 2 interventions for social and academic behaviors, or an intervention team ensuring that the students who are most at risk in your building receive targeted help to master the universal skills of learning, you will find specific tools, templates, and protocols to support your efforts. Following an opening chapter that provides grounding information in the RTI at Work process and the professional learning community (PLC) foundation, the four remaining chapters in *The Big Book of Tools for RTI at Work* mirror the organization of school intervention efforts as detailed by Mike Mattos, Austin Buffum, Janet Malone, Luis F. Cruz,

Nicole Dimich, and Sarah Schuhl (2025) in *Taking Action: A Handbook for RTI at Work, Second Edition*.

- **Chapter 2: Tools for Establishing a Culture of Collective Responsibility**—Aligned with the content covered in the second chapter of *Taking Action: A Handbook for RTI at Work, Second Edition* (Mattos et al., 2025), the resources in this chapter are designed to help your school tackle the essential actions necessary to establish a sustainable foundation for your system of interventions. This chapter includes tools for building strong guiding coalitions, ensuring that your school's faculty believes in every student's ability to learn at grade level or higher, and developing high-functioning teacher teams that use cycles of collective inquiry to improve student outcomes. Readers will also find sorting tasks to gauge their understanding of the RTI at Work process, checklists to evaluate their readiness for implementing a system of interventions, and surveys to gather faculty feedback while implementing new change efforts.

- **Chapter 3: Tools for Building Tier 1 of Your Intervention Pyramid**—Aligned with the content covered in the third and fourth chapters of *Taking Action: A Handbook for RTI at Work, Second Edition* (Mattos et al., 2025), the resources in this chapter are designed to support teacher teams and guiding coalitions who are implementing the essential actions necessary to ensure a guaranteed and viable curriculum is delivered to all students. These resources include tools that teacher teams can use to identify essential grade-level standards and implement the team teaching-assessing-learning cycle, as well as tools that guiding coalitions can use to guarantee universal access to essential grade-level curriculum, identify and teach essential academic and social behaviors, and provide preventions to proactively support student success. Readers will also find criteria for determining which grade-level standards are essential, templates for unpacking those standards once identified, tools for building a master schedule that supports intervention, and checklists for concentrating instruction on social and academic behaviors.

- **Chapter 4: Tools for Building Tier 2 of Your Intervention Pyramid**—Aligned with the content covered in the fifth and sixth chapters of *Taking Action: A Handbook for RTI at Work, Second Edition* (Mattos et al., 2025), the resources in this chapter are designed to support teacher teams and guiding coalitions who are implementing the necessary actions to ensure all students have access to additional time and support for learning grade-level essential standards. These resources include tools that teacher teams can use to design supplemental interventions around academic essentials and to monitor the progress of students receiving additional support for learning. This chapter also includes tools that guiding coalitions can use to schedule time for supplemental interventions, establish a process for schoolwide student intervention identification, and coordinate interventions for students needing support for academic challenges *and* support for behavioral, attendance, and home challenges (what is sometimes known as *skill and will support*). Readers will also find lists of re-engagement strategies that work, suggestions for pretesting students for prerequisite knowledge and skills, surveys to gather staff feedback on the efficacy of supplemental intervention periods, and forms for teachers to recommend students for academic and behavioral support.

- **Chapter 5: Tools for Building Tier 3 of Your Intervention Pyramid**—Aligned with the content covered in the seventh and eighth chapters of *Taking Action: A Handbook for RTI at Work, Second Edition* (Mattos et al., 2025), the resources in this chapter are designed to support guiding coalitions and intervention teams who are implementing the essential actions necessary to implement interventions for students who are two or more grade levels behind in the universal skills of learning. This chapter includes tools that guiding coalitions can use to identify students needing intensive support and to assess the effectiveness of their interventions. It also provides tools that intervention teams can use to diagnose, treat, prioritize, and monitor Tier 3 interventions; to ensure that Tier 3 interventions are delivered at the proper intensity; and to determine whether special education recommendations are justifiable. Readers will also find surveys to gather feedback from teachers about universal screenings, lists detailing the essential function of school intervention teams, action planning templates to support students referred for Tier 3 interventions, and strategies for communicating Tier 3 intervention plans to parents.

Because *The Big Book of Tools for RTI at Work* is a collection of additional resources aimed to support educators exploring the intervention process detailed in *Taking Action: A Handbook for RTI at Work, Second Edition* (Mattos et al., 2025), readers will find that chapters 3 through 5 are divided into separate sections. Each section contains tools designed specifically for the school-level teams charged with leading essential actions at each tier of the intervention process. For example, essential actions are directed by teacher teams and the guiding coalition at Tier 1 in the RTI at Work process. Therefore, chapter 3 of this book—"Tools for Building Tier 1 of Your Intervention Pyramid"—is divided into two sections: one with resources supporting teacher teams and the other with resources supporting the guiding coalition. And, because the essential actions at Tier 3 in the RTI at Work process are carried out by the guiding coalition and the intervention team, chapter 5 of this book—"Tools for Building Tier 3 of Your Intervention Pyramid"—has separate sections with unique resources for both of those critical teams. However, you will not find resources for teacher teams in chapter 5 because teacher teams do not lead any of the essential actions for building Tier 3 in the RTI at Work process.

How to Use This Book

It is worth noting that every tool included in this book can be tied back to an essential action detailed in *Taking Action: A Handbook for RTI at Work, Second Edition* (Mattos et al., 2025). For example, the resource titled "Tool: Eliciting Feedback on Our Master Schedule" (page 146) is tied to Schoolwide Essential Action 1 at Tier 1 in the RTI at Work process, *Ensure Access to Essential Grade-Level Curriculum*, and the resource titled "Tool: Preparing a Prerequisite Pretest" (page 204) is tied to Teacher Team Essential Action 2 in the RTI at Work process, *Identify and Target Immediate Prerequisite Skills*. These connections are intentional; this text is not designed to introduce readers to new essential actions necessary to build a system of interventions but instead to provide additional support to schools working to successfully implement the RTI at Work process (Mattos et al., 2025). To make these connections explicit, we list the essential action, chapter, and page references from *Taking Action* (Mattos et al., 2025) after the title for each tool included in this text. That way, readers looking for additional context on the rationale for essential actions can quickly return to *Taking Action*.

Additionally, the reference following each tool's description in the body text and in the subheading following each reproducible's title—which always includes a decimal number—can serve as a key for readers, pointing them directly to the essential action in the second edition of *Taking Action*. Here is how to read that key: the whole number found before the decimal point of each reference identifies the chapter in the second edition of *Taking Action* that tool is connected to. The fractional number found after the decimal point names the action step found within the chapter for that tool. So, readers interested in learning more about a tool with the reference *Essential Action 3.1—Identify Essential Standards* would turn to chapter 3, essential action 1 in *Taking Action*. Information on a tool with the reference *Essential Action 8.1—Diagnose, Target, Prioritize, and Monitor Tier 3 Reinforcements* can be found in chapter 8, essential action 1 in *Taking Action*. With this key, you will always be able to connect resources in this text to the rationale for those resources found in *Taking Action: A Handbook for RTI at Work, Second Edition* (Mattos et al., 2025).

For every tool in this book, we will use the following symbols to specify which team best positioned to use it along with indicators—1, 2, 3, or F for *foundational*—to denote which tier it is designed to support.

Guiding Coalition

Teacher Teams

Intervention Team

For the RTI at Work process to be seamless, it's important to have the reproducible tools in this book at the ready. Check this book's inside front cover to find a unique access code to enter at **go.SolutionTree.com/RTIatWork/BBTRTI** to digitally access all reproducibles. The code on the inside front cover is unique to your book and can only be used once. After you enter your code, the exclusive reproducibles will be added to your customer dashboard on the Solution Tree website, allowing you access to the reproducibles at any time. Each reproducible in this book indicates if it is free to access or requires the code. Additionally, a selection of the tools is available online only. Each tool's description indicates its page number if it's in the book or "online" if it can be found at the reproducible link.

The Big Book of Tools for RTI at Work has been designed as a working companion to *Taking Action: A Handbook for RTI at Work, Second Edition* (Mattos et al., 2025), the seminal text describing the RTI at Work process. What does that mean for readers? If you are looking to build a better understanding of the RTI at Work process, turn first to *Taking Action*—where core concepts are detailed in depth and where essential links between those concepts are highlighted explicitly by the work's original architects. This text, on the other hand, is designed for readers who have already built an understanding of the RTI at Work process and are looking for additional resources to support specific essential action implementation.

Think of it this way: when auto mechanics train for their careers, they build a broad knowledge of how motor vehicles operate. They study the concepts behind combustion engines and electric motors. They learn about filtering both air and oil. They examine transmissions, water pumps, shock absorbers, and master cylinders. More importantly, they develop a complete understanding of the role each interconnected system in a vehicle—fueling, braking, suspension, cooling, and electrical—plays in the successful functioning of the entire car. Without this understanding, no matter how skilled auto mechanics are with the individual tools of the trade, they cannot keep vehicles running at the highest levels.

Similarly, while developing a wide range of skills and techniques is undoubtedly part of any good culinary program, students interested in becoming chefs are taught more than just how to use knives, double broilers, and deep fryers before starting their own restaurants. Instead, students practice developing cohesive menus that balance colors, flavors, and textures. They examine the risks of foodborne illnesses and strategies for maintaining safe and healthy kitchens. They learn about the core principles of nutrition, explore culinary traditions worldwide, and study business management practices like scheduling employees, conducting inventories, and controlling costs. Why? Because the experts who run culinary schools recognize that success in the food service industry depends on *first* developing expertise in a wide range of integrated areas and *then* finding the right tools to support that work.

The same is true for you. To implement the RTI at Work process, you must understand why interventions must be coordinated across an entire school rather than delivered by individual teachers working in isolation. You must be able to articulate the relationships between teacher teams, guiding coalitions, and intervention teams. You must know the differences between the work done at Tier 1, Tier 2, and Tier 3 in the intervention pyramid and be able to list the essential actions necessary for ensuring your efforts at all three tiers are efficient and effective. We recommend turning first to *Taking Action: A Handbook for RTI at Work, Second Edition* (Mattos et al., 2025) to build that core knowledge and content expertise. Skip that step, and no single set of tools can help you create a successful system of interventions designed to ensure that all students learn at the highest levels.

What *The Big Book of Tools for RTI at Work* can do, however, is provide you with a collection of resources to guide the efforts of teacher teams, guiding coalitions, and intervention teams who are implementing the essential actions necessary for building a solid system of interventions. Think of this text as a professional toolbox—a place to turn when you know *what* to do but are not sure *how* to do it. Take faith in knowing that each tool included has been carefully designed to help you accomplish a specific goal and has been used by other practitioners doing the same work. Choose the right tool at the right time—and use it in the right way with the right team—and *you can move your school forward.*

Here are a few additional tips to help you take full advantage of *The Big Book of Tools for RTI at Work.*

- **Remember that building a system of interventions and filling out worksheets are *not* the same thing:** The tools in this text *can* explicitly structure your efforts to implement the essential actions of the RTI at Work process—and if you use them correctly, you *will* build the capacity of your teacher teams, guiding coalition, and intervention team. However, do not fall into the trap of thinking that you are implementing the RTI at Work process correctly just because you have asked school-level teams to fill out blanks on worksheets. In fact, if your teams start to see the RTI at Work process as nothing more than filling out worksheets, you are probably getting everything wrong! Instead, see the tools in this book as conversation starters prompting teams to think deliberately about the core work necessary to build an effective system of interventions. It is deep and meaningful reflection that we are trying to facilitate with these resources, not simple compliance. As writer Jeff Duntemann (2016) says, "A good tool improves the way you work. A great tool improves the way you *think.*"

- **Remember that your team may not currently need some of the tools in this book:** *The Big Book of Tools for RTI at Work* is the most comprehensive collection of supporting materials available for schools implementing the RTI at Work process. Containing nearly two hundred different tools and templates covering every essential action detailed in *Taking Action: A Handbook for RTI at Work, Second Edition* (Mattos et al., 2025), you are sure to find ideas and resources that you can use right away. However, there are also ideas and resources your teams are not yet ready for. For example, schools just starting to experiment with intervention systems are likely to lean on the tools found in the first chapter, knowing that they need to establish high-functioning guiding coalitions and teacher teams before they begin implementing the technical actions tied to interventions. However, those same schools may wait to pull from the resources in later chapters, recognizing that the key to doing things well is to tackle first things first.

That means you should view *The Big Book of Tools for RTI at Work* as a reference guide that you return to again and again instead of as a book you read from cover to cover. The key to using this text is not to read first and then act. Instead, the key is to find tools that can immediately support the work that your building is ready for.

- **Remember that you can modify these tools to make them more valuable to your school-based teams:** The authors of *The Big Book of Tools for RTI at Work* all have extensive practical experience as practitioners, coaches, and professional development providers in schools working to implement the RTI at Work process. The included resources are tangible expressions of those firsthand experiences—work products developed in the moment to help teacher teams, guiding coalitions, and intervention teams move forward. They reflect the questions we ask teams to answer, the information we recommend collecting, and the documentation we believe teams should generate to build successful systems of intervention. That does not mean, however, that you must use our templates as they are or immediately replace tools you already use to do the same work. Remember: the specific tools you use to implement essential actions are not as important as ensuring that your critical school-based teams are doing the right work.

  So, look at our tools with a critical eye. What do you like about them? How do they compare to the tools that you have developed on your own or adopted from others? What changes would you make to improve them? Maybe the steps outlined on one of our tools are too complex for your teams, and you need to simplify by removing a few questions. Perhaps a specific section of one of our tools would make a great addition to something you already use. You might revise the overall flow of one of our tools, reorganizing questions or sections so they are arranged in a manner that makes more sense to you. All those modifications are possible, and we invite you to see our resources as a starting point for your work instead of a rigid format that you can't change.

Our final recommendation for using *The Big Book of Tools for RTI at Work* may be the most important. Whether you decide to use the included tools as they are or modify them to better meet the unique needs of your teacher teams, guiding coalition, or intervention team, your goal should be to get started *no matter how ready you feel*. Accept that no decision you make, practice you introduce, or process you apply will be perfect from the get-go. Instead, the best decisions, practices, and processes are developed collaboratively through multiple revisions and iterations. Adopting a "let's act and then revise" approach to implementing the RTI at Work process is the only way to ensure your school moves forward. After all, being great at anything is just a function of being good repeatedly (Smith, 2019)—and being good repeatedly *starts with taking action*.

Grasping the Bigger Picture

Big picture dreams broken down into smaller, more manageable parts unveil the steps that lead you to where you want to go.

—Richie Norton

Creating a highly effective system of interventions is like putting together a jigsaw puzzle. Puzzles comprise smaller, specific pieces that collectively create the larger picture. Certain pieces fit together, so the proper placement of each piece is critical. Success requires many discrete tasks, all of which must be completed accurately. And when all the pieces come together, they can create a final product that is far greater than the individual parts.

Similarly, there is no singular intervention—no monumental action or magical tool—that will ensure every student's success. A successful system of interventions is formed from many targeted actions that will collectively meet the diverse academic and behavioral needs of your students. Some tasks are complementary—they fit together to achieve a larger essential outcome. Success requires many targeted actions, completed successfully by different teams on your campus, to create a final product that is more powerful than the individual parts.

Now imagine you and your colleagues are tasked to assemble a jigsaw puzzle. You are given all the individual pieces, and they are randomly placed face up in front of you. Just one problem—you have not been shown the picture on the front of the puzzle box, so you are unclear on what you're trying to build. It is much more difficult to successfully assemble a puzzle if you lack a clear vision of the completed picture and how the pieces fit together.

The goal of this book is to provide more than a toolbox of random resources; it is a targeted set of complementary tools that will help a school create an effective system of supports. Because each tool's designed purpose represents just one piece of the MTSS puzzle—and must fit correctly with other tasks and tools in this book—an understanding of the larger picture is critical. In this book, our guiding graphic organizer is the RTI at Work pyramid (figure 1.1, page 12).

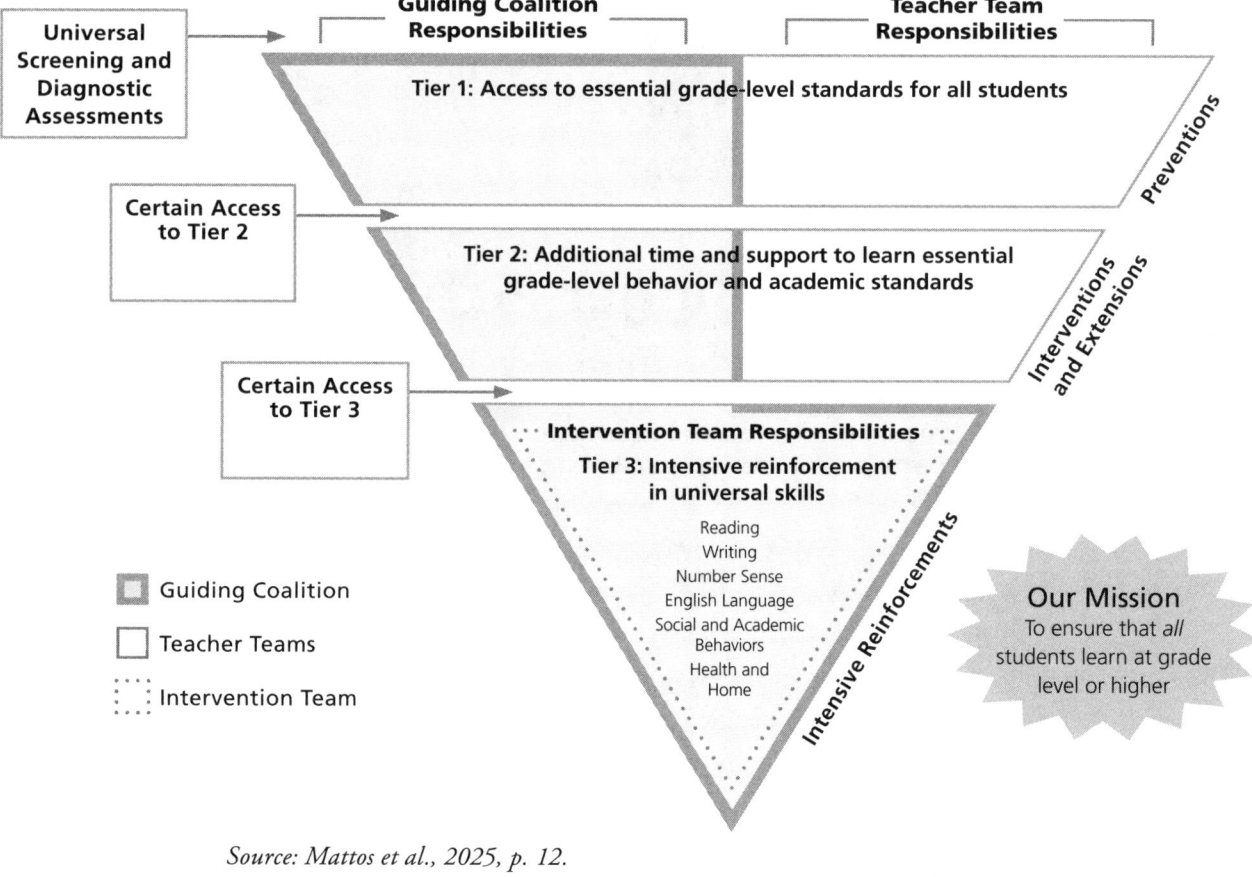

Source: Mattos et al., 2025, p. 12.

Figure 1.1: The RTI at Work pyramid.

In this chapter, we discuss the RTI at Work process and the PLC foundation it is built on.

The RTI at Work Process

Developed by authors Austin Buffum, Mike Mattos, and Janet Malone (2018), the RTI at Work process is based on a school being a PLC. At the top of the pyramid is Tier 1 (see figure 1.2). It is the widest part of the pyramid because it visually represents what *all* students receive as part of their daily instruction—access to grade-level *essential* standards.

Essential standards are the indispensable academic and behavior learning outcomes that students must master each year to be prepared for the next grade or course. Failure to master these standards will cripple a student's future success in school and beyond. While it is possible that some students might miss portions of core instruction to receive interventions, students cannot miss the teaching of this essential curriculum to receive additional help.

Undoubtedly, some students will not master every essential standard by the end of a unit of study. Because these specific learning outcomes are indispensable prerequisite skills for future success, the school must systematically provide targeted interventions to ensure all students master this necessary grade-level curriculum. This additional time and support to master grade-level essential curriculum is the purpose of Tier 2 (see figure 1.3).

Grasping the Bigger Picture   13

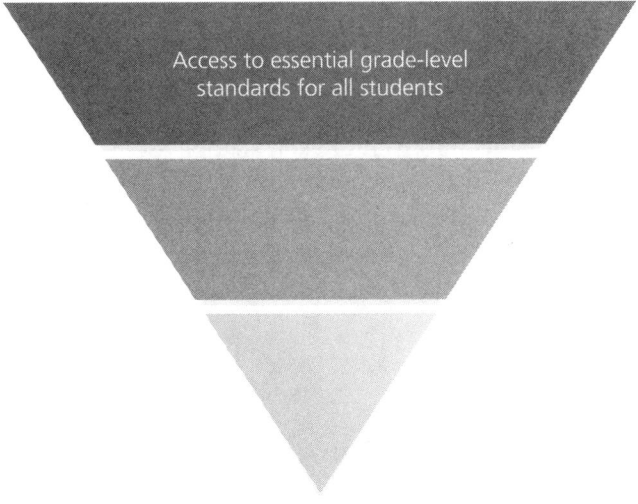

Source: Mattos et al., 2025, p. 14.

Figure 1.2: Tier 1 is the core instruction program.

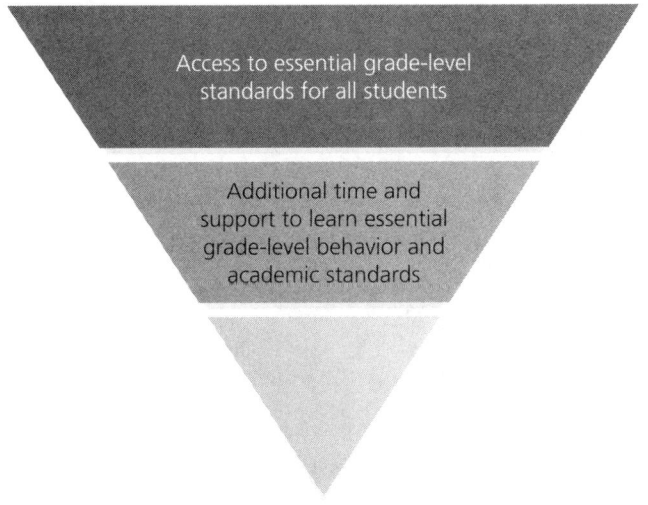

Source: Mattos et al., 2025, p. 15.

Figure 1.3: Tier 2 is supplemental support to master grade-level curriculum.

These Tier 2 interventions must have the following attributes (Mattos et al., 2025).

- Scheduled during the school day, when students are required to be at school and your staff is available because it is during contracted time
- Provided in addition to Tier 1, not in place of it
- Targeted to individual student need
- Directive so students are not allowed to opt out
- Systematic and collaborative—the help a student receives is not dependent solely on the specific teacher or teachers that a student is assigned to for core instruction

Most students will succeed if a school provides access to essential grade-level curriculum and effective initial teaching during Tier 1 core instruction and targeted supplemental academic and behavioral help in meeting these standards at Tier 2.

However, some students inevitably enter each school year lacking the universal skills needed to learn at high levels. This is especially the case when they are significantly below grade level in the following abilities.

- Decoding and comprehending grade-level text
- Writing effectively
- Applying number sense
- Comprehending the English language (or the school's primary language)
- Demonstrating social and academic behaviors consistently
- Overcoming complications due to health or home

Students will struggle in virtually every grade level, course, and subject if they are significantly behind in just one of these areas. These students will need intensive reinforcement to close these gaps. This is the purpose of Tier 3 (see figure 1.4).

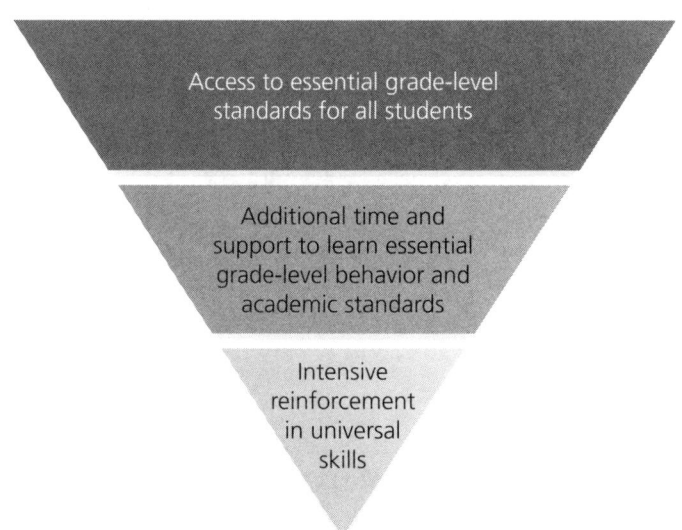

Source: Mattos et al., 2025, p. 16.

Figure 1.4: Tier 3 is intensive reinforcement of universal skills.

The characteristics of Tier 3 include the following.

- Supports are built into a student's daily schedule.
- Help is targeted to individual student need.
- It is not regular education or special education—it is available for any student who has the need.

- Supports are guided or provided by the faculty members who are best trained in each area of need. This means both regular education and special education resources should be used for the benefit of all students who demonstrate the need.
- It is not a "life sentence"—students should be improving at least two years of academic growth within a single school year.

Last, and most important, some students will need all three tiers to learn at high levels—this is why it is called a *multitiered* system of supports. Students are not moved from tier to tier; instead, the tiers are value added. All students need effective initial teaching on grade-level essential standards at Tier 1. In addition to Tier 1, some students will need supplemental support in mastering those standards at Tier 2. And in addition to Tier 1 and Tier 2, some students will need intensive supports to learn essential outcomes from previous years. Students in need of Tier 3 intensive help often also struggle with new essential grade-level curriculum. This means these students need Tier 2 and Tier 3 support, all without missing new essential instruction at Tier 1.

Individual teachers cannot effectively provide all three levels of support in their own classrooms. Such support requires a schoolwide, collective, collaborative, coordinated, all-hands-on-deck mentality. This is why structuring our RTI at Work process is built on a school being a professional learning community.

The PLC Foundation

Because systematic interventions require high levels of faculty collaboration, it is critical that a school functions as a PLC. We specifically advocate for the Professional Learning Communities at Work® framework, originally created by Richard DuFour and Robert Eaker (1998). Mike Mattos, Richard DuFour, Rebecca DuFour, Robert Eaker, and Thomas W. Many (2016) define a *professional learning community* as a "never-ending process in which educators commit to working together to ensure higher levels of learning for every student" (p. 5).

To achieve this goal—an unrelenting focus on learning—educators work collaboratively to *learn together* about the practices proven to increase student learning, apply what they have learned, and gather evidence of student learning to validate their efforts and guide their next steps. This collective learning focuses on the factors that support and hinder student success.

Because individual teachers working in isolation cannot ensure high levels of learning for every student, the PLC at Work process requires a collaborative culture in which educators work in teams and take collective responsibility for student success. Specifically, in the RTI at Work process, we recommend three types of teams to guide the school's MTSS process (Buffum, Mattos, Weber, & Hierck, 2015). The first type is teacher teams, which are composed of teachers who share essential academic learning outcomes. They are usually grade-level teams at the elementary level and course-specific teams at the secondary level. Teacher teams take lead responsibility for identifying, teaching, and reteaching essential academic standards, directing supplemental (Tier 2) academic interventions, and assisting with academic and social behavior supports.

Visually, we capture the lead responsibilities for these three teams in the RTI at Work pyramid. A teacher team's lead responsibilities at Tier 1 and Tier 2 are visually captured in the top right-hand portion of the pyramid (see figure 1.5).

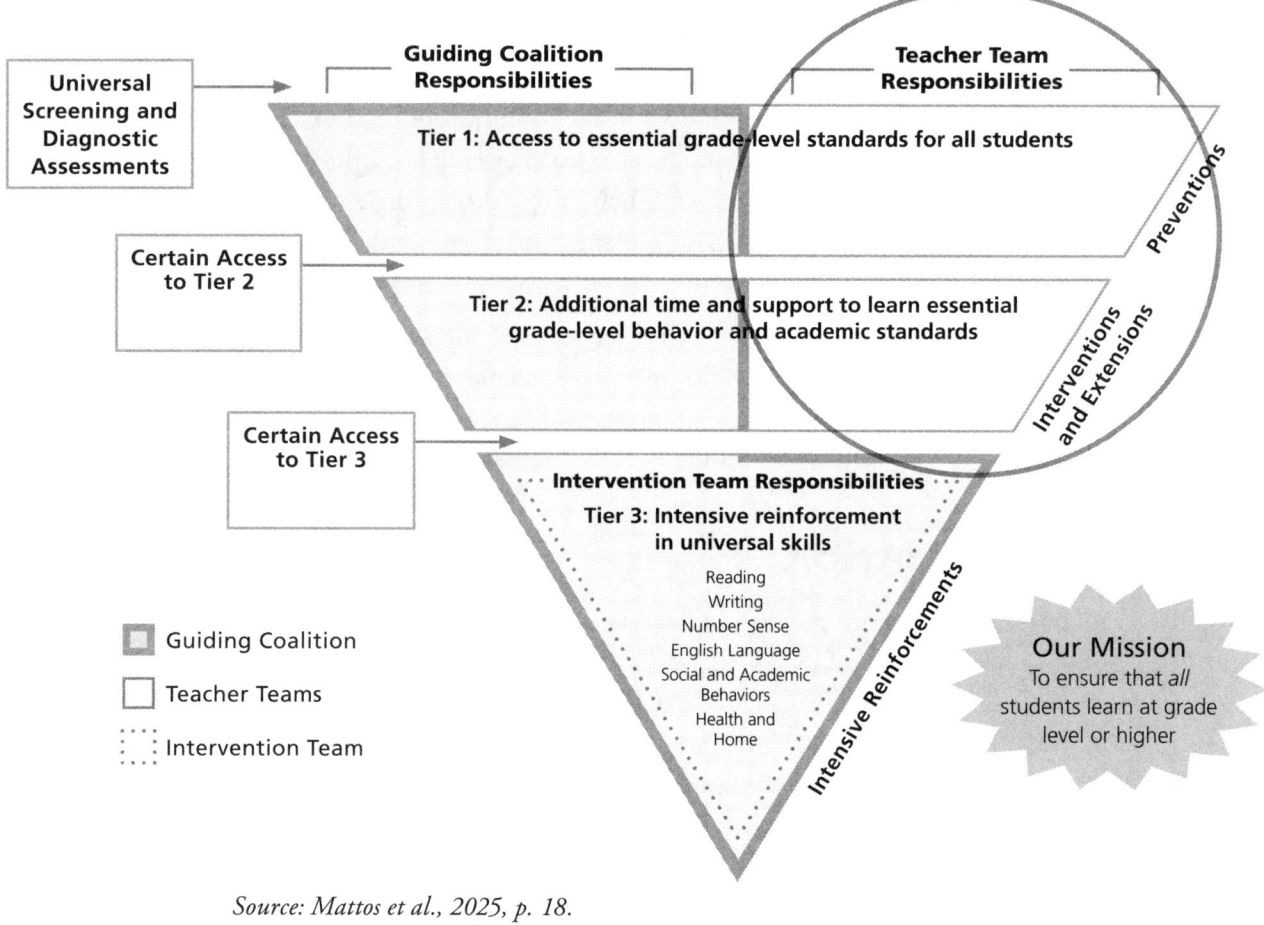

Source: Mattos et al., 2025, p. 18.

Figure 1.5: Tier 1 and Tier 2 responsibilities of collaborative teacher teams.

Collaboration alone within teacher teams will not improve student learning unless these efforts focus on the *right work*. To this end, collaboration in the PLC at Work process is guided by four critical questions:

a. What knowledge, skills, and dispositions should every student acquire as a result of this unit, this course, or this grade level?

b. How will we know when each student has acquired the essential knowledge and skills?

c. How will we respond when some students do not learn?

d. How will we extend the learning for students who are already proficient? (DuFour et al., 2024, p. 44)

Likewise, the lead responsibilities of the two schoolwide teams—the leadership and intervention teams—are represented in the left-hand side of the pyramid (see figure 1.6).

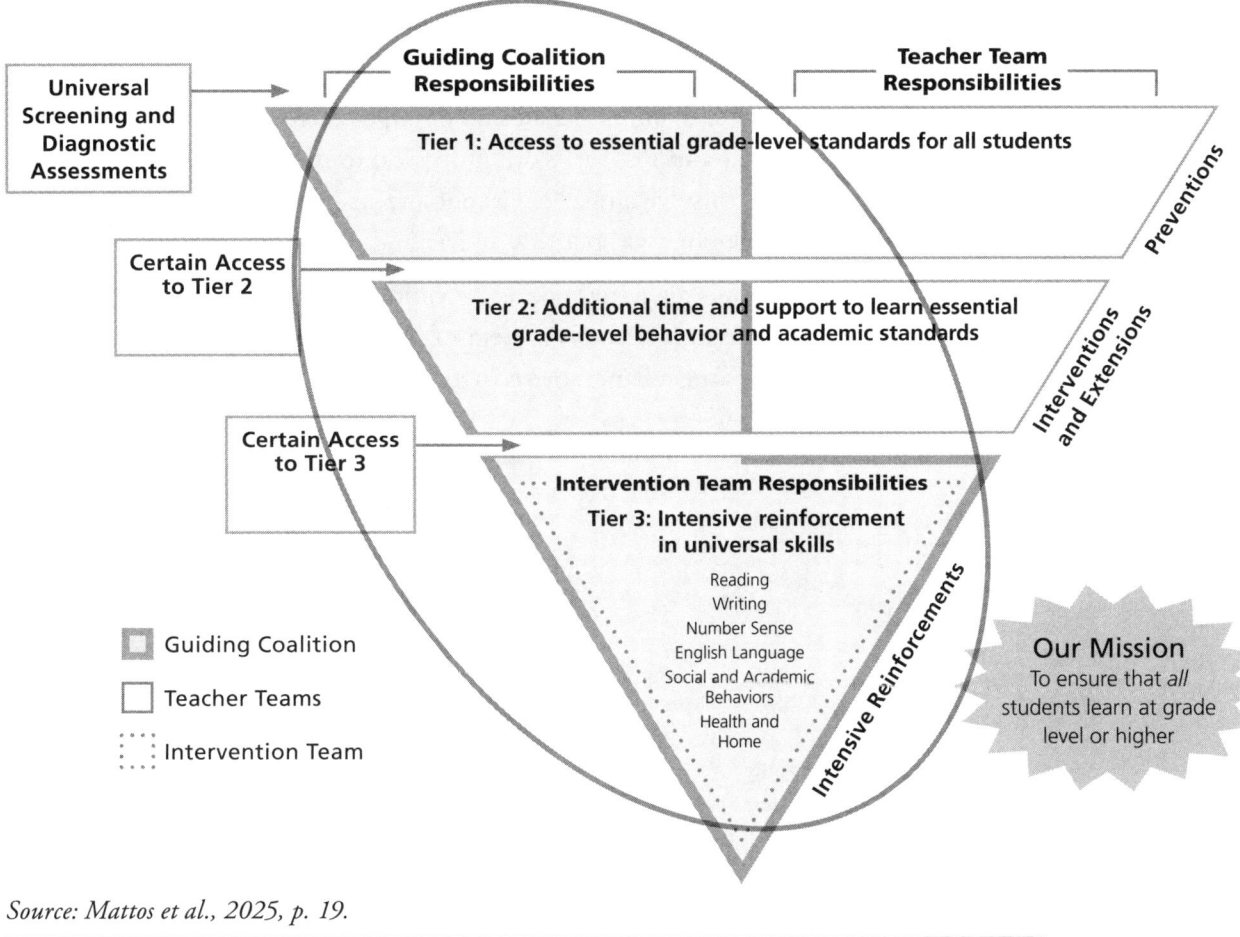

Source: Mattos et al., 2025, p. 19.

Figure 1.6: Tiers 1, 2, and 3 processes that must be coordinated across the entire school.

The guiding coalition—also called a *school leadership team*—has the lead responsibility for efforts that must be coordinated across the school. These include creating a shared school mission, allocating resources to support collaboration and student learning, designing the school master schedule, and leading schoolwide behavior efforts at all three tiers. The intervention team solves problems related to the school's students who are most at risk. Most often, these students have multiple needs in both academics and behavior. Made up of the school's staff best trained in the areas where students often struggle—such as behavior, literacy, and numeracy—this team meets frequently to diagnose, target, coordinate, and monitor the interventions for students requiring Tier 3 intensive supports.

Finally, educators in a PLC purposefully and relentlessly collect evidence that students are learning. Actual proof of practice—instead of merely past practices, preferences, or intentions—drives decisions at every tier.

Conclusion

Hopefully you now have a clear vision of the picture on the puzzle box. Each action in your effort to craft an effective system of interventions, no matter how small, contributes to the larger picture of support and growth for your students. It's not about a single groundbreaking strategy or tool but rather a blend of targeted efforts, coordinated within the frameworks of the RTI and PLC at Work processes, to meet your students' diverse needs. Just as attempting to solve a puzzle without a clear image guide would be challenging, navigating interventions without this understanding would be equally daunting.

Our next step—if this was an actual puzzle—would be to find and put together the edge pieces. When building an effective system of interventions, we start by creating the healthy school culture and collaborative structures needed to successfully intervene.

Tools for Establishing a Culture of Collective Responsibility

> *But here is the critical point: to start the journey, we must accept primary responsibility for what we can control—student mastery of academic skills, knowledge, and dispositions—and assume each student is capable of achieving these outcomes, regardless of their demographic background.*
>
> —Mike Mattos, Austin Buffum, Janet Malone, Luis F. Cruz, Nicole Dimich, & Sarah Schuhl

Interventions are anything a school does—above and beyond what all learners receive—that helps a student succeed in school (Mattos et al., 2025). We can say with confidence that we have never worked with a school that did not have any interventions. Every school offers help when students struggle. But sadly, we rarely find schools that have systematic interventions. *Systematic interventions* are characterized by the following.

- The entire staff takes collective responsibility for every student's success. There is a palpable sense that the faculty has shunned the divisive mindset of "my students versus your students," "my class versus your class," and "regular education versus special education." Instead, learners are viewed as *our* students and the staff works together to ensure every child achieves at high levels.

- Because ensuring every student's success requires a collective effort, the school has purposefully created specific teams to achieve this outcome and scheduled frequent collaborative time to identify students for extra help, determine specific student needs, provide interventions, and evaluate progress.

- The school has developed a healthy culture in which educators focus their collaboration on what they can directly control—effective teaching practices provided within their current school day and school resources.

When done well, a school with systematic interventions can make the following promises to every student—and parent or guardian—who attends their school:

> *It does not matter which teacher or teachers you are assigned to in this school. If you need additional time and support to succeed, we guarantee you will receive it. You will be the beneficiary of the entire staff's collective expertise. This additional time and support will be embedded in the school day, so we can ensure and require that you receive it. And you do not have to qualify—or have a defined disability—to receive help. Any student who needs additional time and support for learning will receive it.*

Creating such a system does not begin with providing interventions. Instead, it starts by creating the right teams, scheduling dedicated time for collaboration, setting adult norms of behavior, and creating the learning-focused school culture required to effectively respond when students need additional help. The tools in this chapter are designed to achieve these foundational outcomes. It would be naive at best—and downright irresponsible at worst—to understand that an MTSS is a schoolwide process impacting every faculty member, but then haphazardly create team structures or not allocate sufficient professional time to do this life-saving work. When done well, systematic interventions should be positive experiences for students and educators. This only happens when staff members are asked to work smarter within their regular work day to collaborate and intervene and are not asked to work beyond contractual hours. Failure to plan for these foundational outcomes will set your staff up to fail.

Resources Designed to Establish a Culture of Collective Responsibility

The resources in this chapter are all designed to help guiding coalitions establish a culture of collective responsibility in their buildings. They are tied to the essential actions detailed in chapter 2 of *Taking Action: A Handbook for RTI at Work, Second Edition* (Mattos et al., 2025).

These resources include the following. Visit **go.SolutionTree.com/RTIatWork/BBTRTI** to access online-only tools.

- **"Tool: Building Your Guiding Coalition"** (page 34)—Creating a guiding coalition is an essential first step toward successfully implementing the RTI at Work process. A *guiding coalition* is a group of people with the skills necessary to lead their colleagues through "the predictable turmoil" that comes with any new change effort in schools (DuFour et al., 2024). Use this tool, which details the four types of organizational power necessary to move change initiatives forward in any organization, to evaluate your guiding coalition's current composition.
  - *Taking Action* reference: Essential Action 2.1—Establish a Guiding Coalition, p. 30

- **"Tool: Ten Considerations for the Guiding Coalition"** (page 36)—The guiding coalition's work is essential in successfully implementing the RTI at Work process. This team takes the lead in establishing the right conditions within the school that other critical teams—teacher teams and the intervention team—will need to successfully build a strong pyramid of interventions. To ensure their work pays dividends, the guiding coalition should review the considerations listed on this quarterly check-in and plan next steps for any not currently in place. These reviews will support the strong implementation of school intervention efforts and ensure that implementation stays strong once it is achieved.
    - *Taking Action* reference: Essential Action 2.1—Establish a Guiding Coalition, p. 30

- **"Tool: Ten Considerations for the Guiding Coalition—Behavior Specific"** (online only): The guiding coalition's work isn't limited to creating the conditions necessary for implementing the academic elements of a pyramid of interventions; it also includes creating the conditions required to implement the behavioral aspects. However, there are specific considerations for the guiding coalition to navigate when considering behavior-related interventions. Use this quarterly check-in to review these considerations and determine if you have created the right conditions to ensure all students master grade-level essential behaviors.
    - *Taking Action* reference: Essential Action 2.1—Establish a Guiding Coalition, p. 30

- **"Tool: Analysis and Action Planning Template for Guiding Coalitions"** (page 38)—Knowing that effective guiding coalitions are essential for successfully implementing both the PLC and RTI at Work processes, Phillip Page and David Chiprany of the Bartow County School System in Cartersville, Georgia, developed an annual survey to monitor the progress of individual schools, identify needed central office supports for each building, and help principals and guiding coalitions determine their professional learning schedule for the year. Use this tool—which is an adapted version of Page and Chiprany's original survey—to do that work in your building.
    - *Taking Action* reference: Essential Action 2.1—Establish a Guiding Coalition, p. 30

- **"Tool: Using Academic Data to Target the Work of Guiding Coalitions"** (online only)—Guiding coalitions conduct annual effectiveness assessments of their schoolwide system of interventions, analyzing available data to determine whether improvements are evident across various subject areas.

This tool offers a straightforward protocol for guiding coalitions to examine data on a subject-by-subject basis, evaluating both schoolwide outcomes and the progress of students who are receiving intensive interventions.

- *Taking Action* reference: Essential Action 2.1—Establish a Guiding Coalition, p. 30

- **"Tool: Using Faculty Survey Data to Target the Work of Guiding Coalitions"** (page 45)—Annual effectiveness assessments of schoolwide systems of interventions, conducted by guiding coalitions, should encompass a comprehensive analysis of available academic data to determine whether progress is evident across all subject areas and grade levels. In addition to quantitative data, it is crucial for guiding coalitions to analyze the perceptions of school faculty. This tool and its companion analysis worksheet, **"Tool: Analyzing Faculty Survey on the Work of Guiding Coalitions"** (page 46), are designed to collect valuable insights into staff perceptions regarding schoolwide intervention efforts. The collected data can be utilized to identify areas for celebration and areas in need of improvement. When collected on an annual basis, these data become valuable for tracking and analyzing school improvements over time.

  - *Taking Action* reference: Essential Action 2.1—Establish a Guiding Coalition, p. 30

- **"Tool: Planning a Cycle of Inquiry for Guiding Coalitions"** (page 49)—Effective guiding coalitions play vital roles in fostering collaborative capacity within a school and ensuring that teacher teams focus on the right work. They achieve this by engaging in recurring cycles of collective inquiry together. These cycles of inquiry are structured around the four critical questions of learning viewed through the lens of collaborative teams: (1) What knowledge and skills do we want teams to acquire, and how will we teach those essentials to teams?, (2) How will we assess team progress toward mastering our essentials?, (3) What actions will we take when a team struggles to master our essentials?, and (4) What actions will we take when a team is prepared to extend its work beyond mastery of our essentials? You can use this tool, along with the accompanying **sample** (page 50), to plan and implement a cycle of inquiry with your guiding coalition.

  - *Taking Action* reference: Essential Action 2.1—Establish a Guiding Coalition, p. 30

- **"Tool: Using AI Tools to Support Collaborative Team Development"** (page 51)—To coach teacher teams effectively, guiding coalitions should approach collaborative skills and behaviors with the same systematic process used to study academic essential standards. This begins by developing a collective understanding of what mastering a collaborative skill or behavior entails and creating a proficiency scale outlining the steps to achieve mastery in these areas. This resource provides a series of prompts to assist your guiding coalition in engaging AI chatbots like ChatGPT (https://chat.openai.com) and Gemini (https://gemini.google.com) in an in-depth exploration of specific collaborative skills or behaviors.

- *Taking Action* reference: Essential Action 2.1—Establish a Guiding Coalition, p. 30

■ **"Tool: Writing a SMART Goal for Team Development"** (online only)—One of the core responsibilities of any guiding coalition is to support teacher teams' continued development (Hall, 2022). The challenge is that the teams in our buildings are as developmentally diverse as the students in our classrooms—bringing a wide-ranging set of skills and experiences to the planning table and requiring differentiated support. That means guiding coalitions committed to working efficiently should write *SMART goals*—strategic and specific, measurable, attainable, results oriented, and time bound—detailing specific plans for moving individual learning teams forward. Doing so ensures that our professional development efforts are targeted "by name and by need"—an essential criterion for effective intervention. Doing so also allows members of the guiding coalition to practice using SMART goals to plan next actions—a core collaborative behavior in a learning community—with one another before leading that same practice on their teacher teams. This tool and its **overview** (online only) will walk you through creating a SMART goal for team development. Readers can also find **samples** of SMART goals for team development online.

- *Taking Action* reference: Essential Action 2.1—Establish a Guiding Coalition, p. 30

■ **"Tool: SWOT Analysis for Guiding Coalitions"** (online only)—Businesses often use SWOT analyses to make more proactive and informed decisions about potential change initiatives (Minsky & Aron, 2021). SWOT is an acronym for strengths, weaknesses, opportunities, and threats. By completing a SWOT analysis, businesses can identify their strengths, improve their weaknesses, take advantage of their opportunities, and mitigate any threats to their success. Conducted in collaboration with organizational leaders from across departments, a SWOT analysis gives a business a complete picture of its current corporate reality before investing fully in new efforts. Guiding coalitions can replicate this process in schools working to establish a system of interventions. This tool can help your guiding coalition complete a SWOT analysis.

- *Taking Action* reference: Essential Action 2.1—Establish a Guiding Coalition, p. 30

- **"Tool: What Should We See in a System of Interventions?"** (online only)—Schools interested in building an effective system of interventions must begin by understanding the essential actions taken by the three critical teams in the RTI at Work model: (1) the collaborative teacher teams, (2) the guiding coalition, and (3) the intervention team. Creating a system of efficient and effective interventions is impossible without a strong understanding of these essential actions. Guiding coalitions interested in evaluating their understanding—or the understanding of their faculties—of the essential actions in the RTI at Work process can complete this sorting task together and then check their answers with the corresponding **key** found online.
    - *Taking Action* reference: Essential Action 2.1—Establish a Guiding Coalition, p. 30

- **"Survey: Rating Our Readiness for RTI"** (page 52)—In *Uniting Academic and Behavior Interventions: Solving the Skill or Will Dilemma*, intervention experts Austin Buffum, Mike Mattos, Chris Weber, and Tom Hierck (2015) argue that successful interventions require teachers to commit to two fundamental assumptions: (1) all students are capable of learning at the highest levels and (2) it is the school staff's responsibility to ensure that the highest levels of learning happen for every student. To assess the current commitment levels in your building to these fundamental assumptions, you can first administer this survey and then use **"Tool: Reflecting on Our Faculty's Readiness for RTI"** (page 53) with your guiding coalition to analyze results and plan next steps.
    - *Taking Action* reference: Essential Action 2.2—Build a Culture of Collective Responsibility, p. 40

- **"Checklist: Simplifying RTI Culture Survey"** (online only)—Many schools implementing the RTI at Work process make the mistake of rushing first to design interventions for students instead of investing time into establishing the cultural beliefs necessary to ensure that interventions pay dividends. While planning interventions is essential, no intervention will produce meaningful results if the building's faculty does not yet believe that all students are capable of learning and that ensuring higher levels of learning is the responsibility of educators. Complete this checklist with your guiding coalition to determine whether your school's culture will support a successful system of interventions.
    - *Taking Action* reference: Essential Action 2.2—Build a Culture of Collective Responsibility, p. 40

- **"Tool: Does Our School Alibi?"** (online only)—Research on what high-performing schools do differently is not new. Author and educator John Holt (1964) was writing about high-performing schools in 1964, and one of his seminal arguments was that the highest-performing schools did not make excuses for why students struggle. He writes, "If the students did not learn, the schools did not blame them, or their families, backgrounds, neighborhoods, attitudes, nervous systems, or whatever. They did not alibi" (Holt, 1964, p. 8). That is a near-perfect description of educators' actions in schools with a strong sense of collective responsibility. Find Holt's (1964) full quote in this tool and use it to evaluate your school's current reality.
    - *Taking Action* reference: Essential Action 2.2—Build a Culture of Collective Responsibility, p. 40

- **"Tool: Exploring Hattie's Research on Response to Intervention"** (online only)—Researcher John Hattie (2023) has been working to quantify the impact of different influences—home circumstances, instructional practices, and school conditions—on students as learners. He ranks 322 different influences, from those that have "the potential to considerably accelerate student achievement" to those "likely to have a negative impact on student achievement" (Hattie, 2023). This research can convince skeptical teachers that, while home circumstances impact a student's ability to succeed, the most impactful influences on student achievement are things we control as educators. Use this sorting task and the accompanying **answer key** (online only) to start a conversation in your building about the importance of school-based factors on student success.
    - *Taking Action* reference: Essential Action 2.2—Build a Culture of Collective Responsibility, p. 40

- **"Tool: Creating a *These Are Our Kids* Slide"** (online only)—One common mistake that schools make when trying to build a culture of collective responsibility is focusing teacher attention on standardized test scores as a motivator. The truth is that teachers are rarely motivated by the percentage of students who are passing end-of-grade exams in their building. What motivates teachers to accept responsibility for helping all students to learn at grade level or higher is knowing that specific students they care about personally are not achieving. To make that point in your school, consider asking teams to use this tool to create a *These Are Our Kids* slide highlighting individual students who are going to require the collective expertise of the entire team to learn at high levels.
    - *Taking Action* reference: Essential Action 2.2—Build a Culture of Collective Responsibility, p. 40

- **"Tool: Evaluating Our Mission Statement"** (page 54)—In the article "Why Are We Here?," corporate coaches Sally Blount and Paul Leinwand (2019) argue, "Purpose is the key to motivation—and motivated employees are the key to realizing your purpose." They detail the critical steps businesses can take to develop purpose statements connecting their employees to their organizational purpose. Known as mission statements in the RTI at Work process, purpose statements like those detailed by Blount and Leinwand (2019) are essential to building an organization's culture of collective responsibility. Use this tool to evaluate the efficacy of your school's mission statement.
    - *Taking Action* reference: Essential Action 2.2—Build a Culture of Collective Responsibility, p. 40

- **"Tool: Developing Collective Commitments"** (page 56)—After developing a mission statement, high-functioning professional learning communities create a clear set of values statements. These values statements are often called collective commitments. They become the promises that community members make to one another—a visible expression of the expectations that each member must live up to. Collective commitments answer the question, How will we act to fulfill our school's mission? Use this tool to develop collective commitments for your faculty.
    - *Taking Action* reference: Essential Action 2.2—Build a Culture of Collective Responsibility, p. 40

- **"Tool: Who Takes Lead Responsibility for Interventions?"** (online only)—Creating successful systems of interventions in a building is a complex task that cannot be left to chance. Instead, the work of the collaborative teacher teams, guiding coalition, and intervention team must be carefully coordinated to produce meaningful results for students. Schools cannot succeed until they have these teams in place and define the essential actions each team oversees. Use this tool to review the lead responsibilities of each of these school-level teams.
    - *Taking Action* reference: Essential Action 2.2—Build a Culture of Collective Responsibility, p. 40

- **"Tool: Site-Based Teams Aligned to the RTI at Work Process"** (page 58)—As detailed in "Tool: Who Takes Lead Responsibility for Interventions?" (online only), schools must establish several different teams with dedicated responsibilities to create effective systems of interventions. This tool can be used to develop an even deeper understanding of the types of teams needed and their critical roles in implementing the RTI at Work process. In addition, this tool provides users with an implementation continuum that can be used to evaluate their current reality.

- *Taking Action* reference: Essential Action 2.2—Build a Culture of Collective Responsibility, p. 40

- **"Tool: Teams Needed in RTI at Work—A Principal's Reflection"** (page 60): While the RTI at Work process requires the coordinated effort of several site-based teams who accept lead responsibility for implementing specific essential actions, it is ultimately the school principal's job first to build and then set these coordinated teams in motion. This tool can help principals determine if they have laid the proper groundwork to ensure these teams succeed.
  - *Taking Action* reference: Essential Action 2.2—Build a Culture of Collective Responsibility, p. 40

- **"Tool: Forming Teacher Teams"** (page 62)—While the critical teams in the RTI at Work process—teacher teams, guiding coalitions, and intervention teams—are essential for creating a successful system of interventions in a school, teacher teams accept lead responsibility for three of the most critical Tier 1 and Tier 2 tasks in the school: (1) identifying grade-level essential standards, (2) providing initial instruction in those essentials, and (3) designing supplemental interventions for students who need additional time and support to master those essentials. The most efficient teacher teams comprise teachers with students at the same grade level or in the same subject area, but that is not the only teaming structure that can work. This tool introduces the four most common teaming structures found in schools. Use it to identify the right composition for teacher teams in your building.
  - *Taking Action* reference: Essential Action 2.3—Form Collaborative Teacher Teams, p. 52

- **"Tool: What Work Is Your Team *Kind of Doing*?"** (online only)—Breez Longwell Daniels (2020), who is both an experienced principal and an expert on collaboration in small schools and rural communities, believes that teacher teams are often tempted to say that they are *doing the right work* when they meet, but, in reality, they are just *kind of doing it*. Teams that are *kind of doing* the work are teams that tackle the right tasks once but do not implement them consistently, teams that know what the right work is but have yet to embrace it fully, or teams that are implementing some parts of the collaborative process but ignoring others. This tool introduces the right work of teacher teams and asks members to identify core collaborative behaviors that they have mastered and those they must improve on.
  - *Taking Action* reference: Essential Action 2.3—Form Collaborative Teacher Teams, p. 52

- **"Tool: Reflecting on the Core Work of Collaborative Teams"** (online only)—Ask most educators to explain the purpose of collaboration and they will likely answer, "To ensure higher levels of learning for all students." While that statement is true, it is also incomplete. The correct answer is, "To ensure higher levels of learning for all students by giving every teacher the opportunity to study their practice together with their peers." Meaningful collaboration promotes intentional experimentation with instruction and shared attempts to amplify teaching strategies. Use this tool to start that conversation with your teachers.
    - *Taking Action* reference: Essential Action 2.3—Form Collaborative Teacher Teams, p. 52

- **"Tool: Understanding Teacher Approaches to Collaboration"** (online only)—A key responsibility for principals in thriving learning communities is building healthy teacher teams. The first step toward building healthy teacher teams is thinking intentionally about the composition of members. One way to evaluate your team's composition is to consider the approach individual members take when faced with conflict or when they are allowed to share thoughts and ideas. Using just those two indicators, organizational psychologist and Wharton professor Adam Grant (2016) argues that you can spot four different types of people in your organization: (1) disagreeable givers, (2) agreeable givers, (3) disagreeable takers, and (4) agreeable takers. Use this tool to understand who those people are in your school and to quickly spot learning teams with an unhealthy composition for productive collaboration.
    - *Taking Action* reference: Essential Action 2.3—Form Collaborative Teacher Teams, p. 52

- **"Survey: Midyear Collaborative Team Check-In"** (page 64)—Providing additional time and support to teams struggling with core collaborative practices depends on gathering evidence of their current reality. That evidence can come from observations conducted by school leaders who attend collaborative meetings and from conducting teacher surveys so they can share their firsthand experiences with the regular work of their collaborative team. This survey—created by Lincoln Heights Middle School in Morristown, Tennessee—is designed to be given annually and to collect information about team performance in broad areas like developing common assessments, analyzing student learning data, and using assessment results to inform instructional practices.
    - *Taking Action* reference: Essential Action 2.3—Form Collaborative Teacher Teams, p. 52

- **"Tool: The Strengths, Weaknesses, Opportunities, and Threats of Collaboration"** (online only)—Transitioning schools to structures where teachers work interdependently to ensure high levels of learning for all students is not always easy for educators used to working in isolation. Those educators need time and space to think through the strengths, weaknesses, opportunities, and threats of collaboration before entirely investing in the new work that you are asking them to do. Use this tool to begin that conversation in teams where teachers question the value of collaboration.
    - *Taking Action* reference: Essential Action 2.3—Form Collaborative Teacher Teams, p. 52

- **"Tool: Team Collaboration Time—Planning Guide and Schedule"** (page 67): In *Taking Action: A Handbook for RTI at Work, Second Edition*, the original architects of the RTI at Work process write, "Collaboration time is essential to the PLC and RTI processes. Without it, the work is virtually impossible" (Mattos et al., 2025, p. 62). What does that mean for school leaders? One of the first tasks you must tackle is to develop a schedule that provides every teacher with job-embedded time to meet with their teacher teams. Use this tool, which is also included in *Taking Action*, to begin sketching out a schedule that includes weekly time for team collaboration.
    - *Taking Action* reference: Essential Action 2.3—Form Collaborative Teacher Teams, p. 52

- **"Tool: Have We Created Time for Teacher Collaborative Teams?"** (page 68)—Schools experienced with the RTI at Work process likely have an established schedule for on-the-clock teacher collaboration. In such cases, the guiding coalition's responsibility is not to create a new schedule but to assess their current approach. This tool can assist you in evaluating your schedule against the non-negotiable elements that facilitate meaningful collaboration outlined in *Learning by Doing: A Handbook for Professional Learning Communities at Work, Fourth Edition* (DuFour et al., 2024).
    - *Taking Action* reference: Essential Action 2.3—Form Collaborative Teacher Teams, p. 52

- **"Tool Overview: Developing Team Norms"** (page 70)—Every group that you belong to—your Sunday school class, your child's sports teams, participants in your family reunion or your fantasy football league, your collaborative teacher team—has common participation patterns. Sometimes, those participation patterns are positive and can move the group forward; other times, those patterns are harmful and can hold the group back. To ensure that their common participation patterns are healthy and productive, teacher teams in schools implementing the RTI at Work process write norms that describe the actions they will take to honor one another's time (Ferriter, 2020). Use this overview and its accompanying template **"Tool: Commit to Team Norms"** (page 71) to write a clear set of norms for your collaborative team.

- *Taking Action* reference: Essential Action 2.4—Commit to Team Norms, p. 63

■ **"Tool: Developing Specific Actions to Address the Needs of Our Peers"** (page 73)—The most common mistake that teams make when writing norms is generating vague statements that leave room for individual interpretation. Norms like *be on time* and *be respectful* are ineffective because notions of punctuality and respect vary among individuals. Effective norms outline *specific* actions teams will take to address common behaviors that are interrupting productive group work. Use this tool and its corresponding set of **sample answers** (page 74) to practice writing better norms.

- *Taking Action* reference: Essential Action 2.4—Commit to Team Norms, p. 63

■ **"Tool: Addressing the Three Common Reasons for Resistance to Change"** (page 76)—In *Time for Change: Four Essential Skills for Transformational School and District Leaders*, school change experts Anthony Muhammad and Luis F. Cruz (2019) argue that successful change efforts require leaders to make cognitive, emotional, and functional investments in faculty members. Doing so addresses the three primary reasons that reasonable people resist change: (1) they struggle to understand the why behind new change efforts, (2) previous negative experiences influence their readiness to move forward with new change efforts, or (3) they lack the skills necessary to successfully implement new change efforts (Muhammad & Cruz, 2019). Use this tool to identify faculty members in need of additional cognitive, emotional, or functional investments and to develop a plan for moving people forward.

- *Taking Action* reference: Essential Action 2.5—Prepare for Staff Resistance, p. 69

■ **"Tool: Rating Your Readiness for Our New Initiative"** (page 78)—Providing differentiated support to teachers struggling with change efforts begins by collecting information on each staff member's readiness. School leaders need to know that they have successfully communicated the rationale behind the change initiative and provided a detailed and doable plan for how the change initiative will be implemented. Use this survey to gather that information from your faculty.

- *Taking Action* reference: Essential Action 2.5—Prepare for Staff Resistance, p. 69

- **"Tool: Does Your School Have an Avoid-at-All-Costs List?"** (online only)—For investor Warren Buffett (as cited in Frontier Research, 2015), success in any endeavor is a matter of prioritization, and struggles are a direct result of an inability to focus on important outcomes. Experienced educators understand that the inability to prioritize is often the root cause of resistance to school change efforts. Skeptical teachers who have been asked to invest in too many ideas for far too long may view chasing new initiatives as nothing more than wasted time. To focus energies on a small handful of priorities, Buffett recommends creating an avoid-at-all-costs list—a process that your school can replicate using this tool.
  - *Taking Action* reference: Essential Action 2.5—Prepare for Staff Resistance, p. 69

Conclusion

Odds are that readers of *The Big Book of Tools for RTI at Work* already acknowledge that the implementation of systematic interventions is not merely an option for schools, but a necessity. No matter how effective our initial instruction is, there will always be students who need additional time and support for learning. It is essential to remember, however, that implementing systematic interventions is not solely about addressing the needs of struggling students. It requires that school leaders build a culture of collective responsibility that unites the entire school community.

Building and sustaining that culture of collective responsibility starts by developing a guiding coalition—a group of dedicated individuals equipped with the skills necessary to navigate the challenges that change inevitably brings. Working with school administrators, the guiding coalition uses evidence gathered from observing school processes and practices to identify strengths, weaknesses, opportunities, and threats within the school environment and to develop systematic, intentional plans for moving collaborative teams, individual teachers, and students forward.

Building and sustaining that culture of collective responsibility also depends on the collective efforts of three critical school-based teams—(1) the guiding coalition, (2) the intervention team, and (3) collaborative teacher teams. Each of these teams accepts lead responsibility for a different set of essential actions necessary for successful implementation of systematic interventions. Schools that "work hard and succeed" (Mattos et al., 2025, p. 312) carefully articulate these responsibilities and ensure that all three critical teams are working intentionally to do the right work together.

The tools presented in this chapter offer a road map for leaders and educators seeking to establish a culture of collective responsibility. From crafting effective mission statements to developing teacher teams that collaborate seamlessly, each tool serves as a compass, guiding educational communities toward the shared goal of providing every student with the support necessary to thrive. Use them to evaluate your readiness, adapt your approaches, and envision a future where everyone believes in the power and potential of interventions that are seamlessly integrated into the fabric of the school day.

Resources Designed to
Establish a Culture of Collective Responsibility

Tool: Building Your Guiding Coalition

Taking Action *reference: Essential Action 2.1—Establish a Guiding Coalition, p. 30*

Instructions: Review the four types of organizational power that should be represented in your guiding coalition. Then, use the quadrants at the end of the tool to identify faculty members with the right leadership skills to drive change in your building.

Members of your guiding coalition should have four essential types of organizational power.

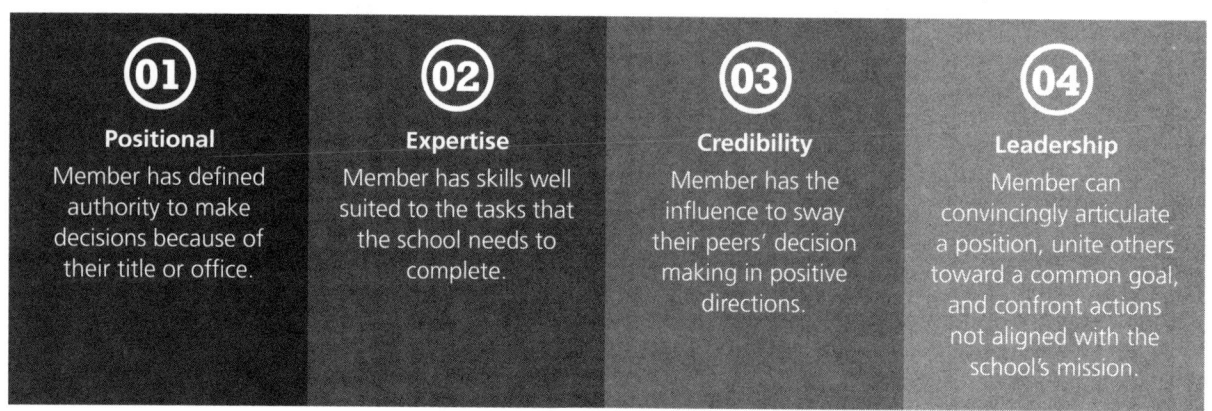

01 Positional — Member has defined authority to make decisions because of their title or office.

02 Expertise — Member has skills well suited to the tasks that the school needs to complete.

03 Credibility — Member has the influence to sway their peers' decision making in positive directions.

04 Leadership — Member can convincingly articulate a position, unite others toward a common goal, and confront actions not aligned with the school's mission.

Source: Kotter, J. P. (1996). Leading change. Boston: Harvard Business School Press.

In the following quadrants, identify the members of your guiding coalition who possess each of the four types of organizational power identified by John Kotter (1996, 2012) in his seminal book Leading Change.

The following members of our guiding coalition possess **positional** power:	The following members of our guiding coalition possess the **expertise** needed to complete our work:

page 1 of 2

The following members of our guiding coalition have the **credibility** necessary to influence their peers:	The following members of our guiding coalition have the **leadership** necessary to unite others:

Questions for Reflection

What patterns do you notice in the current composition of your guiding coalition?

How will those patterns affect—either positively or negatively—the work of our guiding coalition?

Based on the patterns that you notice, what changes do you need to make to your guiding coalition?

What members of your faculty would be good additions to your guiding coalition? Why?

Source: Adapted from Mattos, M., Buffum, A., Malone, J., Cruz, L. F., Dimich, N., & Schuhl, S. (2025). Taking action: A handbook for RTI at Work (2nd ed.). Bloomington, IN: Solution Tree Press.

References

Kotter, J. P. (1996). *Leading change*. Boston: Harvard Business School Press.

Kotter, J. P. (2012). *Leading change*. Boston: Harvard Business Review Press.

Tool: Ten Considerations for the Guiding Coalition

Taking Action *reference: Essential Action 2.1—Establish a Guiding Coalition, p. 30*

Instructions: Read each consideration from the **Guiding Coalition Considerations** column. Reflect on your current reality and write the appropriate number from the rating scale in the **Rating** column. The third column can be used to record evidence of considerations currently in place or to record the next steps for considerations that are not currently or partially in place.

Date of Review	
School	

Rating Scale: 1—Not in place, 2—Partially in place, 3—In place

Guiding Coalition Considerations Note that these tasks may be conducted by a subset of the guiding coalition.	Rating	Evidence This Consideration Is in Place or Steps to Address Implementation
The guiding coalition has led the work of establishing a school mission, vision, collective commitments, and school goals.		
The guiding coalition ensures that all certified staff serve on a collaborative team and that the teams have a regular meeting schedule.		
The guiding coalition ensures that all certified staff understand the three big ideas and the four critical questions of PLCs, laying the foundation for further action.		
The guiding coalition ensures that staff have the understanding and tools to utilize the teaching-assessing-learning cycle.		
The guiding coalition ensures that the school schedule allows students to access all three tiers of intervention without sacrificing one tier of support for another.		

The guiding coalition ensures that schoolwide academic and social behaviors are explicitly taught and monitored.		
The guiding coalition ensures that an intervention team is established to support interventions that are outside the scope of teacher teams.		
The guiding coalition ensures that a referral process is in place for staff to request support for students they believe, via evidence, need tiered support managed by the intervention team or other schoolwide personnel.		
The guiding coalition ensures that all staff have an operational understanding of RTI and how they can best serve students within the model. **Sample:** *Teachers know how to appropriately deliver Tier 2 academic interventions.*		
The guiding coalition has a system to monitor RTI implementation effectiveness schoolwide in order to celebrate successes and address needs.		

Notes:

Tool: Analysis and Action Planning Template for Guiding Coalitions

Taking Action *reference: Essential Action 2.1—Establish a Guiding Coalition, p. 30*

School Name:

Instructions: To move a school forward, guiding coalitions must remain focused on both distributed leadership and the three big ideas of the PLC at Work process. Using the key indicators detailed on pages 3–6 of this tool, analyze your work in each of these four leadership domains. Then, use the following tables to create an action plan to advise your guiding coalition's next steps.

Review the key indicators for each of the four leadership domains on pages 3–6 of this tool. Identify the strengths and weaknesses of your school's current work in each domain.

Leadership Domain	What Are Your Current Strengths and Weaknesses in Each Domain?
Distributed Leadership	
Focus on Learning	
Focus on Collaboration	
Focus on Results	

Our First Semester Priorities:

What three key indicators will be your guiding coalition's *top priorities* for the first semester?

Key Indicators List the leadership domain and the key indicator.	What Needs to Happen to Be Successful in This Indicator? List action steps that will be taken to grow in this area.
Note: It is not necessary to list action steps from all four of the leadership domains. It is possible that you might have three indicators from one domain that your guiding coalition would like to focus on first.	

Our Second Semester Priorities:

What three key indicators will be your guiding coalition's *top priorities* for the second semester?

Key Indicators List the leadership domain and the key indicator.	What Needs to Happen to Be Successful in This Indicator? List action steps that will be taken to grow in this area.
Note: These priorities may change over the course of the first semester—and that's OK. The goal here is to think forward and identify potential growth opportunities, even if those growth opportunities end up changing later.	

Source: Adapted from Chiprany, D. T., & Page, P. (2025). Celebrating in a PLC at Work: A leader's guide to building collective efficacy and high-performing collaborative teams. Bloomington, IN: Solution Tree Press.

Key Leadership Indicators for Guiding Coalitions

Instructions: Key indicators for each leadership domain are detailed in the following tables. Work with your guiding coalition to review these indicators and rate your current reality by circling the number in the **Your Rating** column. Then, use your ratings to complete the action planning template found on pages 1–2 of this tool.

Rating Scale: 1—Not evident, 2—In progress, 3—Embedded in our culture

Domain: Distributed Leadership

"Those who hope to lead the PLC process must begin by acknowledging that no one person will have the energy, expertise, and influence to lead a complex change process until it becomes anchored in the organization's culture without first gaining the support of key staff members" (DuFour et al., 2024, p. 35).

Your Rating	Key Indicator	Next Steps
1 2 3	**L1. Building Collective Teacher Efficacy** The guiding coalition members share the belief that we have the skills and empowerment to positively impact collaborative teams.	
1 2 3	**L2. Supporting the PLC Culture** The guiding coalition is the catalyst for the PLC process. We have a mission, vision, and collective commitments that drive our work.	
1 2 3	**L3. Being Willing and Able** The guiding coalition members have a passion for PLC work and the skill set to implement the "right work."	
1 2 3	**L4. Holding Resisters Accountable** The guiding coalition has a process in place for members to address and hold accountable staff members who resist the PLC process.	
1 2 3	**L5. Clarifying Loose and Tight PLC Expectations** The guiding coalition members know the five "tight" PLC characteristics and understand how to use the "loose" characteristics to build collective teacher efficacy.	
1 2 3	**L6. Monitoring the PLC Process** The guiding coalition fosters a culture that has a clear monitoring plan to determine which collaborative teams are functioning at a high level and which teams need assistance in learning, collaboration, or results.	
1 2 3	**L7. Celebrating the Right Work** The guiding coalition recognizes staff for the "right work" in learning, collaboration, and results.	

Domain: Focus on Learning				
"When a school or district functions as a PLC, educators within the organization embrace high levels of learning for all students as both the reason the organization exists and the fundamental responsibility of those who work within it" (DuFour et al., 2024, p. 18).				
Your Rating			Key Indicator	Next Steps
1	2	3	**FL1. Implementing and Monitoring the Teaching-Assessing-Learning Cycle** The guiding coalition monitors collaborative teams to ensure the use of the teaching-assessing-learning cycle as the unit plan for all essential learning. Collaborative teams do the following. • Screen for prior skills • Use common formative assessments • Give common end-of-unit or summative assessments • Use common end-of-unit or summative assessment proficiency data to assign students to Tier 2 interventions, extensions, or enrichment	
1	2	3	**FL2. Identifying Essential Standards** The guiding coalition monitors collaborative teams to ensure teams have identified all essential learning for the subject or course.	
1	2	3	**FL3. Identifying Learning Targets** The guiding coalition monitors collaborative teams to ensure teams have identified all learning targets associated with the essential learning.	
1	2	3	**FL4. Aligning Instructional Rigor With Proficiency Levels** The guiding coalition monitors collaborative teams to ensure there is evidence that students are exposed to quality, rigorous tasks that allow them to do the following. • Problem solve and communicate effectively, both orally and through writing • Analyze and evaluate information • Show understanding through choice	
1	2	3	**FL5. Extending Learning for Proficient Students** The guiding coalition monitors collaborative teams to ensure students who show proficiency on the common formative assessment, the common end-of-unit or summative assessment, or both have opportunities for extension or enrichment.	

Establish a Culture of Collective Responsibility — F

Domain: Focus on Collaboration		
"The second big idea driving the PLC process is that in order to ensure all students learn at high levels, *educators must work collaboratively and take collective responsibility for the success of each student*" (DuFour et al., 2024, p. 18).		
Your Rating	Key Indicator	Next Steps
1 2 3	**C1. Monitoring High-Functioning Collaborative Teams** The guiding coalition monitors collaborative teams to ensure the following. • The team has a facilitator. • The team has established roles. • The team has established norms. • The agendas for the next meeting are available in advance. • The team works interdependently while committing to teaching every student throughout the collaborative process. • The teachers use student data to adjust student instruction and to improve teaching practices.	
1 2 3	**C2. Committing to a Guaranteed and Viable Curriculum** The guiding coalition monitors to ensure collaborative team members commit to a guaranteed and viable curriculum for *all* students.	
1 2 3	**C3. Identifying and Monitoring SMART Goals** The guiding coalition monitors school SMART goals to focus on students' results. The goals are monitored and used to set the direction for teachers to improve student achievement in a targeted area.	
1 2 3	**C4. Understanding the Characteristics of a High-Functioning Team** The guiding coalition trains all instructional staff in the characteristics of a high-functioning team and monitors all collaborative teams to ensure they progress toward becoming high functioning.	
1 2 3	**C5. Identifying High-Functioning Collaborative Teams** The guiding coalition actively seeks to identify collaborative teams who meet the high-functioning team characteristics.	
1 2 3	**C6. Supporting Future High-Functioning Teams** The guiding coalition provides support and professional development for all collaborative teams to continue progressing toward becoming a high-functioning collaborative team.	

Domain: Focus on Results				
"To assess their effectiveness in helping all students learn, educators in a PLC focus on results—evidence of student learning. They then use the evidence of learning to inform and improve their professional practice and respond to individual students" (DuFour et al., 2024, p. 19).				
Your Rating			Key Indicator	Next Steps
1	2	3	**R1. Using Data to Define Greatest Area of Need and Immediate Feedback for Real-Time Instruction** The guiding coalition monitors collaborative teams to ensure they use multiple common formative assessments to identify specific preventions or extensions by learning targets for individual students.	
1	2	3	**R2. Creating and Implementing Common End-of-Unit or Summative Assessments Using Backward Design** The guiding coalition monitors collaborative teams to ensure they create a common end-of-unit or summative assessment before determining instructional practices and pacing.	
1	2	3	**R3. Monitoring Common Assessments** The guiding coalition monitors common end-of-unit or summative assessment data to identify which collaborative teams to celebrate or provide support to for student success.	
1	2	3	**R4. Identifying Response to Intervention for Tier 2 and Tier 3** The guiding coalition ensures collaborative teams use a common end-of-unit or summative assessment to identify Tier 2 students who did not meet proficiency. The guiding coalition uses a universal screener and diagnostic assessments to identify students for Tier 3 reinforcement.	
1	2	3	**R5. Addressing Students Needing Behavior Supports Within Tier 2** The guiding coalition has established a schoolwide team of experts to work with Tier 2 students who are not proficient on common assessments due to behavior issues.	
1	2	3	**R6. Addressing Tier 3 Students With an Intervention Team** The guiding coalition has established a schoolwide team of experts to work with Tier 3 students.	
1	2	3	**R7. Measuring Response to Intervention Success** The guiding coalition regularly monitors RTI data to measure the success of the Tier 2 and Tier 3 RTI programs. Data include percentage of students entering Tier 2 (less than 20 percent) and Tier 3 (less than 5 percent) and the percentage of students exiting Tier 2 and Tier 3.	

Source: Key indicators adapted from Chiprany, D. T., & Page, P. (2025). Celebrating in a PLC at Work: A leader's guide to building collective efficacy and high-performing collaborative teams. Bloomington, IN: Solution Tree Press.

Reference

DuFour, R., DuFour, R., Eaker, R., Many, T. W., Mattos, M., & Muhammad, A. (2024). *Learning by doing: A handbook for Professional Learning Communities at Work* (4th ed.). Bloomington, IN: Solution Tree Press.

Tool: Using Faculty Survey Data to Target the Work of Guiding Coalitions

Taking Action *reference: Essential Action 2.1—Establish a Guiding Coalition, p. 30*

Instructions: Our guiding coalition conducts an annual evaluation regarding the effectiveness of our system of intervention. To facilitate this evaluation, we are asking for feedback from all faculty members. Please respond to each survey question using the following scale.

Rating Scale: 1—Not at all, 2—A little, 3—Somewhat, 4—Mostly, 5—Absolutely

Survey Question	Your Response (Circle one.)
My collaborative team effectively answers **the first critical question of learning**: What do we want students to know and be able to do? (Determining essential standards, learning targets, common proficiency, scope and sequence planning)	1 2 3 4 5
My collaborative team effectively answers **the second critical question of learning**: How will we know if each student has learned it? (Common end-of-unit assessments, common formative assessments, collaborative scoring, collaborative data analysis)	1 2 3 4 5
My collaborative team effectively answers **the third critical question of learning**: How will we respond when some students do not learn it? (Reteaching Tier 1, Tier 2 grouping and instruction, planning for additional time and support, modifying instruction)	1 2 3 4 5
My collaborative team effectively answers **the fourth critical question of learning**: How will we extend learning for students who have demonstrated proficiency? (Extension and enrichment in Tier 1, Tier 2 grouping and instruction, planning for deeper learning opportunities, modifying instruction)	1 2 3 4 5
My school or site effectively delivers tiered social, emotional, and behavioral interventions using the resources that we have.	1 2 3 4 5
My school or site effectively delivers tiered academic interventions using the resources that we have.	1 2 3 4 5
Comments:	

Tool: Analyzing Faculty Survey on the Work of Guiding Coalitions

Taking Action *reference: Essential Action 2.1—Establish a Guiding Coalition, p. 30*

Instructions: Once all faculty members have completed the faculty survey on the effectiveness of your system of interventions (page 45), use the following chart to analyze the results. In the **Percentage of Respondents** row for each survey question, specify the percentage of faculty members who assigned each rating (1 to 5). In the **Percent Improvement** row for each survey question, indicate the percentage change in the percent of respondents who assigned that rating compared to the previous administration of the survey.* Finally, use the reflection questions at the end of this tool to inform your next actions.

Leave this row blank if this is the first time the survey has been administered.

School:				Date:		
Survey Question	**Data**	**1**	**2**	**3**	**4**	**5**
My collaborative team effectively answers **the first critical question of learning**: What do we want students to know and be able to do? *(Determining essential standards, learning targets, common proficiency, scope and sequence planning)*	Percentage of respondents					
	Percent improvement					
My collaborative team effectively answers **the second critical question of learning**: How will we know if each student has learned it? *(Common end-of-unit assessments, common formative assessments, collaborative scoring, collaborative data analysis)*	Percentage of respondents					
	Percent improvement					
My collaborative team effectively answers **the third critical question of learning**: How will we respond when some students do not learn it? *(Reteaching Tier 1, Tier 2 grouping and instruction, planning for additional time and support, modifying instruction)*	Percentage of respondents					
	Percent improvement					
My collaborative team effectively answers **the fourth critical question of learning**: How will we extend learning for students who have demonstrated proficiency? *(Extension and enrichment in Tier 1, Tier 2 grouping and instruction, planning for deeper learning opportunities, modifying instruction)*	Percentage of respondents					
	Percent improvement					

Survey Question	Data	1	2	3	4	5
My school or site effectively delivers tiered social, emotional, and behavioral interventions using the resources that we have.	Percentage of respondents					
	Percent improvement					
My school or site effectively delivers tiered academic interventions using the resources that we have.	Percentage of respondents					
	Percent improvement					

Where can we find **areas of significant improvement** in our survey results? *Consider the following.* • *Are there any survey questions with growth in the percentage of responses of a 4 or 5?* • *Are there any survey questions with a decrease in the percentage of responses of a 1 or 2?* • *Are there any survey questions with greater than 80 percent of respondents indicating a 4 or 5?* • *Are there any survey questions with less than 20 percent of respondents indicating a 1 or 2?*	
Where can we find **areas of continued challenge** in our survey results? *Consider the following.* • *Are there any survey questions with a decrease in the percentage of responses of a 4 or 5?* • *Are there any survey questions with an increase in the percentage of responses of a 1 or 2?* • *Are there any survey questions with less than 50 percent of respondents indicating a 4 or 5?* • *Are there any survey questions with more than 50 percent of respondents indicating a 1 or 2?*	

Establish a Culture of Collective Responsibility

| How will we **celebrate results** and **address challenges**?
Consider the following.
• How will we share data with the faculty?
• What action steps will we take because of the survey?
• How will we communicate these action steps to the faculty?
• How will we gather additional input from faculty members, including on our action plans? | |

Tool: Planning a Cycle of Inquiry for Guiding Coalitions

Taking Action *reference: Essential Action 2.1—Establish a Guiding Coalition, p. 30*

Instructions: Working with your guiding coalition, identify one essential that you want collaborative teams to master. Then, use team-centered versions of the four critical questions of learning to develop a plan for teaching your identified essential to collaborative teams. Record your plan in the following table.

One Essential That We Want Collaborative Teams to Master Is:	
What is it that we want teams to know and be able to do with this essential? What is our plan for teaching this essential to teams?	How will we assess team progress toward mastery of this essential?
What actions will we take when a team struggles to master our essentials?	What actions will we take when a team is prepared to extend its work beyond mastery of our essentials?

The Big Book of Tools for RTI at Work © 2025 Solution Tree Press • SolutionTree.com
Visit **go.SolutionTree.com/RTIatWork/BBTRTI** to download this free reproducible.

Sample: Planning a Cycle of Inquiry for Guiding Coalitions

Taking Action *reference*: Essential Action 2.1—Establish a Guiding Coalition, p. 30

Instructions: Working with your guiding coalition, identify one essential that you want collaborative teams to master. Then, use team-centered versions of the four critical questions of learning to develop a plan for teaching your identified essential to collaborative teams. Record your plan in the following table.

One Essential That We Want Collaborative Teams to Master Is: Using data to inform both instruction and intervention decisions	
What is it that we want teams to know and be able to do with this essential? What is our plan for teaching this essential to teams? • We want teams to know how to develop a common assessment that will give them reliable information about both teaching and learning. • We want teams to have a protocol to use to guide their conversations about data. • We want teams to have a tool for organizing data sets and recording their learning when analyzing data. • We want teams to recognize that assessment data can give information about both the efficacy of teams' instructional practices and individual students' level of mastery. • We want teams to know that analyzing data isn't about finding effective teachers. Instead, it's about finding effective practices. To teach these essentials, we will do the following. • Select protocols and tools for teams to use when analyzing data • Show a video from Global PD Teams (www.solutiontree.com/globalpdteams) that shows a team analyzing data • Develop a plan for celebrating moments when teams succeed at analyzing data	How will we assess team progress toward mastery of this essential? • We will develop a proficiency scale describing the use of data on collaborative teacher teams. • We will have guiding coalition members on each team use the proficiency scale to give teams initial ratings on their use of data. • We will revisit these initial ratings in our guiding coalition meetings. • We will use our proficiency scale to identify the needs of each individual team, and then address those needs in upcoming grade-level meetings. • We will have our instructional facilitator conduct additional observations of team-based data meetings each quarter.
What actions will we take when a team struggles to master our essentials? While our individual actions will depend on the specific struggles each team is having, we can try some of the following strategies. • We will have the instructional facilitator lead data meetings until teams have well-established routines. • We will give teams sample data sets to analyze before asking them to analyze their own data. • We will encourage teams to begin data analysis efforts with short (three to five questions) common assessments. • We will have high-performing teams conduct a data meeting during a faculty meeting that we can use as a "fishbowl" task for other teams.	What actions will we take when a team is prepared to extend its work beyond mastery of our essentials? • We will encourage teams to experiment with different assessment strategies. • We will encourage teams to create intentional variations of a strategy they believe in and to document which variation worked the best. • We will encourage teams to create a catalog of practices that they know work for different student populations (multilingual learners, students receiving special education services, struggling readers, students on the autism spectrum, introverts, extroverts) in their classes.

Tool: Using AI Tools to Support Collaborative Team Development

Taking Action *reference: Essential Action 2.1—Establish a Guiding Coalition, p. 30*

Instructions: Using an AI chatbot like ChatGPT (https://chat.openai.com) or Gemini (https://gemini.google.com), work with your guiding coalition to develop a shared understanding of a collaborative skill or behavior by posing the prompts in the first column of the following table. Then, assess its responses for accuracy and summarize its thinking in the second column. Remember that you should never rely on AI chatbots for original thinking. Instead, use AI chatbots to give you something to think about. Doing so will accelerate your guiding coalition's work, giving you more time to engage in meaningful conversations.

Collaborative Skill or Behavior We Are Writing a Proficiency Scale For:	
Start a new chat in an AI chatbot. Then, ask these prompts in order.	**Together, review the AI chatbot's response for accuracy. Summarize its thinking here.**
I am evaluating *[collaborative skill or behavior]* on collaborative teacher teams. List five core behaviors that I should be looking for. *Sample: I am evaluating the use of data to inform instruction and intervention on collaborative teacher teams. List five core behaviors that I should be looking for.*	
Can you list the common mistakes that collaborative teacher teams make when they are *[collaborative skill or behavior]*? *Sample: Can you list the common mistakes that collaborative teacher teams make when they are trying to use data to inform instruction and intervention?*	
Can you write a proficiency scale describing the effective use of *[collaborative skill or behavior]* on collaborative teams? *Sample: Can you write a proficiency scale describing the effective use of data to inform instruction and intervention on collaborative teams?*	
Can you give me three activities I can use to teach collaborative teacher teams how to *[collaborative skill or behavior]*? *Sample: Can you give me three activities I can use to teach collaborative teacher teams how to use data to inform instruction and intervention?*	

Survey: Rating Our Readiness for RTI

Taking Action reference: Essential Action 2.2—Build a Culture of Collective Responsibility, p. 40

Instructions: Our guiding coalition is gathering information about our current reality in preparation for our upcoming implementation of a system of interventions in our building. Please complete the following survey to help with those efforts. Your responses will help us plan meaningful next steps for our faculty's intervention efforts.

Teacher Name:	Grade Level and Department:

Rate Your Level of Agreement With the Following Statements

1. A student's ability to succeed in school is influenced by their aptitudes and inherent abilities.

Strongly Disagree	1	2	3	4	5	Strongly Agree

2. Circumstances beyond the school's control (such as poverty, lack of parental support, and unsafe communities) prevent some students from succeeding.

Strongly Disagree	1	2	3	4	5	Strongly Agree

3. All students want to succeed in school.

Strongly Disagree	1	2	3	4	5	Strongly Agree

4. It is the school's responsibility to ensure that all students learn academic skills and content.

Strongly Disagree	1	2	3	4	5	Strongly Agree

5. It is the school's responsibility to ensure that all students learn behaviors like responsibility, respect, and motivation.

Strongly Disagree	1	2	3	4	5	Strongly Agree

6. Students learn at higher levels when they are grouped by ability.

Strongly Disagree	1	2	3	4	5	Strongly Agree

7. Our school needs more special education support for struggling students.

Strongly Disagree	1	2	3	4	5	Strongly Agree

8. What is the greatest barrier to helping more students learn at higher levels in our school?

Tool: Reflecting on Our Faculty's Readiness for RTI

Taking Action *reference: Essential Action 2.2—Build a Culture of Collective Responsibility, p. 40*

Instructions: The guiding coalition's job is to design systematic plans to create the right cultural conditions for learning in a school building. While reviewing your faculty's responses to "Survey: Rating Our Readiness for RTI" (page 52), use the following reflection questions to identify any cultural gaps that must be addressed before implementing your school's system of interventions.

Questions for Reflection

What patterns can we spot in the responses that we have received to this survey?

Why do those patterns exist here in our school?

What impact will those patterns have on our efforts to implement an effective system of interventions?

What actions must we take to build a stronger cultural foundation for our RTI efforts?

Tool: Evaluating Our Mission Statement

Taking Action *reference: Essential Action 2.2—Build a Culture of Collective Responsibility, p. 40*

Instructions: Work with your guiding coalition to review your school's mission statement. Use the questions in the first column to guide your discussion. Record your reactions, reflections, and next actions in the second column.

Our School's Mission Statement:	
Questions to Consider	**Our Responses**
What makes our mission statement unique from other schools in our district and state? A mission statement answers the question, Why do we exist? It is essential for setting direction and growing investment in a building's faculty. As such, it must be more than a general slogan filled with platitudes that teachers will largely ignore. <ul><li>What parts of our mission statement can generate commitment from our classroom teachers?</li><li>What parts of our mission statement are too generic to generate commitment from our classroom teachers?</li><li>If we put our mission statement alongside mission statements from other schools, could our teachers identify which was ours?</li></ul>	
How do our teachers feel about our mission statement? If a mission statement is going to drive actions by this building's educators, it must share sentiments that teachers can embrace and believe in. <ul><li>Can our teachers clearly articulate our mission statement?</li><li>Can our teachers explain how our mission statement is unique?</li><li>Can our teachers explain how achieving our mission statement will benefit our students?</li><li>How do our teachers demonstrate a commitment—or a lack thereof—to our mission in both their words and actions?</li><li>Do we see a difference in commitment to our mission across grade levels or departments? What explains those differences and how will we address them?</li></ul>	

What actions would we have to take to deliver on the promises articulated in our mission statement?

Mission statements are only practical tools for building commitment in educators when every action and decision a school makes connects to ideas expressed in the mission. Stated differently, actions and decisions disconnected from the mission undermine efforts to build faculty commitment to a shared direction.

- How would we act differently if we were to deliver on the promises in our mission statement?
- Would there be changes in the way we deliver instruction, build our master schedule, or assign teachers and students?
- Would there be changes in the way we allocate resources, make purchases, or spend our professional development time?
- What actions have we taken recently to advance our mission? Have we clearly articulated to our teachers the connections between those decisions and advancing our mission?
- What actions have we taken recently that prevent us from advancing our mission? How can we revise, rethink, or replace those decisions?

Source: Questions adapted from Blount, S., & Leinwand, P. (2019). Why are we here? Accessed at https://hbr.org/2019/11/why-are-we-here on March 21, 2023.

Tool: Developing Collective Commitments

Taking Action *reference*: Essential Action 2.2—Build a Culture of Collective Responsibility, p. 40

Instructions: The guiding coalition should complete the two steps detailed in this tool to develop collective commitments that define necessary community member actions to advance the school's mission.

Step 1: List Your Mission Statement

Collective commitments are the specific actions community members must take to fulfill your school's mission. Everyone needs to know exactly what your mission statement says to write collective commitments.

Step 2: Develop Collective Commitments

Now, develop a series of *we will* statements describing how individual members of your school community would have to act to fulfill your school's mission.

Question	Sample	Your Response (Formatted as *we will* statements)
What would our **interactions with one another** need to look like if we were going to fulfill our mission statement?	We will see one another as partners to learn from rather than peers to compete with.	

What would our **collaborative work** need to look like if we were going to fulfill our mission statement?	We will adopt a spirit of inquiry in our collaborative work, committed to flunking unsuccessful practices together.	
What would our **instruction** need to look like if we were going to fulfill our mission statement?	We will encourage experimentation with instructional practices until we identify strategies that help more students learn at higher levels.	
What would our **use of data** need to look like if we were going to fulfill our mission statement?	We will see data as evidence of our instruction's efficacy instead of as evidence of individual teachers' effectiveness.	
What **core beliefs** would we have to hold if we were going to fulfill our mission statement?	We will believe in the ability of every student to learn at the highest levels.	

Tips for Writing Collective Commitments

- **Limit your total number of collective commitments:** While there is no right number of collective commitments for your school, limiting your entire list to eight to ten items ensures that you are prioritizing only the most essential behaviors. What's more, people are more likely to lean into a smaller number of promises than they are to lean into a long list of promises that are difficult for everyone to maintain.

- **Write every collective commitment as a *we will* statement:** Doing so turns your collective commitment into a specific action that people will take to move your mission forward—and specific actions are exactly what collective commitments are supposed to be.

- **Regularly review your collective commitments:** Collective commitments are only helpful when they begin to drive the day-to-day actions of your faculty members. It would be best if you built regular opportunities to revisit your collective commitments into the ongoing work of your teams and faculty. Celebrate people and teacher teams you see honoring your commitments and care enough to confront people and teams violating them.

Tool: Site-Based Teams Aligned to the RTI at Work Process

Taking Action *reference: Essential Action 2.2—Build a Culture of Collective Responsibility, p. 40*

To create effective intervention systems, schools must establish several teams with dedicated responsibilities for moving intervention efforts forward. This tool can be used to develop a deeper understanding of the needed teams and their critical roles in implementing the RTI at Work process. In addition, this tool provides users with an implementation continuum to evaluate their current reality.

Instructions: Read the description for each site-based team aligned to the RTI at Work process. Then, use the **Implementation Continuum** table found on page 2 of this tool to rate the work done by each site-based team in your building. Doing so will provide you with an understanding of your site's current reality.

Team	Description
Guiding Coalition	"A guiding coalition is an alliance of key members of an organization who are specifically charged with leading a change process through predictable turmoil. Members of the coalition should include opinion leaders—people who are so respected within the organization that others are likely to follow their lead" (Mattos et al., 2016, p. 21). **The guiding coalition does the following.** • Meets regularly to support the school's mission, vision, collective commitments, and goals • Has a deep understanding of the PLC process and can support and lead that work • Is not simply a team of representatives that gets or disseminates information

Intervention Team	An intervention team serves to diagnose, target, prioritize, and monitor students' intervention needs beyond the expertise of a content-area teacher or collaborative team. This includes providing struggling students with behavioral and academic support (Mattos et al., 2025).
	The intervention team does the following.
	• Meets regularly and is made up of specialists or those with expertise
	• Maintains a focus on the following essential functions:
	  • Identifies students needing intensive support in social-emotional learning, behaviors (Tier 2 and 3), or academics (Tier 3) using relevant data
	  • Determines specific interventions and establishes intervention goals for each student, prioritizing resources based on greatest needs
	  • Establishes and utilizes a student referral process, allowing staff to recommend students to the school intervention team for consideration and support
	  • Regularly monitors intervention success at the student level using relevant data
	  • Makes intervention adjustments (entrance, exit, and intensity) based on need during and after intervention cycles
	  • Assesses the effectiveness of interventions offered and learns from, celebrates, and adjusts interventions based on those assessments

Tier 1 Behavior Team	The Tier 1 behavior team, which may be a subset of the guiding coalition, focuses on a schoolwide system of support and prevention regarding students' behavioral and social needs (Hannigan, Hannigan, Mattos, & Buffum, 2021). **The Tier 1 behavior team does the following.** • Meets regularly and comprises a general representation of the faculty • Establishes the expectations for student academic and behavioral skills • Develops plans to ensure that each student and teacher understands the expectations

	• Monitors data at least monthly to gauge success, develop a current problem statement, and devise a plan to address the current problem statement; this may include targeted reteaching
Collaborative Teacher Teams	"The collaborative team is made up of educators who share students or content and who work interdependently to achieve common SMART goals for which members are mutually accountable" (Mattos et al., 2016, p. 38). **The collaborative teacher team does the following.** • Meets weekly (or as frequently as possible when there are special circumstances) • Has a common SMART goal that will impact educator practice and student achievement • Utilizes the four critical questions of a PLC and the teaching-assessing-learning cycle to conduct cycles of inquiry around grade-level essential standards

Implementation Continuum

Team	Learning	Planning	Implementing	Refining
Guiding Coalition	We do not have this team in place, but we are learning about its roles and responsibilities.	We do not have this team in place, but we are laying the groundwork to establish it.	We have this team in place and are focusing on developing our processes.	This team is in place and focuses on small adjustments to maximize its effectiveness.
Intervention Team	We do not have this team in place, but we are learning about its roles and responsibilities.	We do not have this team in place, but we are laying the groundwork to establish it.	We have this team in place and are focusing on developing our processes.	This team is in place and focuses on small adjustments to maximize its effectiveness.
Tier 1 Behavior Team	We do not have this team in place, but we are learning about its roles and responsibilities.	We do not have this team in place, but we are laying the groundwork to establish it.	We have this team in place and are focusing on developing our processes.	This team is in place and focuses on small adjustments to maximize its effectiveness.
Collaborative Teacher Teams	We do not have this team in place, but we are learning about its roles and responsibilities.	We do not have this team in place, but we are laying the groundwork to establish it.	We have this team in place and are focusing on developing our processes.	This team is in place and focuses on small adjustments to maximize its effectiveness.

References

Hannigan, J., Hannigan, J. D., Mattos, M., & Buffum, A. (2021). *Behavior solutions: Teaching academic and social skills through RTI at Work*. Bloomington, IN: Solution Tree Press.

Mattos, M., Buffum, A., Malone, J., Cruz, L. F., Dimich, N., & Schuhl, S. (2025). *Taking action: A handbook for RTI at Work* (2nd ed.). Bloomington, IN: Solution Tree Press.

Mattos, M., DuFour, R., DuFour, R., Eaker, R., & Many, T. W. (2016). *Concise answers to frequently asked questions about Professional Learning Communities at Work*. Bloomington, IN: Solution Tree Press.

Tool: Teams Needed in RTI at Work—A Principal's Reflection

Taking Action reference: Essential Action 2.2—Build a Culture of Collective Responsibility, p. 40

Site		Principal		Date	

Instructions: Read each readiness indicator in the following table and then rate your school using the 1–3 rating scale. Use your rating to list the next steps worth taking or celebrations worth holding in the **Notes** column.

Rating Scale: 1—Not yet in place, 2—On its way, 3—In place

Descriptor	Rating	Notes
My school site has collaboratively developed and committed to the following foundations for teams to be successful. • A shared mission that provides the school's fundamental purpose • A shared vision that provides a compelling future status • A shared set of collective commitments that guide adult behaviors • A shared set of goals to target and monitor our success		
My school site has established a guiding coalition that does the following. • Meets at least monthly • Focuses on supporting the school's mission, vision, collective commitments, and goals • Has a deep understanding of the PLC and RTI processes • Supports and leads adult learning • Is not simply a team of representatives that disseminates information		

My school site has organized all certified staff into teacher teams that do the following. • Meet weekly • Have a common SMART goal that will impact adult practice and student achievement • Utilize the four critical questions of a PLC in a unit-by-unit or otherwise ongoing process through the teaching-assessing-learning cycle		
My school site has established a Tier 1 behavior team (which may be the guiding coalition or subset) that does the following. • Meets at least monthly • Is made up of a general representation of the staff • Establishes expectations for student academic and behavioral skills • Develops plans to ensure that each student and teacher understands the expectations • Uses data to monitor success, develop a current problem statement, and devise a plan to address the current problem statement		
My school site has established an intervention team that does the following. • Meets regularly • Is made up of specialists or those with relevant expertise • Focuses on diagnosing, targeting, prioritizing, and monitoring the students' intervention needs that go beyond the expertise of the individual teacher or collaborative team		

Tool: Forming Teacher Teams

Taking Action *reference:* Essential Action 2.3—Form Collaborative Teacher Teams, p. 52

Instructions: The most efficient teacher teams are composed of educators teaching students in the same grade level or subject area, but that is not the only teaming structure that can work. This tool introduces the four most common teaming structures found in schools. Use it to identify the best composition for your building's teacher teams. There is no one right structure for collaborative teams.

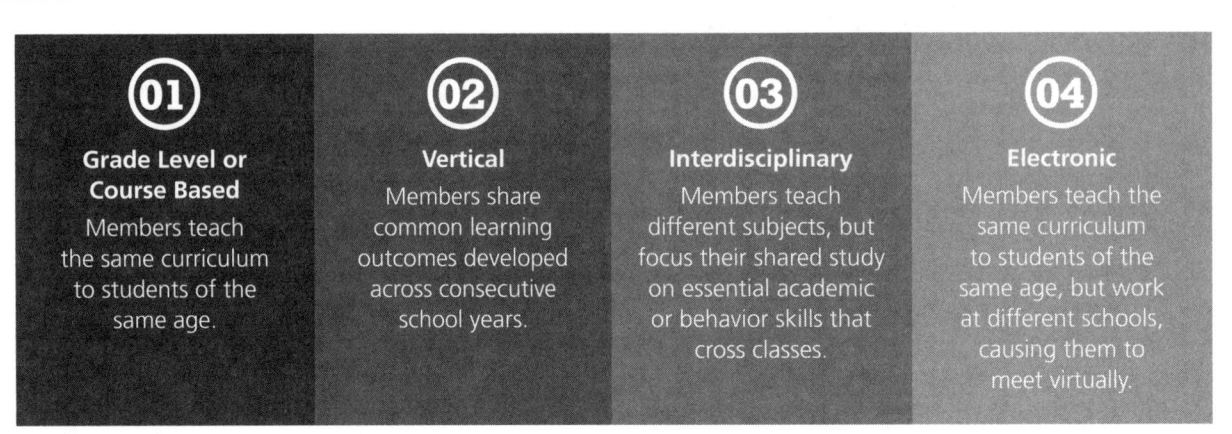

In the following quadrants, list the advantages and disadvantages of each teaming structure recommended in the diagram.

The advantages and disadvantages of **grade-level or course-based** teacher teams are:	The advantages and disadvantages of **vertical** teacher teams are:

The advantages and disadvantages of **interdisciplinary** teacher teams are:	The advantages and disadvantages of **electronic** teacher teams are:

Questions for Reflection

Which teaming structures have you already tried in your building? What were the results?

Which teaming structures would have the *greatest* impact on student learning? Which would have the *least* impact on student learning? Explain your rankings.

Which teaming structures would be the *hardest* to implement? Which would be the *easiest* to implement? Explain your rankings.

Which teaming structures would resonate the *most* with your teachers? Which would resonate the *least*? Explain your rankings.

Can you think of any additional teaming structures that might be worth considering?

Survey: Midyear Collaborative Team Check-In

Taking Action *reference: Essential Action 2.3—Form Collaborative Teacher Teams, p. 52*

Instructions: Working on your own, answer the following questions about your collaborative team's work. The information gathered here will remain confidential and be used to identify the next steps for each team in our building.

Your Name	

PLC Goal 1: Collaborative planning—*Identify and make sense of standards for the unit. Establish pacing and student learning goals.*

Indicator	Not Yet	Sometimes	Most of the Time	Consistently
We collaboratively identify the pacing of standards.	☐	☐	☐	☐
We collaboratively identify and discuss what proficiency entails for each standard.	☐	☐	☐	☐
We collaboratively identify and discuss what strategies we will use to get students to proficiency.	☐	☐	☐	☐
We collaboratively identify dates for common formative and summative assessments.	☐	☐	☐	☐

PLC Goal 2: Common formative assessment—*Develop common formative and end-of-unit assessments.*

Indicator	Not Yet	Sometimes	Most of the Time	Consistently
We collectively determine which standards are essential for common assessment.	☐	☐	☐	☐
We collectively discuss the criteria for success (proficiency) before giving an assessment.	☐	☐	☐	☐
We collectively give our common formative assessments at the same time and under the same circumstances to ensure validity.	☐	☐	☐	☐

PLC Goal 3: Reviewing our instructional practices—*Discuss the effectiveness of our instructional practices and try new practices together.*

Indicator	Not Yet	Sometimes	Most of the Time	Consistently
When planning, we collaboratively identify research-based practices to use during instruction.	☐	☐	☐	☐

Indicator	Not Yet	Sometimes	Most of the Time	Consistently
When planning, we collaboratively identify ways to differentiate and scaffold specific lessons for multilingual learners and students receiving special education services.	☐	☐	☐	☐
When planning, we discuss common misconceptions students may have *before* teaching a lesson and plan to address each one.	☐	☐	☐	☐

PLC Goal 4: Data analysis and response—*Analyze common assessment data and develop a plan to re-engage learners.*

Indicator	Not Yet	Sometimes	Most of the Time	Consistently
When disaggregating data, common formative assessments are scored the same way and use the same criteria for proficiency.	☐	☐	☐	☐
When disaggregating data, we identify students who are not yet proficient by name and need.	☐	☐	☐	☐
When disaggregating data, we discuss the effectiveness of our chosen instructional strategies based on evidence in student work samples.	☐	☐	☐	☐
After disaggregating data, we develop a plan to target students who are not yet proficient.	☐	☐	☐	☐

PLC Goal 5: Student ownership—*Students analyze data and set learning goals.*

Indicator	Not Yet	Sometimes	Most of the Time	Consistently
We collaboratively discuss how to give students feedback on assessments.	☐	☐	☐	☐
We collaboratively develop opportunities for students to fix errors on assessments and to identify what they have learned and not yet learned.	☐	☐	☐	☐
We collaboratively engage students in goal setting based on evidence of learning.	☐	☐	☐	☐

Questions for Reflection

What would you rate the work of your collaborative team on a scale from 1 to 5, where 1 represents *not very productive* and 5 represents *very productive*? Explain your rating.

What work does your collaborative team do well?

What work does your collaborative team struggle with?

What support does your collaborative team need to move your work forward?

Source: © 2022 by Lincoln Heights Middle School, Morristown, TN. Used with permission. Adapted from Kanold, T. D., Toncheff, M., Larson, M. R., Barnes, B., Kanold-McIntyre, J., & Schuhl, S. (2018). Mathematics coaching and collaboration in a PLC at Work. Bloomington, IN: Solution Tree Press; Kramer, S. V. (Ed.). (2021). Charting the course for leaders: Lessons from priority schools in a PLC at Work. Bloomington, IN: Solution Tree Press.

Tool: Team Collaboration Time—Planning Guide and Schedule

Taking Action *reference: Essential Action 2.3—Form Collaborative Teacher Teams, p. 52*

Collaborative time is essential to the PLC and RTI processes. Without it, the work is virtually impossible. It is the guiding coalition's responsibility to ensure frequent collaboration for schoolwide and teacher teams. This time should be:

- **Frequent**—Each team should meet weekly, or once every other week at a minimum.
- **Scheduled**—Meetings should last at least forty-five to sixty minutes per week.
- **Embedded**—Time must be embedded in the professional and contractual work week.

Site Collaboration Schedule

Schoolwide Teams	Time and Day	Location
Guiding coalition		
Intervention team		

Teacher Teams	Time and Day	Location

Source: Mattos, M., Buffum, A., Malone, J., Cruz, L. F., Dimich, N., & Schuhl, S. (2025). Taking action: A handbook for RTI at Work (2nd ed.). Bloomington, IN: Solution Tree Press, p. 62.

Tool: Have We Created Time for Teacher Collaborative Teams?

Taking Action *reference: Essential Action 2.3—Form Collaborative Teacher Teams, p. 52*

Instructions: Work with your school's guiding coalition to review each descriptor in the **Descriptor** column of the following table. Use the **Rating** column to assess your school's current reality. Utilize your rating to identify potential **Next Steps and Noteworthy Achievements** in the third column.

Site		Completed By		Date	

Rating Scale: 1—Not yet in place, 2—On its way, 3—In place

Descriptor	Rating	Next Steps and Noteworthy Achievements
Team Composition My school site has ensured that *all* educators are organized into logical collaborative teams including the following (DuFour et al., 2024). • **Same-course or grade-level teams** in which teachers share the same curriculum • **Vertical teams** in which teachers share content in grade levels above or below • **Electronic teams** in which teachers connect virtually with educators who are not on their site in a same-course, grade-level, or vertical team • **Interdisciplinary teams** in which teachers of differing content areas develop a common overarching goal • **Logically linked teams** in which teachers have a common goal based on their areas of expertise		
Time for Collaboration My school site has established a time for *every* team to meet each week for forty-five to sixty minutes through the following (DuFour et al., 2024). • Building a master schedule that provides **common preparation** time for teacher teams • Using **parallel scheduling** where specialists provide instruction when a team meets • **Adjusting start and end times** of the work or student day • **Sharing classes** by combining grade levels for a period of instruction, allowing a team to meet • Using group **activities, events, or testing** as an opportunity to have nonteaching staff members support students while teacher teams meet		

• **Banking time** used for instruction to open opportunities for student release • Using **in-service and faculty meeting time** for teacher teams to meet		
Clear Focus My school site has clarified the focus of collaborative team time by ensuring each team understands the following four critical questions and their associated actions (DuFour et al., 2024). • **Critical question 1:** What do we want students to know and be able to do? 　• Determine essential standards and unwrap those standards for clarity. • **Critical question 2:** How will we know if they learned it? 　• Create common assessments to monitor learning, calibrate scoring on those assessments, and analyze the data together. • **Critical question 3:** How will we respond when some students do not learn? 　• Create a team plan to support students who were not proficient on the common assessment. • **Critical question 4:** How will we extend learning for students who are already proficient? 　• Create a team plan to support students who have demonstrated proficiency on the common assessment.		
Supporting Teams My site has a plan to support collaborative team time by providing the following. • Regular opportunities for teams to reflect on their current practices and determine next steps for growth • Observational feedback to teams • Ongoing professional development to deepen understanding • Tools and resources, such as agenda templates, that teams will need to use for effective collaborative time		

Reference

DuFour, R., DuFour, R., Eaker, R., Many, T. W., Mattos, M., & Muhammad, A. (2024). *Learning by doing: A handbook for Professional Learning Communities at Work* (4th ed.). Bloomington, IN: Solution Tree Press.

Tool Overview: Developing Team Norms

Taking Action *reference: Essential Action 2.4—Commit to Team Norms, p. 63*

Instructions: According to learning community expert Daniel R. Venables (2011), developing norms can be done in two steps.

1. **Sharing pet peeves and essential traits:** Venables (2011) recommends that teams begin their norm-setting process by allowing members to share both the kinds of behaviors that drive them crazy while working in groups and the key traits that others will notice about them. He calls those our "peeves and traits." Sharing our peeves and traits early in a norm-setting process can help to make individual needs and expectations transparent to everyone.

2. **Brainstorming four to six norms:** After identifying individual members' peeves and traits, Venables (2011) recommends that teams brainstorm a list of four to six expectations that will govern the shared work of a learning team. Limiting a list of norms to fewer than six expectations accomplishes two goals: (a) it forces teams to prioritize the behaviors they hope to see from each other and (b) it makes it easier for individuals to adhere to their colleagues' expectations. Longer lists of norms quickly become irrelevant or ignored because they are impossible to remember.

Use "Tool: Commit to Team Norms" on page 71 to guide your team as you develop norms that define common patterns of participation for your collaborative work.

Reference

Venables, D. R. (2011). *The practice of authentic PLCs: A guide to effective teacher teams*. Thousand Oaks, CA: Corwin Press.

Tool: Commit to Team Norms

Taking Action *reference: Essential Action 2.4—Commit to Team Norms, p. 63*

Instructions: Use this tool to guide your team as you develop norms that define common participation patterns for your collaborative work.

Step 1: Share Our Pet Peeves and Essential Traits

Each member should share one pet peeve that they have while working in groups with others and one essential trait that others will notice while working in a group with them. These peeves and traits will be used to develop norms in step 2.

Team Member	Pet Peeve That I Have While Working in Groups With Others	Essential Trait You Will Notice While Working in Groups With Me
Sample: Bill Ferriter	**Sample:** It drives me nuts when people are on their devices while we are engaged in important conversations.	**Sample:** I make decisions quickly and am almost always ready to move on. That can drive people who need more think time crazy.

Questions for Reflection

What patterns in your own behavior are likely to bother other members of your learning team? Why?

What patterns in the behavior of other team members are likely to bother you? Why?

What are some common actions we need to take if we're going to make sure that our meetings feel productive for all our individual members?

Step 2: Brainstorm Our Norms

Now, brainstorm four to six norms that will govern the work of your learning team. Remember that norms are explicit statements that describe how your team will act in individual situations. If followed, norms should create environments that address the peeves and traits of individual members of your learning team detailed in step 1.

Team Behavior and Process	Our Norms
Making Shared Decisions **Sample:** We will use our fist-to-five rating tool to give everyone the opportunity to express their level of agreement with shared decisions.	
Handling Disagreements **Sample:** We won't move forward with important decisions until everyone has had the chance to be heard and to offer alternatives to the ideas we are considering.	
Showing Respect to One Another **Sample:** We will be active contributors in every meeting—adding thoughts, offering suggestions, and sharing our opinions.	
Structuring Our Meetings **Sample:** We will have a clear agenda for every meeting that includes no more than three items.	

Questions for Reflection

Which of our group's norms will be the easiest for you to follow? Which will be the hardest?

Based on our team's unique set of peeves and traits, which of our group's norms will be the most important to ensuring that our collaborative work feels productive for everyone?

How will we hold each other accountable for adhering to our team's norms? How will we celebrate moments when team members are following our team's norms?

Tool: Developing Specific Actions to Address the Needs of Our Peers

Taking Action *reference: Essential Action 2.4—Commit to Team Norms, p. 63*

Instructions: Working with your learning team, examine the statements listed in the first column of the following table. These statements outline ten of the most common behaviors that interrupt collaborative teams' productive work. Then, in the second column, craft a specific action that teams can implement to address each behavior. Use the following format to write your norms: "To ensure that *[insert desired pattern of participation]*, we will *[insert specific action]*."

Common Behaviors That Derail Collaborative Teams	Norm Designed to Address This Behavior (Written as a specific action statement)
Sample: *One person dominates the conversation.*	**Sample:** *To ensure everyone has an equal voice in our conversations, we will ask everyone to speak once before anyone speaks twice.*
People are distracted by their digital devices rather than tuned in to the team's ongoing conversations.	
Team meetings are unfocused.	
Team never gets anything done.	
There is a lot of complaining about problems and very little time spent finding solutions.	
Members come to meetings unprepared.	
Members show up to meetings late.	
Members engage in sidebar conversations.	
Members have negative attitudes about the team's collective work.	
Decisions are made before everyone has enough time to think about the options.	
Members don't share their thoughts during team meetings.	

Establish a Culture of Collective Responsibility

The Big Book of Tools for RTI at Work © 2025 Solution Tree Press • SolutionTree.com
Visit **go.SolutionTree.com/RTIatWork/BBTRTI** and enter the unique access code found on the book's inside front cover to access this reproducible.

Sample: Developing Specific Actions to Address the Needs of Our Peers

Taking Action reference: Essential Action 2.4—Commit to Team Norms, p. 63

Instructions: Review the sample actions detailed in the second column of the following table. Compare them to the actions that your team generated while working together on the previous page. What do you like best about your own answers? What do you like best about the sample answers? Does your team need to borrow any norms from either of these two lists?

Common Behaviors That Derail Collaborative Teams	Norm Designed to Address This Behavior (Written as a specific action statement)
Sample: One person dominates the conversation.	**Sample:** To ensure everyone has an equal voice in our conversations, we will ask everyone to speak once before anyone speaks twice.
People are distracted by their digital devices rather than tuned in to the team's ongoing conversations.	To ensure everyone is tuned in to our team's conversations, we will turn our devices off or over unless we are working on a shared document together.
Team meetings are unfocused.	To ensure our work stays focused, our team's facilitator will share our agenda two days before our meetings, and we will assign a "team rounder" who will hold us accountable for sticking to it during our meeting.
Team never gets anything done.	To ensure we complete work together, we will set a timer whenever we are creating a shared product. When the timer goes off, our shared product is finished. Our timekeeper will remind us of the timer whenever we get bogged down in wordsmithing or conversations that seem to be going in circles.
There is a lot of complaining about problems and very little time spent finding solutions.	To ensure our work is focused on finding solutions, we will list all our concerns at the beginning of each meeting and generate "what if we tried" statements for each one. Example: Concern—We don't have enough time to collaborate. "What if we tried" statement—What if we tried collaborating around just one essential until we establish positive work routines?
Members come to meetings unprepared.	To ensure we all arrive with the materials we need to participate in our meetings, our team encourager will send a text message reminder on the morning of our meetings listing the items we need to bring with us.
Members show up to meetings late.	To ensure all members show up to our meetings on time, we will leave a ten-minute buffer at the beginning of our planning period to allow members to get any last-minute things finished before we start our work together. That way, unexpected changes to our personal schedules won't interfere with our collaborative work.

Members engage in sidebar conversations.	To ensure we can fully invest in thinking together, we will begin every meeting with a moment of sharing—each member can share one thought that is at the forefront of their minds and likely to prevent them from giving their complete attention during our shared conversations.
Members have negative attitudes about the team's collective work.	To ensure we all see the positives in the work we are doing together, we will add an "our latest win" item to every agenda when we celebrate something positive we have accomplished together.
Decisions are made before everyone has enough time to think about the options.	To ensure everyone has had enough time to process, we will never make important decisions in one meeting. Instead, we will talk through the decision together, table it, and finish the discussion at the beginning of the next meeting.
Members don't share their thoughts during team meetings.	To ensure everyone shares their thoughts about important decisions, we will create a Padlet (www.padlet.com) and ask members to share a post with their thoughts before our meetings begin. Then, our facilitator will summarize the ideas shared at the beginning of our team meetings.

Establish a Culture of Collective Responsibility

Tool: Addressing the Three Common Reasons for Resistance to Change

Taking Action *reference: Essential Action 2.5—Prepare for Staff Resistance, p. 69*

Instructions: Use the first column in the following table to review the three investments that leaders must make in their faculty to address reasonable resistance to change. In the second column, list faculty members that you believe need each of these additional investments. Finally, use the third column to develop a plan for making these investments.

Investments Leaders Must Make in Faculty Members	Faculty Members in Need of Additional Investments	Action Plan for Making Additional Investments in Faculty Members
Cognitive Investments Answers the question *Why should I change?* by communicating the rationale for change to teachers. **Quote to Consider** "To understand why something is important and reach a logical and beneficial conclusion requires examining evidence, weighing options, and engaging in a dialogue, both internally and externally. We believe that leaders often deny educators these opportunities to logically understand the why of change, and this frustrates them, leading to pessimism and withdrawal from change." —Muhammad & Cruz, 2019, p. 19		
Emotional Investments Answers the question *Who is asking me to change?* by establishing trust with teachers. **Quote to Consider** "Past experiences leave an emotional imprint on a person . . . . Leaders must consider emotions when trying to create intrinsic commitment to change in a staff. When leaders ignore people's emotions and experiences, that alone can stimulate a pessimistic view of change." —Muhammad & Cruz, 2019, pp. 19–20		

Functional Investments		
Answers the question *How do I change?* by building capacity in teachers. **Quote to Consider** "Leaders cannot fairly require someone to complete a task that they have not properly prepared him or her to complete. . . . Poorly constructed professional learning experiences, inadequate resources, and little time for full implementation can be enough to give teachers a negative view of change." —Muhammad & Cruz, 2019, p. 20		

Reference

Muhammad, A., & Cruz, L. F. (2019). *Time for change: Four essential skills for transformational school and district leaders.* Bloomington, IN: Solution Tree Press.

Tool: Rating Your Readiness for Our New Initiative

Taking Action *reference: Essential Action 2.5—Prepare for Staff Resistance, p. 69*

Instructions: Over the last few professional development sessions, you have been introduced to _____, a new initiative that we are going to invest our collective energies into this year. Please answer the following questions to help school leadership better understand your readiness for tackling this initiative. Your name is optional, but including it would give us the opportunity to reach out to you for more information as we plan our building's next steps.

Teacher name: _____

Rate your current understanding of the *why* behind our new initiative.						
I'm open to this initiative, but I still don't fully understand why it is the right work for our school at this time.	1	2	3	4	5	I fully understand why we are pursuing this initiative and believe it is the right work for our school at this time.

Rate your current understanding of the *how* behind our new initiative.						
I'm still not sure exactly what I will need to do to move this initiative forward. I will need support to accomplish this work.	1	2	3	4	5	I know exactly what I am being asked to do to move this initiative forward, and I have the capacity to do that work well.

Questions for Reflection

What new opportunities do you see in this initiative? How will this change benefit teachers? How will this change benefit students?

What makes you skeptical about this initiative? Why are you hesitant to fully embrace it?

What would you need—from the guiding coalition, administration, and the district—to fully embrace this initiative?

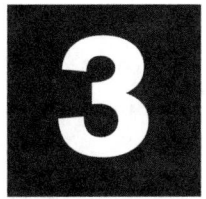

Tools for Building Tier 1 of Your Intervention Pyramid

If we are to build a solid foundation of essential skills and knowledge for students at Tier 1, we must be crystal clear about what those skills and knowledge are.

—Mike Mattos, Austin Buffum, Janet Malone, Luis F. Cruz, Nicole Dimich, & Sarah Schuhl

Most schools do not have an intervention problem. Instead, they have a *what they are doing all day* problem (Mattos, 2018). Interventions cannot make up for a school where educators work in isolation and are expected to meet the diverse learning needs of the students assigned to their individual classrooms. Likewise, Tier 2 interventions will not make up for generally ineffective initial teaching, and Tier 3 interventions will not work if students are labeled "low achieving" based on their ability to learn grade-level essential curriculum and are subsequently placed in remedial coursework for core instruction. It is nearly impossible to target behavior interventions unless a faculty has clarity on the most essential behaviors all students must learn and is systematically and consistently teaching these behaviors across the school. A successful system of interventions starts at Tier 1.

Consider the prerequisite conditions necessary for a school to successfully provide interventions for students who require additional support to master essential grade-level curriculum. Asking an individual teacher to meet all these needs in their classroom would be unrealistic. Educators who have formed the collaborative teams of a PLC can respond collectively when students need additional time for reinforcement or extended learning. Yet, teachers on the same team could not collectively provide these supports unless they first agreed on essential learning outcomes and the kind of ongoing common formative assessment information necessary to identify both student needs and the effectiveness of initial instruction. Creating a guaranteed and viable curriculum and ongoing common formative assessment processes are the foundational building blocks of an effective Tier 1 core instructional program (Gregory, Kaufeldt, & Mattos, 2016). These practices do not reduce teachers to the role of instructional facilitators but instead empower teacher teams to make critical decisions regarding curriculum, instruction, and assessment. It is just as essential that these PLC practices don't restrict an individual teacher's ability to practice the art of teaching. The first set of tools in this chapter focuses on supporting teacher teams in these critical Tier 1 essential actions.

Equally important, students cannot miss initial instruction on essential grade-level curriculum to receive interventions. Teacher teams lack the authority to unilaterally create sacred time in a school's master schedule to ensure all students have access to grade-level essential curriculum—this must be coordinated across the school. This is one of the most important Tier 1 essential actions of the school's guiding coalition. Likewise, the actions needed to identify and teach essential behaviors are best achieved when they are a schoolwide, coordinated effort. The tools in the second half of the chapter will assist a school's guiding coalition with Tier 1 master schedule decisions, core behavioral processes, and preventive steps to ensure most students are succeeding without the need for constant Tier 2 and Tier 3 support.

The resources in this chapter facilitate the work done at Tier 1 in a system of interventions, and they are divided into two separate sections. The resources in the first section are designed to support teacher teams and are tied to the recommendations in chapter 3 of *Taking Action: A Handbook for RTI at Work, Second Edition* (Mattos et al., 2025): "Tier 1 Teacher Team Essential Actions." The resources in the second section are designed to support guiding coalitions. They are tied to the recommendations made in chapter 4 of *Taking Action* (Mattos et al., 2025): "Tier 1 Guiding Coalition Essential Actions."

Section 1: Resources Designed to Support Tier 1 Teacher Team Essential Actions

Visit **go.SolutionTree.com/RTIatWork/BBTRTI** to access online-only tools.

- **"Tool: Using REAL to Identify Essential Standards"** (page 99)—The first step that teacher teams take together when building a system of interventions may be the most important: they systematically identify a small handful of essentials to focus their collaborative time and energy on, knowing that it is impossible to ensure all students learn every standard in their required curriculum given the time available for instruction and intervention during the school year. Determining which standards are essential is commonly done using three criteria, first detailed by Douglas B. Reeves (2002): (1) readiness, (2) endurance, and (3) leverage. Assessment experts, including Larry Ainsworth (2013), Thomas W. Many and Ted Horrell (2014), and Kim Bailey and Chris Jakicic (2021), have recommended adding a fourth criterion to Reeves's (2002) original list: How frequently is a standard assessed? This tool details those four criteria and suggests a process for using them to evaluate standards for inclusion on a list of essential standards for a grade level or course.

    - *Taking Action* reference: Essential Action 3.1—Identify Essential Standards, p. 85

- **"Tool: Essential Standards Chart"** (page 100)—After identifying essentials for their grade level or course, teacher teams collaborate to rewrite each standard in student-friendly language, determine the level of rigor the standard requires, identify prerequisite knowledge and vocabulary that can help students master the standard, decide on the best strategies for assessing mastery, and develop extensions for students working beyond grade-level expectations. These actions develop shared clarity in a collaborative team before members begin instruction around their essentials. Teams can use this tool to record shared decisions while tackling these tasks for their essential standards.
  - *Taking Action* reference: Essential Action 3.1—Identify Essential Standards, p. 85

- **"Tool: Developing a Shared Pacing Guide"** (online only)—If teachers are going to collaborate around instruction and intervention in a meaningful way, they must teach roughly the same thing at roughly the same time. Otherwise, collaborative team time will feel forced and unproductive. While that may come across as common sense to some, others have spent their careers in schools where pacing decisions have always been left to individual teachers' professional discretion. The result: different teachers of the same grade level or course in the same school may be teaching the same units at different times—or may spend different numbers of instructional days on the same units. If that sounds like your team, know that meaningful collaborative conversations start only after you develop a shared pacing guide for your units of study. Use this tool to guide your team through that process.
  - *Taking Action* reference: Essential Action 3.2—Design a Unit Assessment Plan, p. 94

- **"Tool: Essential Standards Unit Plan"** (page 101)—In *Taking Action: A Handbook for RTI at Work, Second Edition* (Mattos et al., 2025), the original architects of the RTI at Work process recommend that teacher teams create a unit plan for each essential standard by completing a four-step process: (1) discussing the type of learning required in the essential standard, (2) deconstructing the essential standard into learning targets, (3) converting learning targets into student-friendly language, and (4) identifying assessments to measure mastery of each learning target. They write, "The process of creating unit assessment plans positions teachers to intentionally teach, assess, and proactively respond to student learning struggles prior to the conclusion of any unit" (Mattos et al., 2025, p. 96). You can use this template and **samples** (online and on page 102) to create a unit plan for one of your essential standards.
  - *Taking Action* reference: Essential Action 3.2—Design a Unit Assessment Plan, p. 94

- **"Tool: Deconstructing Essential Standards"** (online only)—We want readers to know that the templates we provide in *The Big Book of Tools for RTI at Work* are not the only ways to accomplish individual tasks. In fact, the tool itself is not what matters most to moving your intervention efforts forward. What matters most are the conversations that these tools are designed to facilitate. To demonstrate that, we offer this tool and **sample** (online only) for you to consider. Notice that while it has a different format from "Tool: Essential Standards Unit Plan" (page 101), it facilitates the same conversation by helping teachers build a shared understanding of the skills and concepts students are expected to master. We are not suggesting that teams use both tools. Instead, we are emphasizing the point that readers can modify any of our tools to create something that resonates with them or aligns with their current work.
  - *Taking Action* reference: Essential Action 3.2—Design a Unit Assessment Plan, p. 94

- **"Tool: Using AI Tools to Deconstruct an Essential Standard"** (page 104)—Regardless of the chosen approach, building a shared understanding of the skills and concepts that students are expected to master is an essential first step in crafting a targeted instructional plan. Failing to deconstruct an essential standard before planning instruction is akin to overlooking a recipe before preparing a special family dinner. While the meal will eventually get cooked, you are bound to waste time making repeated trips to the grocery store for forgotten ingredients. The good news for teachers is that deconstructing standards has gotten a lot easier now that artificial intelligence tools like ChatGPT (https://chat.openai.com) and Gemini (https://gemini.google.com) have become widely available. This tool can show you how to use an AI chatbot to help your team deconstruct an essential standard in sixty minutes or less.
  - *Taking Action* reference: Essential Action 3.2—Design a Unit Assessment Plan, p. 94

- **"Tool: Using AI Tools to Develop a Proficiency Scale"** (page 105)—Teams can also enhance their shared understanding of essential standards by creating proficiency scales. These scales outline the sequential steps a student must take to master an essential, which helps teams develop instructional sequences with that goal in mind. Additionally, proficiency scales assist in targeting interventions and extensions for students struggling with or exceeding grade-level expectations. Teams can use the prompts in this tool with an AI chatbot like ChatGPT (https://chat.openai.com) or Gemini (https://gemini.google.com) to accelerate the creation of a proficiency scale.

- *Taking Action* reference: Essential Action 3.2—Design a Unit Assessment Plan, p. 94

■ **"Tool: Tier 1 Instructional Strategies to Consider"** (online only)—The best intervention starts by ensuring that teachers incorporate research-based instructional strategies into their initial instruction. This proactive approach can prevent students from falling behind in the first place. There is good news for school leaders interested in increasing the effectiveness of their initial instruction—there is extensive research on strategies that yield significant gains in student achievement. The challenge is that teachers may not always be aware of this research. To enhance your teachers' instructional expertise, consider encouraging them to explore the six practices outlined in this resource, which represent some of the most effective strategies highlighted in *The New Classroom Instruction That Works: The Best Research-Based Strategies for Increasing Student Achievement* (Goodwin & Rouleau, 2022).

- *Taking Action* reference: Essential Action 3.2—Design a Unit Assessment Plan, p. 94

■ **"Tool: Using AI as a Thought Partner or Content Creator"** (online only)—One of the most valuable roles that AI tools can play in the work of collaborative teams is as a thought partner—making recommendations, generating ideas, and creating content for teachers to consider. This tool provides a collection of thought-provoking AI prompts that can help teachers learn more about their curriculum, create content for their classrooms, and think creatively about how they can use AI to improve their teaching.

- *Taking Action* reference: Essential Action 3.2—Design a Unit Assessment Plan, p. 94

■ **"Tool: Examining Your Work With the Team Teaching-Assessing-Learning Cycle"** (page 106)—In *Taking Action*, Mattos and colleagues (2025) detail the steps teacher teams take when working through a cycle of inquiry around their practice with one another. They call this process the team teaching-assessing-learning cycle. Use this tool to examine how closely the current work of your collaborative team aligns with this cycle.

- *Taking Action* reference: Essential Action 3.2—Design a Unit Assessment Plan, p. 94

■ **"Tool: Common Formative Assessment Pretest"** (page 108)—Despite the widespread use of the term *common formative assessment* in education, there's often a lack of clarity among teachers regarding what these assessments are and how they should be integrated into collaborative team efforts. School leaders can use this pretest and its corresponding **answer key** (page 109) to establish a shared understanding of how common formative assessments can be utilized to inform Tier 1 instruction and Tier 2 intervention efforts.

- *Taking Action* reference: Essential Action 3.3—Create Common Assessments and Begin Instruction, p. 114

- **"Tool: Assessment Design Checklist"** (page 111)—When developing common formative assessments and common end-of-unit assessments, teams should evaluate the quality of their final product against two criteria: (1) the accuracy of their design and (2) the intentionality of their use (Mattos et al., 2025). When evaluating the accuracy of an assessment's design, teams ensure that the assessment items are tied to specific learning targets, are written at the appropriate level of rigor, and are formatted in a way that enables students to demonstrate mastery without confusion (Mattos et al., 2025). When evaluating the intentionality of an assessment, teams analyze results by student, by standard, and by target; discuss the common understandings, misunderstandings, and misconceptions demonstrated by students; and develop a plan for responding to the collected results (Mattos et al., 2025). This checklist, included in the second edition of *Taking Action: A Handbook for RTI at Work* (Mattos et al., 2025), can help collaborative teams evaluate an existing assessment for accuracy and intentionality.

  - *Taking Action* reference: Essential Action 3.3—Create Common Assessments and Begin Instruction, p. 114

- **"Tool: Matching Assessment Strategies With Essential Standards"** (online only)—Gathering accurate information from common formative assessments relies on choosing an assessment method that matches the required standard's complexity. Using a multiple-choice assessment to determine mastery of a performance outcome is as ineffective as using a performance assessment to determine mastery of basic content knowledge. Use this tool and its corresponding **sample answers** (online only) to enhance your understanding of how best to align your assessment strategies to the rigor of the standards you are assessing.

  - *Taking Action* reference: Essential Action 3.3—Create Common Assessments and Begin Instruction, p. 114

- **"Tool: Building a Common Formative Assessment"** (page 114)—Teams using the teaching-assessing-learning cycle as part of Tier 1 of a system of interventions gather evidence from common formative assessments to inform their next actions. Unlike common end-of-unit assessments, common formative assessments are intentionally short, tied to specific learning targets, given throughout a cycle of instruction, and designed to lead to in-the-moment adjustments in classroom instruction. Use this template to develop a short common formative assessment for one of your upcoming learning targets.

- *Taking Action* reference: Essential Action 3.3—Create Common Assessments and Begin Instruction, p. 114

- **"Tool: Performance Tracking Table"** (page 115)—Observations are a valuable source of information about student progress toward mastery that teacher teams often overlook because they are challenging to collect and document. To make that work more manageable, education professors Douglas Fisher and Nancy Frey (2012) recommend using simple tracking tables for two purposes: (1) detail the common errors teachers expect students to make and (2) include the initials of students that teachers observe making those errors. Your team can use this template and **samples** (page 116) to turn observations into instructionally actionable data.

  - *Taking Action* reference: Essential Action 3.3—Create Common Assessments and Begin Instruction, p. 114

- **"Tool: Vet Your Current Assessment With the Three Design Qualities"** (online only)—The original architects of the PLC at Work process describe assessment as "one of the most powerful weapons in an educator's arsenal" (DuFour, DuFour, Eaker, Mattos, & Muhammad, 2021, p. 191). Teams use common formative assessments to check progress throughout a unit of study and end-of-unit assessments to identify students who need additional time and support for learning. This tool—drawn from the second edition of *Design in Five: Essential Phases to Create Engaging Assessment Practice* (Dimich, 2024)—provides an overview of assessment design and implementation criteria that can inform teams as they create assessments together, evaluate assessments that they have already created, or adapt assessments provided by curriculum resources.

  - *Taking Action* reference: Essential Action 3.3—Create Common Assessments and Begin Instruction, p. 114

- **"Tool: Evaluating Classroom Feedback Practices"** (online only)—Nothing has greater potential to influence a student's motivation and long-term success in school than the feedback that we give them. When feedback is tied to specific learning outcomes and designed to prompt action from learners, it empowers students to become partners in the learning process. Conversely, feedback that overwhelms students, lacks clarity, or comes across as a directive command does little to progress learning. Use this tool and its companion **work samples** (online only) to examine the characteristics of effective feedback practices.

  - *Taking Action* reference: Essential Action 3.4—Foster Student Investment, p. 129

- **"Student Tool: Student Survey on Classroom Feedback"** (online only)—Your students are an invaluable source of information about your school's feedback practices. They interact with teachers from various grade levels and subjects, making them well informed about the feedback they receive. By gaining an understanding of your students' perspectives on feedback, you can assess whether your practices are creating an environment that fosters student investment in their learning. Use this survey to gather more information from your learners about the feedback practices in your building.
  - *Taking Action* reference: Essential Action 3.4—Foster Student Investment, p. 129

- **"Tool: Reflecting on the Role Grades Can Play as Feedback"** (page 119)—An essential conversation for all teams to have when assessing student learning is how to give students meaningful feedback once an assessment is complete. The most common type of feedback students receive—grades—can often be utterly useless as a form of actionable feedback (Wiggins, 2012). However, that does not mean teachers *cannot* use grades as actionable feedback. In an article in *Kappan Magazine* titled "Can Grades Be an Effective Form of Feedback?," assessment expert Thomas R. Guskey (2022) details four necessary conditions that must be in place for grades to serve as a meaningful form of feedback to students. Use this tool to explore and compare those criteria to how your team currently uses grades.
  - *Taking Action* reference: Essential Action 3.4—Foster Student Investment, p. 129

- **"Sample: Assessment Wrapper for Primary Students"** (page 121)—Teachers can empower primary students to take an active role in their learning by administering brief assessments with questions directly aligned with specific essential outcomes. When the assessment is over, students can work alongside the teacher to identify their correct and incorrect responses. This collaborative analysis helps primary students identify the essentials they have mastered and those they are still struggling with. Diane Kerr, Tracey A. Hulen, Jacqueline Heller, and Brian K. Butler (2021), experts in primary education, advocate the use of *assessment wrappers* for facilitating this work with students. This tool offers a sample assessment wrapper for second graders studying measurement.
  - *Taking Action* reference: Essential Action 3.4—Foster Student Investment, p. 129

- **"Tool: Practice Test Tracking Template for Secondary Students"** (page 124)—Secondary teachers can encourage student engagement in the assessment process by administering practice tests a few days before end-of-unit assessments and asking students to analyze their responses. This analysis involves identifying patterns in both the concepts they have successfully grasped and the mistakes they are continuing to make. This practice provides students with tangible proof of their progress and aids in developing a personalized, evidence-based study plan for the end-of-unit assessment. Use this tool, adapted from the work of Rick Stiggins and Jan Chappius (Stiggins, Arter, Chappuis, & Chappius, 2007), and accompanying **sample** (page 125) as a resource for students to perform this self-analysis.

- *Taking Action* reference: Essential Action 3.4—Foster Student Investment, p. 129

- **"Tool: Teaching Primary Learners About Short-Term Goal Setting"** (page 126)—One academic skill students should learn is short-term goal setting. For third-grade teacher Stephanie Van Horn (2014), short-term goal setting starts by asking students to complete two sentence starters on sticky notes to create WOW (working on weekly) goals. Once students have completed their WOW goals, their sticky notes are displayed on a chart in the back of the classroom and revisited during daily morning meetings. You can replicate this work in your classroom by making copies of this template and asking students to create their own WOW goals at the beginning of every week.

  - *Taking Action* reference: Essential Action 3.4—Foster Student Investment, p. 129

- **"Tool: Teaching Secondary Learners to Set SMART Goals"** (online only)—The best way to introduce older students to goal setting is to ask them to write SMART goals much like the ones teacher teams set in buildings that have implemented the RTI and PLC at Work processes (Brown & Ferriter, 2021). Teaching students to write SMART goals should be an approachable practice for teachers already well versed in using these goals with one another. More important, teaching students to write SMART goals will give them a structure they can use for personal and professional goal setting long after leaving school. Use this template to guide students through the thinking necessary to set and achieve a SMART goal.

  - *Taking Action* reference: Essential Action 3.4—Foster Student Investment, p. 129

- **"Tool Overview: Creating Next-Step Checklists to Involve Students in the Intervention Process"** (page 127)—Differentiated learning experiences are almost impossible to pull off when teachers are the sole providers of feedback to learners. There are too many students to give timely and directive feedback to everyone as needed. Teacher teams can address this challenge by creating next-step checklists for every unit of study. Next-step checklists provide students a simple tool to monitor their progress toward mastering important outcomes, turning them into active learning partners. Use this overview, **student tool** (page 128), and **sample** (page 129) to create a next-step checklist for one of your upcoming units.

- *Taking Action* reference: Essential Action 3.4—Foster Student Investment, p. 129

■ **"Tool: Developing Exemplars to Make Learning Intentions Explicit"** (online only)—To cultivate student engagement in the assessment process, consider crafting exemplars that clearly convey learning objectives to students. This approach helps students gain a deeper understanding of what a successful result should entail. When students have the chance to look for success criteria in exemplars, they become more adept at recognizing these criteria in their own work. Use this tool and accompanying **template** (online only) and **sample** (online only) to begin developing an exemplar for an upcoming task that your students will have to complete.

- *Taking Action* reference: Essential Action 3.4—Foster Student Investment, p. 129

■ **"Tool: Team Protocol for Analyzing Assessment Results"** (page 130)—Like every step in the PLC and RTI at Work processes, common formative assessments promote reflection. After gathering student responses and work samples, teams analyze the results and look for patterns they can learn from. While that analysis should never feel overwhelming and should never take more than one collaborative planning period, *it must be focused and intentional*—drawing the team's attention to both the students who need additional time and support for learning *and* the impact that instructional choices and assessment designs may have had on student mastery. Use this set of questions developed by assessment experts Kim Bailey and Chris Jakicic (2023) to make intentional assessment analysis a regular part of your team's collaborative work.

- *Taking Action* reference: Essential Action 3.5—Analyze and Respond to Common Assessment Data, p. 138

■ **"Tool: Looking at End-of-Unit Assessment Data"** (page 132)—While developing and delivering quality end-of-unit assessments are essential to plan grade-level essential interventions using evidence of learning, assessments do not become "one of the most powerful weapons in an educator's arsenal" until teams work together to analyze the assessment results (DuFour et al., 2021, p. 191). The questions we ask and the patterns we spot while reflecting on end-of-unit assessments provide us with the necessary information to act on behalf of struggling learners. Use this tool to guide your analysis of end-of-unit assessment results.

- *Taking Action* reference: Essential Action 3.5—Analyze and Respond to Common Assessment Data, p. 138

- **"Tool: Targeting Tier 2 Interventions"** (page 135)—One common mistake teacher teams make after giving common formative assessments is rushing first to generate lists of students needing intervention. While generating these lists is essential, designing supplemental interventions for academic essentials begins by examining student work for common understandings, misunderstandings, errors, and misconceptions. Doing so ensures that Tier 2 intervention efforts target specific student needs. Teacher teams can use this tool, adapted from the work of assessment expert Sarah Schuhl (as cited in Sonju, Kramer, Mattos, & Buffum, 2019), and accompanying **sample** (page 137) to design supplemental interventions that intentionally target identified student needs after giving a common formative assessment.

  - *Taking Action* reference: Essential Action 3.5—Analyze and Respond to Common Assessment Data, p. 138

- **"Tool: Essential Standards Student Tracking Chart"** (page 138)—Successful Tier 2 interventions begin by gathering detailed evidence of student mastery during Tier 1 instruction. Teams must track progress "by student, by standard, and by learning target" (Mattos et al., 2025, p. 176). Teams can use this tracking chart from *Taking Action: A Handbook for RTI at Work, Second Edition* (Mattos et al., 2025) to record the standards and learning targets that individual students struggle to master. Teams cannot target their intervention efforts on identified student needs without this information, therefore decreasing the likelihood that the additional time and support will lead to new learning.

  - *Taking Action* reference: Essential Action 3.5—Analyze and Respond to Common Assessment Data, p. 138

- **"Tool: Reflecting on Our Cycle of Instruction"** (page 139)—One of the most common mistakes that teacher teams make when working through the team teaching-assessing-learning cycle is forgetting that studying instruction is an essential element of any sound system of interventions. That means the evidence we collect from assessments can tell us as much about the efficacy of our professional practices as it does about our students as learners—and if we use that evidence to inform our professional practice, we will have fewer students in need of future intervention because our initial instruction of grade-level essentials improves. This tool encourages teams to reflect on their practices after completing a team teaching-assessing-learning cycle.

  - *Taking Action* reference: Essential Action 3.5—Analyze and Respond to Common Assessment Data, p. 138

- **"Tool: Record of Instructional Strategies Used"** (online only)—Professionals in any field intentionally study the connection between their practices and performance. For teachers, that means examining the impact their instructional choices—the questions they ask, the activities they design, the videos they share, and the groups they create—have on student learning. Teacher teams can use this tool to deliberately record and reflect on the strategies they use to teach one essential standard.
  - *Taking Action* reference: Essential Action 3.5—Analyze and Respond to Common Assessment Data, p. 138

Section 2: Resources Designed to Support Tier 1 Schoolwide Essential Actions

Visit **go.SolutionTree.com/RTIatWork/BBTRTI** to access online-only tools.

- **"Tool: Ensuring Access to Essential Grade-Level Curriculum"** (page 141)—A robust system of interventions begins by ensuring that *all students* have access to initial instruction in grade-level essential standards. That means we must stop pulling elementary students out of class to work with interventionists during grade-level essential instruction or placing secondary students in "remedial classes" teaching below grade level. Here is why: students who miss instruction in grade-level essentials will always fall behind and need interventions. Ensuring access to essential grade-level curriculum is a prevention strategy designed to keep students from needing intervention. Use this tool from *Taking Action: A Handbook for RTI at Work, Second Edition* (Mattos et al., 2025) to determine whether you have ensured all students have access to essential grade-level curriculum.
  - *Taking Action* reference: Essential Action 4.1—Ensure Access to Essential Grade-Level Curriculum, p. 154

- **"Tool: Developing a Master Schedule for Three Tiers of Instruction"** (page 142)—The most common question schools have when implementing the RTI at Work process is, How do you build a schedule to provide additional time and support for learning? The bad news is that there is no one correct answer to that question. Schools implementing the RTI at Work process use a range of bell schedules to deliver solid Tier 1 instruction, Tier 2 supplemental interventions, and Tier 3 intensive interventions in universal skills of learning. The good news is that all those schools created their schedules using a straightforward process—and all those schools used the same considerations to ensure that individual students could receive interventions without missing instruction in new grade-level essentials. Use this tool and **template** (page 145) to review those considerations, examine potential solutions, and reflect on the strengths and weaknesses in your current bell schedule.

- *Taking Action* reference: Essential Action 4.1—Ensure Access to Essential Grade-Level Curriculum, p. 154

■ **"Tool: Eliciting Feedback on Our Master Schedule"** (page 146)—In "From Theory to Practice: A Jigsaw Approach to an Elementary Master Schedule," Claire Springer (2021) recommends that guiding coalitions begin their efforts to develop a master schedule that facilitates meaningful instruction and intervention by surveying faculty members about the strengths and weaknesses of the current schedule. After all, teachers have firsthand experience with scheduling decisions impacting their instruction and intervention efforts. Use this tool to gather feedback from the teachers in your building as you begin to develop a master schedule for the next school year.

- *Taking Action* reference: Essential Action 4.1—Ensure Access to Essential Grade-Level Curriculum, p. 154

■ **"Tool: Reflecting on Your Master Schedule"** (page 147)—For a school to create an effective system of interventions, it will need a master schedule that ensures students can access initial instruction in grade-level essential standards as well as additional time and support for learning those essentials and intensive support in the universal skills of learning. Creating this master schedule starts when schools reflect on their current schedule's strengths and weaknesses. Use the questions included in this tool to begin that reflection in your building.

- *Taking Action* reference: Essential Action 4.1—Ensure Access to Essential Grade-Level Curriculum, p. 154

■ **"Checklists: Establishing Common Expectations, Targeting Instruction, and Reinforcing Positive Behaviors"** (page 148)—The steps for identifying and teaching essential academic and social behaviors are the same regardless of the skill or behavior that a guiding coalition decides to prioritize. First, the team must develop shared expectations for the behavior. Then, it must create a plan for targeting instruction for the behavior. Finally, it must implement strategies for reinforcing the behavior. Use these three checklists from *Taking Action: A Handbook for RTI at Work, Second Edition* (Mattos et al., 2025) to direct your guiding coalition through these steps.

- *Taking Action* reference: Essential Action 4.2—Identify and Teach Essential Academic and Social Behaviors, p. 166

- **"Tool: Reflecting on the Recipe for a Successful Learner"** (page 151)—While teacher teams take lead responsibility for identifying and teaching grade-level academic standards, the guiding coalition takes lead responsibility for identifying academic and social behaviors all students must learn. Unfortunately, due to the pressures of standardized testing, many schools fail to fully recognize the importance of developing a plan to teach essential academic and social behaviors, even though educators inherently know those behaviors significantly impact their students' successes or struggles. Use this tool to remind teachers in your school that skills and dispositions are essential too.
  - *Taking Action* reference: Essential Action 4.2—Identify and Teach Essential Academic and Social Behaviors, p. 166

- **"Tool: Reviewing the Skills Necessary to Succeed in the Modern Workplace"** (page 153)—A responsibility of the guiding coalition at Tier 1 in the RTI at Work process is to identify essential skills and dispositions that all students should master (Mattos et al., 2025). Doing so ensures that students graduate with a firm grasp of the concepts required to succeed in the workplace and the capacity to take action in the ever-shifting environments most modern businesses face. Use this tool to start conversations about the skills and dispositions that your building will prioritize at Tier 1 of your system of interventions.
  - *Taking Action* reference: Essential Action 4.2—Identify and Teach Essential Academic and Social Behaviors, p. 166

- **"Tool: Identifying Essential Knowledge, Skills, and Dispositions"** (online only)—Answering the first critical question in the PLC at Work process—What knowledge, skills, and dispositions should students acquire as a result of this unit of study?—forces teacher teams to identify essentials. Teams are generally comfortable working together to systematically identify essential standards in their required curriculum but need to be more systematic about identifying essential skills and dispositions. Use this tool to practice identifying essential skills and dispositions with your team members.
  - *Taking Action* reference: Essential Action 4.2—Identify and Teach Essential Academic and Social Behaviors, p. 166

- **"Checklist: Concentrating Instruction on Social and Academic Behaviors"** (page 155)—It is not enough for schools *to identify* social and academic behaviors they expect every student to master. Instead, schools must create a specific plan *to teach* students social and academic behaviors, work that is led by the guiding coalition. In *Pyramid of Behavior Interventions: Seven Keys to a Positive Learning Environment*, authors Tom Hierck, Charlie Coleman, and Chris Weber (2011) introduce readers to three criteria that schools can use to determine whether they have effectively concentrated instruction on social and academic behaviors. Guiding coalitions can use this checklist to rate their school's efforts against these criteria.

- *Taking Action* reference: Essential Action 4.2—Identify and Teach Essential Academic and Social Behaviors, p. 166

- **"Student Tool: What Do Successful People Do Differently?"** (page 157)—An essential step toward teaching students about the skills and dispositions of successful learners is establishing and communicating clear criteria for what exactly successful learners do differently. This tool—which includes five characteristics of successful learners detailed by Allen N. Mendler (2021) in the second edition of *Motivating Students Who Don't Care: Proven Strategies to Engage All Learners*—is useful to introduce students to the skills and dispositions of successful learners, to give students opportunities to evaluate themselves against those characteristics, and to encourage students to set goals to improve their work with the skills and dispositions of successful learners.

  - *Taking Action* reference: Essential Action 4.2—Identify and Teach Essential Academic and Social Behaviors, p. 166

- **"Tool: Teaching Students About Self-Regulation"** (online only)—*Self-regulation* is a learner's ability to respond to both the demands and surprises they face when working on a challenging task. Successful students can often self-regulate throughout learning experiences (Willis, 2022; Winne & Hadwin, 1998). What does that mean for classroom teachers? They need to teach students the steps to self-regulate when completing complex assignments. Use the questions found in this tool and the accompanying **student tool** (online only) to start conversations about self-regulation in your classroom.

  - *Taking Action* reference: Essential Action 4.2—Identify and Teach Essential Academic and Social Behaviors, p. 166

- **"Tool: Helping Students Identify the Connections Between Perseverance and Performance"** (online only)—Academic perseverance is one of the most critical skills and dispositions to teach students. Students who can identify the connection between their effort and performance quickly recognize that hard work is essential to succeeding as a learner. Use this tool and its companion **student tool** (online only)—which ask students to reflect on the connection between the grades they earn on major assignments and the effort they put into those tasks—to help students identify the connections between perseverance and performance.

  - *Taking Action* reference: Essential Action 4.2—Identify and Teach Essential Academic and Social Behaviors, p. 166

- **"Tool: Six-Question Guiding Coalition Assessment Inventory"** (online only)—When schools are in the process of creating a balanced assessment approach, it is beneficial to start by taking an inventory of assessments currently used within the system. This inventory can serve as a valuable resource for analyzing the appropriate course of action and identifying potential next steps. This might involve adding assessments to gather essential data or removing assessments that yield redundant or unreliable information. This tool is designed to assist teams in making informed decisions about the assessments they will use going forward.
    - *Taking Action* reference: Essential Action 4.3—Create a Balanced Assessment Approach, p. 174

- **"Tool: Assessment Purpose Map"** (page 159)—Assessments are a crucial component of every educational system. Because assessment information plays an important role in a system of interventions, it is imperative for guiding coalitions, intervention teams, and teacher teams to cultivate a comprehensive understanding of the assessments they administer and their intended purposes as well as the ways in which they use assessment data. Armed with this knowledge, teams can establish a clear road map for harnessing the insights they glean from each assessment. Use this tool to gain a better understanding of the assessments that your school is giving.
    - *Taking Action* reference: Essential Action 4.3—Create a Balanced Assessment Approach, p. 174

- **"Tool: Assessment Stoplight Analysis"** (page 161)—School sites employ data from team-created common formative assessments to address individual students' unique needs. However, data from state assessments and district benchmarks provide feedback at the systems level. These assessments and associated data can identify areas of strength and pinpoint opportunities for schoolwide improvement. The reflection questions in this tool can help school-based teams formulate actionable plans from these large-scale assessments.
    - *Taking Action* reference: Essential Action 4.3—Create a Balanced Assessment Approach, p. 174

- **"Tool: Assessment Reflection by Type"** (page 162)—Assessments administered at school sites take various forms, encompassing large-scale data, benchmark assessments, end-of-unit evaluations, common formative assessments, and ongoing formative assessments. Each of these assessment types contributes essential information to an RTI system. Guiding coalitions can use this tool to evaluate how effectively they utilize each assessment type and plan for improvements moving forward.
    - *Taking Action* reference: Essential Action 4.3—Create a Balanced Assessment Approach, p. 174

- **"Tool: Grading Reflection and Planning"** (page 164)—*Taking Action: A Handbook for RTI at Work, Second Edition* (Mattos et al., 2025) emphasizes co-creating schoolwide grading practices as a crucial step in the RTI at Work process. This involves defining the purpose of grading, using research-based evidence to guide changes in grading practices, and determining the evidence that teachers should include in a student's grade. This tool is designed to assist guiding coalitions in evaluating their current grading system and planning steps to utilize practices that have a positive impact on student learning.
  - *Taking Action* reference: Essential Action 4.4—Co-Create Schoolwide Grading Practices, p. 184

- **"Tool: Standards-Based Mindset Reflection and Planning"** (page 165)—As schools begin to co-create schoolwide grading practices, they often explore elements of standards-based grading. Assessment author and expert Tom Schimmer (2016) has identified key components of a standards-based mindset that underpin effective grading practices. This tool offers sites the chance to gain insight into these components, assess their current implementation, and devise strategies for improvement. All these efforts are aimed at enhancing grading practices to support student success.
  - *Taking Action* reference: Essential Action 4.4—Co-Create Schoolwide Grading Practices, p. 184

- **"Tool: Grading Practices Implementation"** (page 166)—Schools that are aligning grading practices to enhance learning outcomes should focus on building their understanding of research-based practices, establishing a shared and clear grading purpose, and creating an actionable plan for necessary improvements. This tool assists in comprehensively assessing essential components for the successful implementation of schoolwide grading practices and monitoring team progress.
  - *Taking Action* reference: Essential Action 4.4—Co-Create Schoolwide Grading Practices, p. 184

- **"Tool: Desired State for Grading Plan"** (online only)—As emphasized in *Taking Action: A Handbook for RTI at Work, Second Edition* (Mattos et al., 2025), co-creating schoolwide grading practices is a complex process. This tool serves as a valuable resource for sites, helping them define their desired state, evaluate their current circumstances, and devise a strategic action plan to achieve their envisioned grading practices.
  - *Taking Action* reference: Essential Action 4.4—Co-Create Schoolwide Grading Practices, p. 184

- **"Tool: Preventions to Proactively Support Student Success"** (page 168)—In *Taking Action: A Handbook for RTI at Work, Second Edition* (Mattos et al., 2025), the architects of the RTI at Work process argue that teachers can almost always predict the students who will struggle before instruction even begins. Why? Because most students who struggle have one of four needs: (1) gaps in prerequisite skills, (2) predictable developmental needs, (3) transitional needs, or (4) previous personal or academic struggles that are well known to their teachers before moving on to the next grade level. Rather than waiting to reidentify these students year after year, guiding coalitions can use this tool to develop a prevention plan to proactively support the students who are most likely to struggle.
  - *Taking Action* reference: Essential Action 4.5—Provide Preventions to Proactively Support Student Success, p. 192

- **"Tool: Creating a Predictable-Is-Preventable Plan"** (page 170)—Proactively supporting the students most likely to struggle does not just mean that guiding coalitions should begin planning interventions. Instead, proactively supporting students who are most likely to struggle means guiding coalitions should also develop specific actions for addressing the unique needs of both the teachers working with and the parents caring for students at risk. Use this tool, its **overview** (page 169), and **sample** (page 172) to design a plan for supporting all stakeholders when students arrive at your school with predictable challenges that will interfere with their ability to master grade-level essentials.
  - *Taking Action* reference: Essential Action 4.5—Provide Preventions to Proactively Support Student Success, p. 192

Conclusion

Tier 1 intervention efforts in the RTI at Work process begin with developing a guaranteed and viable curriculum supported by ongoing common formative assessments. By systematically identifying essential standards and creating shared pacing guides, collaborative teacher teams can ensure that all students receive consistent, high-quality initial instruction. This work, when done well, *prevents students from needing intervention to begin with*. In fact, developing a guaranteed and viable curriculum may be the most important step to building a sustainable system of interventions. Why? Because there are rarely enough resources available in a school to rely solely on Tier 2 and Tier 3 interventions to address all academic and behavioral challenges students will present.

Equally important to a school's Tier 1 intervention efforts in the RTI at Work process is the guiding coalition's work to identify essential academic and social behaviors that all students are expected to master and to build a bell schedule that provides access to essential grade-level curriculum while enabling interventions for students who need additional time and support for learning. By identifying and systematically teaching academic and social behaviors to all students, guiding coalitions create positive learning environments that support student success. And by developing a bell schedule that coordinates the actions of school personnel, guiding coalitions ensure all students access to initial instruction in essential grade-level curriculum *and* interventions when necessary.

By using the tools in this chapter to focus the work of your collaborative teacher teams and your guiding coalition, your school can build a strong Tier 1 foundation that ensures students' needs are met, reduces the need for Tier 2 and Tier 3 interventions, and promotes overall student success.

Resources Designed to
Support Tier 1 Teacher Team Essential Actions

Tool: Using REAL to Identify Essential Standards

Taking Action *reference: Essential Action 3.1—Identify Essential Standards, p. 85*

Instructions: As one of their first steps, teacher teams identify a few essential outcomes to study together. Use the following process to determine whether a standard you are considering is truly essential.

1. Work as a team to generate a list of standards you believe should be considered for your list of grade-level essentials.
2. Provide each team member with one copy of this tool for each standard you evaluate.
3. One standard at a time, ask team members to independently rate each standard using the REAL criteria and rating scale detailed in this tool.
4. Share your ratings; look for standards that earned universally high ratings. Add those to your list of essentials for this unit of study.
5. Share your ratings; look for standards that earned universally low ratings. Remove those from your list of essentials for this unit of study.
6. If you find areas of disagreement in your ratings, turn to outside evidence or experts to resolve those disagreements. Examples: What do your principals or instructional coaches think about this standard? Is this standard considered necessary by national curriculum experts or organizations?

Standard for Consideration:

Rate the standard we are considering against the following criteria using a scale from 1 to 5, where 1 represents not important *and 5 represents* very important.

Criteria		Description	Your Rating
R	Readiness	How important is this standard for student success in the **same subject** in the **next grade level**?	
E	Endurance	How important is this standard for student success **long after they have left school**?	
A	Assessed	How important is this standard for student success on **end-of-grade exams**?	
L	Leverage	How important is this standard for student success in **multiple subject areas**?	
Total Points for This Standard:			

Will this standard go on your list of essentials for this unit?	Yes	No

Tool: Essential Standards Chart

Taking Action reference: Essential Action 3.1—Identify Essential Standards, p. 85

Instructions: Working in collaborative teams, examine all relevant documents, Common Core standards, state standards, and district power standards, and then apply the criteria of endurance, leverage, and readiness to determine which standards are essential for all students to master. Remember, *less is more*. For each standard selected, complete the remaining columns. Complete this chart by the second or third week of each instructional period (semester).

Grade	Subject	Semester		Team Members	
		What Is It We Expect Students to Learn?			
Description of Standard	Example of Rigor	Prerequisite Skills	When Taught?	Common Summative Assessment	Extension Standards
What is the essential standard to be learned? Describe in student-friendly vocabulary.	What does proficient student work look like? Provide an example or description.	What prior knowledge, skills, or vocabulary are needed for a student to master this standard?	When will this standard be taught?	What assessments will be used to measure student mastery?	What will we do when students have already learned this standard?

Source: Mattos, M., Buffum, A., Malone, J., Cruz, L. F., Dimich, N., & Schuhl, S. (2025). Taking action: A handbook for RTI at Work (2nd ed.). Bloomington, IN: Solution Tree Press, p. 93. Adapted from Buffum, A., Mattos, M., & Weber, C. (2012). Simplifying response to intervention: Four essential guiding principles. Bloomington, IN: Solution Tree Press.

Tool: Essential Standards Unit Plan

Taking Action reference: *Essential Action 3.2—Design a Unit Assessment Plan, p. 94*

Instructions: Use the four-step process (page 81) to complete the following plan.

Essential standard:	☐ Knowledge ☐ Reasoning	☐ Performance skills ☐ Product
End-of-unit assessment:	When taught:	
	Instructional days needed:	

Knowledge Targets	Reasoning Targets	Performance Skills Targets	Product Targets

Student-friendly learning targets:

Assessment Which target or targets are being assessed? How will the assessment be used? Is it a common or individual assessment?	Connection to Standard How will this assessment set up students for successful mastery of the standard?	Student Involvement How will students engage in the assessment process?	Timeline
1.			
2.			
3.			

Source: Buffum, A., Mattos, M., & Malone, J. (2018). Taking action: A handbook for RTI at Work. Bloomington, IN: Solution Tree Press, p. 97.

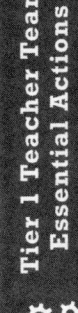

Tier 1 Teacher Team Essential Actions

Tier 1 Teacher Team Essential Actions 1

Sample: Mathematics Essential Standards Unit Plan

Taking Action reference: *Essential Action 3.2—Design a Unit Assessment Plan, p. 94*

This is a sample essential standards unit plan for grade 4 mathematics.

Essential standard: Student will represent multiplication of two-digit by three-digit numbers and describe how that representation connects to the related number sentence.	☐ Knowledge ☑ Reasoning	☐ Performance skills ☐ Product
End-of-unit assessment: Twenty-five-item test with five items—one digit × two to three digits, five items with two digits × two digits, five items with two digits × three digits, and ten points for problem solution with description	**When taught:** March **Instructional days needed:** Sixteen	

Knowledge Targets	Reasoning Targets	Performance Skills Targets	Product Targets
• Know basic facts 0–10. • Know and use several models to represent number sentences.	• Explain how the representation matches the number sentence. • Identify and explain strategies used to solve problems. • Compute multiple-digit problems accurately.		

Student-friendly learning targets:

- I can recall basic facts, 0–10, quickly and accurately.
- I can set up multiplication problems.
- I can use two ways to solve multiplication problems.
- I can use effective strategies to solve problems and find a workable solution.
- I can explain my thinking and strategies.

page 1 of 2

The Big Book of Tools for RTI at Work © 2025 Solution Tree Press • SolutionTree.com
Visit **go.SolutionTree.com/RTIatWork/BBTRTI** and enter the unique access code found on the book's inside front cover to access this reproducible.

Assessment Which target or targets are being assessed? How will the assessment be used? Is it a common or individual assessment?	Connection to Standard How will this assessment set up students for successful mastery of the standard?	Student Involvement How will students engage in the assessment process?	Timeline
1. Ongoing daily quizzes of basic multiplication facts 0–10; one summative quiz—that the student chooses—per week (individual)	Students develop accurate and fluent recall of multiplication facts to successfully compute multiple-digit problems.	Students track daily progress and determine when they are ready for a summative quiz each week.	Ongoing, daily
2. Single digit × two to three digits using two different models and with explanation of models (formative and summative, common formative)	Students develop fluency with multiple algorithms and mathematical language to explain their thinking.	Students self-assess and peer-assess the pretest and make corrections.	Day three: Pretest (formative) Day six: Summative test
3. Two digits × two digits using different models and with explanation of models (formative and summative, individual)	Students develop fluency with multiple algorithms and mathematical language to explain their thinking with problems that have two-digit multipliers.	Students self-assess the pretest, make corrections, and set goals for the summative test.	Day nine: Formative Day twelve: Summative
4. Two-digit × three-digit numbers (mysterious multiplication) (formative, common)	Students use multiplication understanding to solve problems and identify workable solutions.	Students self-assess, select appropriate practice activities, and set goals for final summative test.	Day fourteen: Formative Day sixteen: Final summative

Source: Buffum, A., Mattos, M., & Malone, J. (2018). Taking action: A handbook for RTI at Work. Bloomington, IN: Solution Tree Press, p. 100.

Tool: Using AI Tools to Deconstruct an Essential Standard

Taking Action reference: Essential Action 3.2—Design a Unit Assessment Plan, p. 94

Instructions: When deconstructing your next essential standard, use an AI chatbot like ChatGPT (https://chat.openai.com) or Gemini (https://gemini.google.com) as a collaborative thought partner by posing the prompts in the first column of the following table. Then, assess the responses from your AI chatbot for accuracy and summarize its thinking in the second column of the table. Remember, you should never rely on AI chatbots for original thinking. Instead, use them to give you something to think about. Doing so will accelerate your collaborative work, giving your team more time for meaningful conversations.

Standard We Are Deconstructing:	
Start a new chat in your AI chatbot. Then, ask these prompts in order.	**Together, review your AI chatbot's response for accuracy. Summarize its thinking here.**
Can you unpack this standard? *[Paste standard]* **Sample:** *Can you unpack this standard? "Choose a variety of transition words, phrases, and clauses to convey sequence, to signal shifts from one time or setting to another, and/or to clarify the relationships among ideas" (CCSS.ELA-Literacy.W.6.3.C).*	
List the three most important prerequisites that *[insert grade level]* students should know before learning this standard. **Sample:** *List the three most important prerequisites that sixth-grade students should know before learning this standard.*	
What are the three most common mistakes that *[insert grade level]* students make when learning this standard? **Sample:** *What are the three most common mistakes that sixth-grade students make when learning this standard?*	
Can you give me a learning progression for teaching this standard to *[insert grade level]* students? **Sample:** *Can you give me a learning progression for teaching this standard to sixth-grade students?*	
Describe two resources that I can create to help *[insert grade level]* students master this standard. **Sample:** *Describe two resources that I can create to help sixth-grade students master this standard.*	

Source for standard: National Governors Association Center for Best Practices & Council of Chief State School Officers. (2010a). Common Core State Standards for English language arts and literacy in history/social studies, science, and technical subjects. Washington, DC: Authors. Accessed at https://learning.ccsso.org/wp-content/uploads/2022/11/ADA-Compliant-ELA-Standards.pdf on December 14, 2023.

Tool: Using AI Tools to Develop a Proficiency Scale

Taking Action reference: Essential Action 3.2—Design a Unit Assessment Plan, p. 94

Instructions: When writing your next proficiency scale, use an AI chatbot like ChatGPT (https://chat.openai.com) or Gemini (https://gemini.google.com) as a collaborative thought partner by posing the prompts in the first column of the following table. Then, assess the responses from your AI chatbot for accuracy and summarize its thinking in the second column of the following table. Remember, you should never rely on AI chatbots for original thinking. Instead, use them to give you something to think about. Doing so will accelerate your collaborative work, giving your team more time for meaningful conversations.

Standard We Are Writing a Proficiency Scale For:	
Start a new chat in your AI chatbot. Then, ask these prompts in order.	**Together, review your AI chatbot's response for accuracy. Summarize its thinking here.**
Please create two bulleted lists describing what *[grade level or subject area]* students should know and be able to do if they have mastered this standard: *[paste standard]*. **Sample:** *Please create two bulleted lists describing what sixth-grade students should know and be able to do if they have mastered this standard: "Choose a variety of transition words, phrases, and clauses to convey sequence, to signal shifts from one time or setting to another, and/or to clarify the relationships among ideas" (CCSS.ELA-Literacy.W.6.3.C).*	
Can you give me two bulleted lists describing what students who are **working below grade level** might know and be able to do with this standard?	
Can you give me two bulleted lists describing what students who are **working above grade level** might know and be able to do with this standard?	
Can you summarize this information in a three-column table: one describing performance below grade level, one describing it on grade level, and one describing it above grade level? Include five bullets per column.	
Can you write a proficiency scale describing the steps that students must take to master this standard? Use bullets and make sure that each item is a specific action step.	

Source for standard: National Governors Association Center for Best Practices & Council of Chief State School Officers. (2010a). Common Core State Standards for English language arts and literacy in history/social studies, science, and technical subjects. *Washington, DC: Authors. Accessed at https://learning.ccsso.org/wp-content/uploads/2022/11/ADA-Compliant-ELA-Standards.pdf on December 14, 2023.*

Tool: Examining Your Work With the Team Teaching-Assessing-Learning Cycle

Taking Action *reference: Essential Action 3.2—Design a Unit Assessment Plan, p. 94*

Instructions: In *Taking Action: A Handbook for RTI at Work, Second Edition*, Mattos and colleagues (2025) detail the steps that teacher teams take when working through a cycle of inquiry around their practice with one another. They call this process the team teaching-assessing-learning cycle. Use this tool to examine how closely the current work of your collaborative team aligns with this cycle.

The Team Teaching-Assessing-Learning Cycle

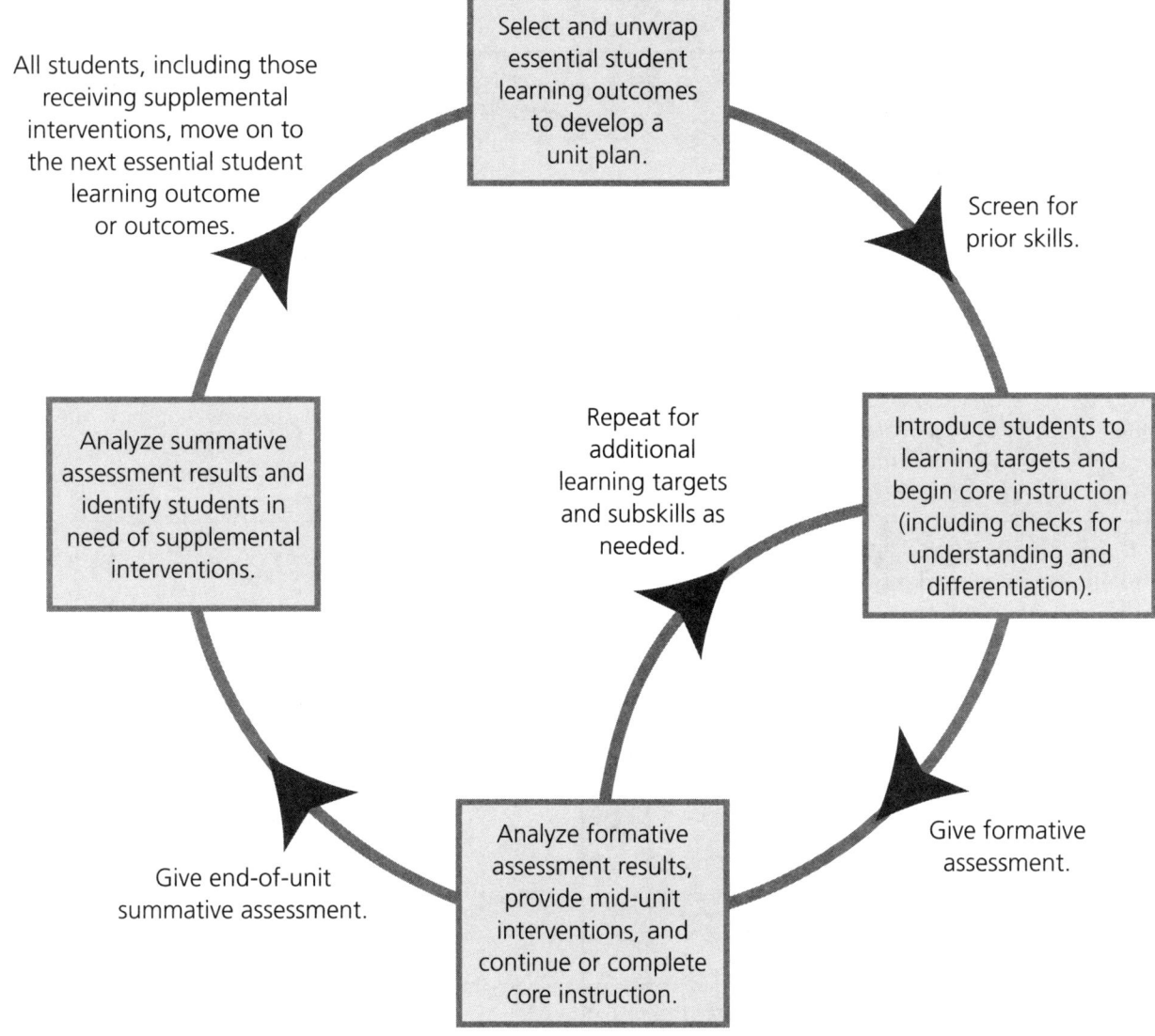

Source: Mattos, M., Buffum, A., Malone, J., Cruz, L. F., Dimich, N., & Schuhl, S. (2025). Taking action: A handbook for RTI at Work (2nd ed.). Bloomington, IN: Solution Tree Press, p. 83. Adapted from Buffum, A., Mattos, M., & Weber, C. (2012). Simplifying response to intervention: Four essential guiding principles. Bloomington, IN: Solution Tree Press.

Questions for Reflection

Which steps in the team teaching-assessing-learning cycle does your collaborative team already take?

Which steps in the team teaching-assessing-learning cycle would be new for your collaborative team?

Are there any steps in the team teaching-assessing-learning cycle that you have experimented with but aren't implementing consistently?

What changes would you need to make to align your work with the team teaching-assessing-learning cycle?

What support will you need to make those changes?

Tool: Common Formative Assessment Pretest

Taking Action *reference: Essential Action 3.3—Create Common Assessments and Begin Instruction, p. 114*

Instructions: While the term *common formative assessment* (CFAs) is widely used in schools, it is often widely misunderstood, preventing teams from fully leveraging CFAs to move student learning forward. Take the following pretest to evaluate your understanding of CFAs. Then, use the corresponding answer key (page 109) to check your answers.

Statement	Your Initial Answer	Your Notes	The Correct Answer
CFAs should be given at the end of an instruction unit.	☐ True ☐ False		☐ True ☐ False
The only purpose of a CFA is for teams to collect student learning data.	☐ True ☐ False		☐ True ☐ False
Assessments are only formative if teachers and students take action or change course after the assessment is given.	☐ True ☐ False		☐ True ☐ False
CFAs must be team designed. That means district benchmarks and standardized tests don't count as CFAs.	☐ True ☐ False		☐ True ☐ False
Every question on a CFA should be directly tied to an individual learning target or grade-level essential.	☐ True ☐ False		☐ True ☐ False
Classroom quick-checks done during the flow of a lesson (examples: fist-to-five ratings, thumbs-up/thumbs-down) can be used as CFAs.	☐ True ☐ False		☐ True ☐ False
Exit tickets done at the end of a lesson can be used as a CFA.	☐ True ☐ False		☐ True ☐ False
For a CFA to be reliable, it should have at least twenty-five questions.	☐ True ☐ False		☐ True ☐ False
Prewritten questions from district-provided resources should never be used on a CFA given by a learning team.	☐ True ☐ False		☐ True ☐ False
A CFA's primary purpose is to generate grades for report cards.	☐ True ☐ False		☐ True ☐ False

Answer Key: Common Formative Assessment Pretest

Taking Action reference: Essential Action 3.3—Create Common Assessments and Begin Instruction, p. 114

Instructions for facilitators: Following the direct instruction of essential concepts regarding common formative assessments (CFAs), utilize the following answer key to emphasize assessment principles that are crucial for your faculty's comprehension.

Statement	The Correct Answer	Explanation
CFAs should be given at the end of an instruction unit.	☐ True ☑ False	The goal of a CFA is to provide teams with just-in-time information that they can use to inform daily instruction. That means teams should give CFAs frequently throughout the instruction cycle. Waiting until the end of a unit prevents teams from taking action before intervention.
The only purpose of a CFA is for teams to collect student learning data.	☐ True ☑ False	While collecting data that teams can use to respond to student needs in the moment is the primary purpose for giving CFAs, it is not the sole purpose. Teams should also be using the results of CFAs to gather evidence of the efficacy of their instruction.
Assessments are only formative if teachers and students take action or change course after the assessment is given.	☑ True ☐ False	CFAs should always inform the next steps for teachers and students. Any assessment given by a teacher that leads to a change in course by teachers or students is formative. Any assessment given that does not result in a change in course is summative.
CFAs must be team designed. That means district benchmarks and standardized tests don't count as CFAs.	☑ True ☐ False	While district benchmarks and standardized assessments can point schools to broad patterns in student performance, they are given too infrequently to lead to meaningful action by teachers and students. Furthermore, writing CFAs together is a valuable learning opportunity for classroom teachers that leads to shared clarity around mastery expectations.
Every question on a CFA should be directly tied to an individual learning target or grade-level essential.	☑ True ☐ False	If CFAs are going to lead to informed action by classroom teachers, questions should be intentionally designed to provide information about what students have—or have not—mastered. Tying each question to specific learning targets or grade-level essentials allows teams to quickly identify the specific needs of students who have not yet mastered grade-level expectations.
Classroom quick-checks done during the flow of a lesson (examples: fist-to-five ratings, thumbs-up/thumbs-down) can be used as CFAs.	☐ True ☑ False	CFAs must lead to the production of a permanent product that can be examined by a team. Classroom quick-checks don't provide that permanent product. These types of activities are called *checks for understanding*, and they provide individual teachers with valuable in-the-moment information about their class's readiness to move forward in instruction, but they are not CFAs.

Exit tickets done at the end of a lesson can be used as a CFA.	☑ True ☐ False	If they are developed by a team and result in a permanent product that can be examined together, exit tickets count as a CFA. The lesson here is that the key in determining whether something can be used as a CFA is the team's ability to examine, learn from, and act on the information collected from students.
For a CFA to be reliable, it should have at least twenty-five questions.	☐ True ☑ False	Shorter assessments given more frequently are generally more effective as CFAs than longer assessments given less frequently. Here's why: shorter assessments are faster to write, faster to deliver, faster to score, and faster to analyze. That makes it more likely for teams to act on the information they collect. A good rule of thumb is that teams should be giving CFAs roughly once every two weeks and that each should have no more than ten questions covering no more than two or three essentials.
Prewritten questions from district-provided resources should never be used on a CFA given by a learning team.	☐ True ☑ False	When looking for questions to add to CFAs, teams should always refer to their district curriculum resources. Doing so can help teams build their assessment knowledge by gaining a better sense for the level of rigor required in a standard. What's more, finding questions for a CFA in district curriculum resources can be faster than creating questions from scratch. The only thing that teams shouldn't do is use questions from district curriculum resources without ensuring that those questions align with their instruction.
A CFA's primary purpose is to generate grades for report cards.	☐ True ☑ False	The primary purpose of a CFA is to provide teachers and students with the necessary information to move their learning forward. Progressive schools often establish policies that CFA scores aren't graded and then added to student averages—or that scores are reported as information, but not weighted in final grade calculations. The goal of these policies is to acknowledge that students need the space to practice without penalty.

Tool: Assessment Design Checklist

Taking Action *reference: Essential Action 3.3—Create Common Assessments and Begin Instruction, p. 114*

Instructions: Review the statements in the following checklist for creating, critiquing, and revising assessments. The statements in this checklist fall into two categories.

1. The design statements reflect qualities or criteria that lead to accurate information from the assessment evidence.
2. The use statements capture the assessment qualities that lead both students and teachers to take action based on what they learn from assessment evidence.

Next to each statement, record your comments on the quality of the design or use of your assessments.

Accurate Design	
Statement	**Response and Comments**
1. The team clarifies the standards, targets, and skills being assessed and determines grade- or course-level expectations for each.	
2. The team matches the assessment method to the learning targets. This means the items or tasks ask students to "do" the verb to show mastery. For example, if the verb in the target is *explain*, the item ensures students produce an explanation and don't just select one.	
3. The team ensures there are enough items to determine with confidence the level of proficiency.	
4. The team determines the cognitive level and grade- or course-level expectations for each item. (If critiquing or revising an already designed assessment, identify the cognitive level and learning target for each item to be sure it reflects the cognitive demand in the standards.)	
5. The team ensures the structure, layout, and setup of the questions create the best possible conditions for students to show their understanding, and revises what might contribute to student confusion.	

Statement	Response and Comments
6. The team ensures directions are present, clear, and concise and the visual layout of the assessment is easy to understand and read.	
7. If utilizing a technology tool, the team ensures that students have the training needed to use the tool in a meaningful way and that they have access to and an understanding of what they need to utilize the tool.	
8. The team ensures the tasks, items, and questions or exercises are written well. • The assessment is clear, succinct, and generally not confusing. • The team identifies the vocabulary and background knowledge needed to engage successfully in the assessment.	
9. The team collaborates with colleagues who have expertise in special education, language learning, and any other specialized expertise to ensure appropriate accommodations or modifications are made for students who need them so they have equitable access and can demonstrate grade- or course-level learning.	
10. The team ensures scores communicated directly on the assessment are provided by learning targets or standards. Or, the scoring rubric indicates the qualities of the work.	
11. The team agrees on how to administer the assessment to students (for example, which resources students can use, what posters can be on the walls, and the length of time given to complete the assessment).	
12. The team creates a tool or plan for students to reflect and, as needed, learn from their assessment results and feedback.	

Intentional Use	
Statement	**Response and Comments**
13. The team analyzes data from the common assessment (formative or end-of-unit) by standard, target, or skill and by student to determine effective instructional practices and identify next steps for students. The team also identifies who needs intervention and extension to achieve the targeted essential standard and learning target.	
14. The team analyzes student work from the common assessment to identify the strengths, errors, and next steps for students related to the essential standard, target, or skill.	
15. The team develops an agreed-on instructional plan for intervention and extension from data analysis and student work. This plan may be executed as a Tier 1 prevention or Tier 2 intervention and extension based on the common assessment the team is analyzing.	
16. The team determines how it will know whether students learned through Tier 1 or Tier 2 responses. In other words, when and how will the team reassess the essential learning that is the focus of the response?	
17. The team agrees on how to evaluate student learning on the assessment (how to score student work for consistent feedback and grading).	

As a team, discuss the following.
- What are the strengths of your team's common assessment based on your alignment to the design-quality checklist?
- What, if any, revisions to the assessment are needed based on your alignment to the design-quality checklist? Decide how those revisions will be made.

Source: Mattos, M., Buffum, A., Malone, J., Cruz, L. F., Dimich, N., & Schuhl, S. (2025). Taking action: A handbook for RTI at Work (2nd ed.). Bloomington, IN: Solution Tree Press, p. 122.

Tool: Building a Common Formative Assessment

Taking Action *reference: Essential Action 3.3—Create Common Assessments and Begin Instruction, p. 114*

Instructions: This template is designed to help you write a short common formative assessment for one essential standard. Start by writing down the learning target you will assess and then checking one box in each column. Fill in your potential assessment questions, expected answers, and common mistakes. Three reminders about the characteristics of high-quality common formative assessments can be found at the bottom of this template.

Essential Learning Target to Be Assessed:			
Depth of Knowledge Level of Target	**Best Strategy for Assessing This Target**	**Percentage of Questions on District Benchmarks and Standardized Tests That Cover This Target**	**How Important This Target Is for Future Success in and Beyond School**
☐ Recall and Reproduction ☐ Skills and Concepts ☐ Strategic Thinking ☐ Extended Thinking	☐ Selected response ☐ Constructed response ☐ Performance task ☐ Other:	☐ 0–5 percent ☐ 6–10 percent ☐ 11–15 percent ☐ More than 15 percent	☐ Not important ☐ Somewhat important ☐ Very important ☐ Essential

Potential Assessment Questions		
Question	**Expected Answer**	**Common Mistakes We Might See**

Three Important Common Formative Assessment Reminders

1. A good common formative assessment will cover no more than three essential learning targets. Limiting the length of a common formative assessment makes it possible for teachers to analyze and then act on collected data in a timely manner.
2. A good common formative assessment should include at least three questions for each learning target that is being tested. That protects data sets against the impact of poorly written questions.
3. The complexity of a question should align with the complexity of the learning target it is designed to measure. That means performance tasks are unnecessary for lower-order learning targets that require recall and reproduction but essential for higher-order learning targets that require strategic or extended thinking.

Source: Ferriter, W. M. (2020). The big book of tools for collaborative teams in a PLC at Work. Bloomington, IN: Solution Tree Press, p. 102.

Tool: Performance Tracking Table

Taking Action *reference: Essential Action 3.3—Create Common Assessments and Begin Instruction, p. 114*

Instructions: Work with your learning team to brainstorm a list of the common mistakes that students are likely to make in your upcoming unit of study; enter the items from that list in the **Errors We Expect to See** column. Then, every time that you assess student performance (*grading papers*, *looking at student work samples*, *making observations during class*, *listening to student reasoning during classroom conversations*, and so on), write the initials of students making common errors in the columns titled **Attempts 1** to **4**. Finally, use the reflection questions to help you determine how to move forward.

Task: _____

Errors We Expect to See	Attempt 1	Attempt 2	Attempt 3	Attempt 4

Questions for Reflection

What conclusions can you draw about next steps worth taking from the data that you have collected? Do similar patterns appear in the data of other members of your learning team?

What do these data suggest about your own instructional strengths and weaknesses? Are there specific subgroups of students that you are struggling or excelling with? Are there specific concepts that you are struggling or excelling at teaching? How do you know?

Which students need targeted reinforcement? Which students need extra practice? Which students need extension?

Source: Ferriter, W. M. (2020). The big book of tools for collaborative teams in a PLC at Work. Bloomington, IN: Solution Tree Press, p. 105. Adapted from Fisher, D., & Frey, N. (2012). Making time for feedback. Educational Leadership, 70(1), 42–47.

Sample: Performance Tracking Table—Elementary School Mathematics

Taking Action reference: Essential Action 3.3—Create Common Assessments and Begin Instruction, p. 114

Instructions: Work with your learning team to brainstorm a list of the common mistakes that students are likely to make in your upcoming unit of study; enter the items from that list in the **Errors We Expect to See** column. Then, every time that you assess student performance (*grading papers, looking at student work samples, making observations during class, listening to student reasoning during classroom conversations*, and so on), write the initials of students making common errors in the columns titled **Attempts 1** to **4**. Finally, use the reflection questions to help you determine how to move forward.

Task: Area Method of Multiplication for Fourth-Grade Students

Errors We Expect to See	Attempt 1	Attempt 2	Attempt 3	Attempt 4
Student adds too many zeros when multiplying multiples of ten.	XP, JM, SA, AK	XP, AK	AK	AK
Student does not line up place values correctly when adding partial products to find the solution.	XP, JM, HH, DL, AK, TD, IG, DD, MP, SP, DP	XP, JM, DL, AK, IG, DD, MP, SP	XP, AK, MP, IG, SP	AK, IG
Student does not expand numbers correctly when recording the hundreds, tens, and ones.	MP, SP, DP	DP		
Student makes a multiplication fact error.	DMT, DD, XP	DMT, DD, XP	DMT, DD, XP	DMT, DD

Questions for Reflection

What conclusions can you draw about next steps worth taking from the data that you have collected? Do similar patterns appear in the data of other members of your learning team?

I am optimistic about these results. Here's why: the most common error—lining up place values correctly when adding partial products—is not fundamentally connected to the mathematics involved in using the area method of multiplication to solve problems. Instead, in most cases, it is a simple factor of not being careful when writing out problems. I notice many of the students in this list are also still developing gross and fine motor skills. Their handwriting, not their mathematical understanding, could be causing the problems that I am seeing. My solution will be to give these students large-grid graph paper and encourage them to write individual numbers into individual boxes on the graph paper. My prediction is that this will help students line up place values correctly.

What do these data suggest about your own instructional strengths and weaknesses? Are there specific subgroups of students that you are struggling or excelling with? Are there specific concepts that you are struggling or excelling at teaching? How do you know?

Something that I'm doing to teach students to expand their place value numbers when setting up their initial grids is working well. That's interesting to me largely because my students are still struggling to line up their place values when adding partial sums. It is surprising that they can do one task but not the other. The pattern that I notice the most, though, is that the students who repeat mistakes time and again in all these areas are students who came to my class behind by a grade level or two in mathematics. This fits a pattern for me: my strategies generally work for students who are on grade level to begin with, but I struggle with students who have gaps in prerequisite knowledge. I need to find someone on my team who is good at teaching grade-level concepts to students who are behind and ask him or her for ideas.

Which students need targeted reinforcement? Which students need extra practice? Which students need extension?

I need to meet with Anya, Diego, Xavion, and Jared sometime during our intervention time to give them some additional reteaching. They continue to appear repeatedly in my observations. I am going to put together a few additional practice activities for the rest of my students as an initial intervention to see if that works.

Source: Ferriter, W. M. (2020). The big book of tools for collaborative teams in a PLC at Work. Bloomington, IN: Solution Tree Press, pp. 106–107. Adapted from Fisher, D., & Frey, N. (2012). Making time for feedback. Educational Leadership, 70(1), 42–47.

Common errors adapted from Roose, T. (2015, December 6). Multiplying with the area model error analysis [Blog post]. Accessed at https://tarheelstateteacher.com/blog/multiplying-with-the-area-model-error-analysis on August 5, 2019.

Sample: Performance Tracking Table—Middle School Science

Taking Action *reference: Essential Action 3.3—Create Common Assessments and Begin Instruction, p. 114*

Instructions: Work with your learning team to brainstorm a list of the common mistakes that students are likely to make in your upcoming unit of study; enter the items from that list in the **Errors We Expect to See** column. Then, every time that you assess student performance (*grading papers, looking at student work samples, making observations during class, listening to student reasoning during classroom conversations*, and so on), write the initials of students making common errors in the columns titled **Attempts 1** to **4**. Finally, use the reflection questions to help you determine how to move forward.

Task: Lab Report for a Sixth-Grade Science Student

Errors We Expect to See	Attempt 1	Attempt 2	Attempt 3	Attempt 4
Hypothesis includes more than one testable variable.	MR, LR, HS, GT, JT	MR, LR, HS	HS	
Procedures are missing critical steps and could not be accurately followed by another scientist.	MR, LR, HS, GT, JT, JE, DD, NE	MR		
Graph or table fails to effectively communicate findings (sloppy; inaccurate information is included; unit labels are missing; scale on y-axis is laid out incorrectly).	DQT			
Conclusion doesn't include specific references to data collected in lab.	MR, LR, HS, SC, JL, KP, AA, DC, SS, KA, EW, JC, NP, KR, JS	MR, LR, HS, SC, JL, KP, AA, DC, KA, JC, NP, KR, JS, PP	MR, LR, HS, SC, JL, KP, DC, KA, JC, NP, KR, JS, PP	MR, LR, HS, SC, JL, KP, DC, KA, JC, NP, KR, JS, PP

Questions for Reflection

What conclusions can you draw about next steps worth taking from the data that you have collected? Do similar patterns appear in the data of other members of your learning team?

One of the things that we noticed across all our performance tracking templates is that we are all struggling to teach students to write proper conclusions for their labs. They don't see the connection between the data that we are collecting in the lab and the conclusions that they are drawing as scientists. One of the things that we can do to help with that is to continue to focus on our "Claim-Evidence-Reasoning" tasks in class. If we do those frequently, students should start to see that all claims need to be backed up with evidence, and that in a lab, collected data are the best evidence for supporting conclusions.

What do these data suggest about your own instructional strengths and weaknesses? Are there specific subgroups of students that you are struggling or excelling with? Are there specific concepts that you are struggling or excelling at teaching? How do you know?

Something that I'm doing to teach students to create graphs is really working. All my students, regardless of class, are making good graphs. I think it might be because we do a bunch of "body graphs" at the beginning of the year. That strategy is always engaging to the students, and I think that it helps them remember components of a good graph when they are asked to make one later.

Which students need targeted reinforcement? Which students need extra practice? Which students need extension?

I've got a whole handful of students who need help integrating data into their conclusion paragraphs. Henry also needs help with hypotheses. I can deliver that intervention during our next schoolwide intervention period.

Source: Ferriter, W. M. (2020). The big book of tools for collaborative teams in a PLC at Work. Bloomington, IN: Solution Tree Press, p. 108. Adapted from Fisher, D., & Frey, N. (2012). Making time for feedback. Educational Leadership, 70(1), 42–47.

Tool: Reflecting on the Role Grades Can Play as Feedback

Taking Action *reference: Essential Action 3.4—Foster Student Investment, p. 129*

Instructions: In an article in *Kappan Magazine* titled "Can Grades Be an Effective Form of Feedback?," assessment expert Thomas R. Guskey (2022) details four *necessary conditions* that must be in place for grades to serve as a meaningful form of feedback to students. Explore the following criteria and consider them against how grades are typically used in your school.

Necessary Condition	Supporting Quote From Article
Grades must be assigned to performances rather than to students.	"Beginning at the earliest levels, teachers must help students and their families understand that grades do not reflect who you are as a learner, but where you are in your learning journey" (Guskey, 2022).
Grades must be criterion based, not norm based.	"Norm-based grades assess students' relative standing among classmates . . . . Criterion-based or task-involving grading describes how well students have met learning goals" (Guskey, 2022).
Grades must be seen as temporary.	"Students' level of performance is never permanent. As students study and practice, their understanding grows and their performance improves. To accurately describe how well students have learned, grades must reflect students' current performance level" (Guskey, 2022).
Grades must be accompanied by guidance for improvement.	"Students need guidance and direction on how to make better progress, reach the goals, and achieve success. This is true of all forms of feedback" (Guskey, 2022).

Questions for Reflection

How closely do school grading practices align with the necessary conditions outlined by Guskey (2022)?

Which necessary condition are you most likely to find in schools? Which necessary condition are you least likely to find? Why?

What barriers keep your school from implementing these necessary conditions in your grading practices? What steps would you have to take to overcome those barriers?

How closely do your current grading practices align with Guskey's (2022) necessary conditions? What are you doing well? What could you improve on?

Reference

Guskey, T. R. (2022, October 24). *Can grades be an effective form of feedback?* Accessed at https://kappanonline.org/grades-feedback-guskey on April 17, 2023.

Sample: Assessment Wrapper for Primary Students

Taking Action *reference: Essential Action 3.4—Foster Student Investment, p. 129*

Instructions: Review your assessment and shade the questions green that you answered correctly. Shade the questions red that you answered incorrectly.

Measuring the Length of Objects

I can accurately use a measurement tool to measure the length of an object.	Question 1	Question 2	Question 3

I can estimate the length of objects (units of inches, feet, centimeters, and meters).	Question 4	Question 5

I can measure to figure out how much longer one object is than another.	Question 6	Question 7

What have you learned so far?

_____

_____

What do you still need to learn?

_____

_____

What is your new learning plan?

_____

_____

Telling Time

I can tell and write time from analog and digital clocks to the nearest five minutes, using a.m. and p.m.	Question 8	Question 9	Question 10

What have you learned so far?
_____
_____

What do you still need to learn?
_____
_____

What is your new learning plan?
_____
_____

Problem Solving

I can use addition and subtraction to solve word problems involving lengths.	Question 11	Question 12	Question 13

I can solve word problems involving dollar bills, quarters, dimes, nickels, and pennies and correctly use $ and ¢ symbols.	Question 14	Question 15	Question 16

What have you learned so far?
_____
_____

What do you still need to learn?

_____

_____

What is your new learning plan?

_____

_____

Source: Kerr, D., Hulen, T. A., Heller, J., & Butler, B. K. (2021). What about us? The PLC at Work process for grades preK–2 teams. Bloomington, IN: Solution Tree Press, pp. 132–134.

Tier 1 Teacher Team Essential Actions

Tool: Practice Test Tracking Template for Secondary Students

Taking Action *reference: Essential Action 3.4—Foster Student Investment, p. 129*

Instructions: While *taking* our practice test, use the left-hand side of the following table to keep track of the questions that are hard for you to answer. Then, while *reviewing* our practice test, use the right-hand side of the table to identify concepts you have mastered and concepts you will need to study before our end-of-unit exam.

		While you are taking your practice test, place an *X* in the column that best represents your feelings about your answer to each question.			While you are reviewing your practice test, place an *X* in the column that best represents your feelings about your answer to each question.			
Question Number	Concept or Skill Covered in This Question	This question was easy.	I have doubts about this answer.	I guessed on this question.	I got this question right.	I got this question wrong. Here is why.		
						I made a simple mistake.	I misread this question.	I need to study this again.
1								
2								
3								
4								
5								
6								
7								
8								
9								
10								
11								
12								
13								
14								
15								

What patterns can you spot in your responses on this practice test?

Source: Adapted from Brown, T., & Ferriter, W. M. (2021). You can learn! Building student ownership, motivation, and efficacy with the PLC at Work process. Bloomington, IN: Solution Tree Press. Table drawn from classroom materials in Chappuis, J., & Stiggins, R. (2020). Classroom assessment for student learning: Doing it right—using it well (3rd ed.). Upper Saddle River, NJ: Pearson Education. Adapted with permission from Paula Gerwig.

Sample: Practice Test Tracking Template for Secondary Students

Taking Action reference: Essential Action 3.4—Foster Student Investment, p. 129

Instructions: While *taking* our practice test, use the left-hand side of the following table to keep track of the questions that are hard for you to answer. Then, while *reviewing* our practice test, use the right-hand side of the table to identify concepts you have mastered and concepts you will need to study before our end-of-unit exam.

		While you are taking your practice test, place an *X* in the column that best represents your feelings about your answer to each question.			While you are reviewing your practice test, place an *X* in the column that best represents your feelings about your answer to each question.			
Question Number	**Concept or Skill Covered in This Question**	This question was easy.	I have doubts about this answer.	I guessed on this question.	I got this question right.	I got this question wrong. Here is why.		
						I made a simple mistake.	I misread this question.	I need to study this again.
1	Food webs	X			X			
2	Energy pyramids	X						X
3	Photosynthesis	X					X	
4	Food webs		X		X			
5	Producers and consumers		X		X			
6	Photosynthesis		X				X	
7	Photosynthesis	X						X
8	Cellular respiration			X	X			
9	Energy pyramids		X					X
10	Cellular respiration			X	X			
11	Food webs	X			X			
12	Flowering plants	X			X			
13	Energy pyramids		X					X
14	Flowering plants	X			X			
15	Flowering plants		X		X			

What patterns can you spot in your responses on this tracking sheet?

I noticed that I am having trouble with energy pyramids. That was something I thought I had mastered already. I will practice a few of those questions before our unit test. I also noticed that I got all the questions about cellular respiration correct, but I'm still going to study those. I guessed at two of the questions and had doubts about the other. I got them right, but that doesn't mean I knew what I was doing.

Source: Adapted from Brown, T., & Ferriter, W. M. (2021). You can learn! Building student ownership, motivation, and efficacy with the PLC at Work process. Bloomington, IN: Solution Tree Press. Table drawn from classroom materials in Chappuis, J., & Stiggins, R. (2020). Classroom assessment for student learning: Doing it right—using it well (3rd ed.). Upper Saddle River, NJ: Pearson Education. Adapted with permission from Paula Gerwig.

Tool: Teaching Primary Learners About Short-Term Goal Setting

Taking Action *reference: Essential Action 3.4—Foster Student Investment, p. 129*

For third-grade teacher Stephanie Van Horn (2014), short-term goal setting starts by asking students to complete two sentence starters on sticky notes to create what she calls WOW—*working on weekly*—goals. Once students have completed their WOW goals, they add their sticky notes to a chart in the back of the classroom and revisit during daily morning meetings. You can replicate this work in your own classroom by making copies of the following WOW goal templates and asking students to fill one out at the beginning of every week.

MY WOW GOAL:

In one week, I will:

I will know that I have made my goal when:

MY WOW GOAL:

In one week, I will:

I will know that I have made my goal when:

MY WOW GOAL:

In one week, I will:

I will know that I have made my goal when:

MY WOW GOAL:

In one week, I will:

I will know that I have made my goal when:

Source: Brown, T., & Ferriter, W. M. (2021). You can learn! Building student ownership, motivation, and efficacy with the PLC at Work process. Bloomington, IN: Solution Tree Press, p. 72.

Reference

Van Horn, S. (2014, November 7). *Working on weekly class SMART goals* [Blog post]. Accessed at www.3rdgradethoughts.com/2014/11/working-on-weekly-class-smart-goals.html on April 18, 2023.

Tool Overview: Creating Next-Step Checklists to Involve Students in the Intervention Process

Taking Action reference: Essential Action 3.4—Foster Student Investment, p. 129

Instructions: Next-step checklists can help students monitor their progress toward mastering important outcomes, turning them into active learning partners. Use this template to create a next-step checklist for one of your upcoming units.

Checklist development instructions for learning teams:

1. In the first column, list three to five essential outcomes for this upcoming unit of study written in student-friendly language. Consider creating questions students can answer with a clear *yes* or *no* response.
2. In the second column, list three to five tasks students can use as evidence to assess their progress toward mastering the essential outcomes covered on this checklist.
3. In the third column, list three to five specific actions students can take to move their learning forward when they struggle to master the essential outcomes being studied. Students should clearly understand these actions and require no additional direction from the teacher in the classroom.
4. In the fourth column, list three to five specific actions that students can take to move their learning forward when they demonstrate grade-level mastery of the essential outcomes before initial instruction ends. Students should clearly understand these actions and require no additional direction from the teacher in the classroom.

Source: The concept of next-step checklists originally appeared in Ferriter, W. M., & Cancellieri, P. J. (2017). Creating a culture of feedback. Bloomington, IN: Solution Tree Press. Additional thinking was contributed by the mathematics team at MacArthur Junior High School, Jonesboro, Arkansas.

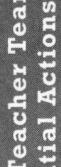

Student Tool: Next-Step Checklist

Over the past few weeks, we have worked on a new unit. Use this next-step checklist sheet to track your progress.

What Do I Need to Know and Be Able to Do?	How Will I Know if I Am Making Progress?	What Steps Should I Take When I Struggle?	What Steps Should I Take When I Excel?
What content and skills do I need to master during this unit? What key questions have I been wrestling with?	What evidence can I collect to track my progress toward mastering essential content and skills?	How can I relearn the content that I am struggling with? How can I get extra practice?	How can I extend my learning? What related topics can I explore? How can I challenge myself to go beyond the basics?
☐	☐	☐	☐
☐	☐	☐	☐
☐	☐	☐	☐

Source: The concept of next-step checklists originally appeared in Ferriter, W. M., & Cancellieri, P. J. (2017). Creating a culture of feedback. Bloomington, IN: Solution Tree Press. Additional thinking was contributed by the mathematics team at MacArthur Junior High School, Jonesboro, Arkansas.

The Big Book of Tools for RTI at Work © 2025 Solution Tree Press • SolutionTree.com

Visit **go.SolutionTree.com/RTIatWork/BBTRTI** and enter the unique access code found on the book's inside front cover to access this reproducible.

Sample: Next-Step Checklist—Sixth-Grade Matter Unit

Taking Action reference: Essential Action 3.4—Foster Student Investment, p. 129

Over the past few weeks, we have worked on a new unit. Use this next-step checklist to track your progress.

What Do I Need to Know and Be Able to Do? What content and skills do I need to master during this unit? What key questions have I been wrestling with?	How Will I Know if I Am Making Progress? What evidence can I collect to track my progress toward mastering essential content and skills?	What Steps Should I Take When I Struggle? How can I relearn the content that I am struggling with? How can I get extra practice?	What Steps Should I Take When I Excel? How can I extend my learning? What related topics can I explore? How can I challenge myself to go beyond the basics?
☐ Can I name the measurable properties of matter?	☐ My score on the Matter Unit Vocabulary Test:	☐ Review classroom Edpuzzle tutorials on heat and characteristic properties of matter.	☐ Explore the classroom Edpuzzle tutorial titled "The Quest to Discover Absolute Zero."
☐ Can I accurately measure the mass, volume, and density of a solid and a liquid?	☐ My score on the States of Matter Research Project:	☐ Meet with a peer tutor during our intervention period to review my density calculations for our Mystery Liquid Lab.	☐ Extend my learning about heat's impact on objects by studying thermal expansion gaps in bridges and buildings.
☐ Can I explain how the structures of solids, liquids, and gases are similar and different?	☐ My score on the Ice Cube to Water Illustration:	☐ Use our Matter Unit Quizlet to review vocabulary from this unit.	☐ Study the design of Yeti coolers and cups. Use what I know about matter to explain why that design works to keep things cool for so long.
☐ Can I detail the effect of heat on different states of matter?	☐ Other evidence of your learning (questions answered in class, contributions to group projects, or comparisons with partners' thoughts):	☐ Ask this question in class to clarify something that I'm wondering/confused about:	☐ Offer to teach a friend something I have learned from this unit of study during peer tutoring time.

Source: The concept of next-step checklists originally appeared in Ferriter, W. M., & Cancellieri, P. J. (2017). Creating a culture of feedback. Bloomington, IN: Solution Tree Press. Additional thinking was contributed by the mathematics team at MacArthur Junior High School, Jonesboro, Arkansas.

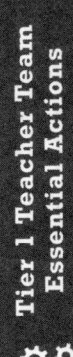

Tier 1 Teacher Team Essential Actions

Tool: Team Protocol for Analyzing Assessment Results

Taking Action reference: Essential Action 3.5—Analyze and Respond to Common Assessment Data, p. 138

Team Data Analysis Protocol

Use results from common formative or end-of-unit assessments.

Note: Enter data prior to the meeting and have access to student work for the discussion. Designate a timekeeper and a notetaker for the conversation.

Question One: What? (Ten minutes)

- What targets seem to have been well established? Not well established?
- Are we seeing some common errors or misunderstandings?
- Is there a common group of students who are not scoring well?
- Do we see significantly different results among our classes?
- Are there any "fuzzy" areas in the scoring of student work? Do we need to calibrate and clarify?
- What student groupings emerge from the data (such as not proficient, close, and beyond proficient)?
- Which students have not achieved proficiency? On what targets do they need support?
- Which students have gone beyond proficiency and may benefit from extended learning opportunities?

Question Two: So What? (Seven minutes)

- What is our hypothesis for these results?
- Did we actually teach what we intended?
- What might be the obstacle for students who are struggling?
- Are our resource materials actually aligned to our targeted learning outcomes?
- What instructional strategies appeared to be highly effective when we were examining our different results?
- Are there any practices we need to research or learn about in order to better support student learning?

Question Three: Now What? (Intervention and extension plan; twenty minutes)

- What concepts or skills need to be retaught to the whole class (based on our data)?
- What short-term interventions and reteaching will we provide to help students reach proficiency?
- Given the errors or misconceptions we see, what strategies will we use? How will these interventions be delivered? Who will deliver them?
- What evidence will we gather throughout the interventions to monitor student learning?
- How might we provide reinforcement or extend student learning for those who demonstrate proficiency (for example, what may we implement within the class or during Tier 2 support)?
- How will we provide students feedback on a timely basis? How are they expected to engage with this feedback?

Sample Organizer

Students Needing Intervention (They may be subdivided into more than one group.)	Support Plan
Students Needing Reinforcement or Minimal Support	**Support Plan**
Students Needing Extension	**Support Plan**

Question Four: What Have We Learned? (Five minutes)

- Are there any changes we would make to our assessments, pacing, or instructional strategies the next time we teach this unit?

Source: Bailey, K., & Jakicic, C. (2023). Common formative assessment: A toolkit for Professional Learning Communities at Work (2nd ed.). Bloomington, IN: Solution Tree Press, pp. 149–150.

Tool: Looking at End-of-Unit Assessment Data

Taking Action *reference: Essential Action 3.5—Analyze and Respond to Common Assessment Data, p. 138*

Instructions: Recently, your students took an end-of-unit assessment. Now, it is time to learn from those results. Spend your next team meeting answering the following questions and developing a plan to take action as a result of the collected data.

Step 1: Engage in Initial Reflection

Look back at your assessment together to spot broad trends in the results.

Questions for Reflection	Your Responses	Your Next Actions Do you need to reteach or reassess? Do you need to research a new instructional strategy?
Looking at your whole class: What questions were answered correctly by *more than* 80 percent of your students? What standards do those questions cover? Why do you think students did so well on those questions?		
Looking at your whole class: What questions were answered correctly by *fewer than* 50 percent of your students? What standards do those questions cover? Why do you think students struggled with those questions?		
Looking at your whole class: What patterns can you spot in questions that cover the same standards? Did students perform similarly on all questions that cover the same standards? Did students perform better on some questions than others?		
Looking at struggling students: What patterns can you spot in questions that struggling students got wrong? Are there similar concepts covered by those questions? Did students give the same wrong answer to those questions? What do those wrong answers suggest about student misunderstandings and gaps in knowledge?		

Step 2: Find Point of Comparison Data

As a team, find the five questions missed most frequently by students on your most recent end-of-unit assessment. Then, list the percentage of students who answered those questions correctly in each teacher's classroom.

The Five Most Commonly Missed Questions on Our End-of-Unit Assessment					
Teacher Name	**Question ___**	**Question ___**	**Question ___**	**Question ___**	**Question ___**
Sample: Mr. Nowak	56	68	73	58	80
Overall Averages					

Questions for Reflection

Are there individual teachers who have identified instructional practices that are particularly effective at teaching the concepts and skills covered in this assessment? What strategies are they using in their classrooms? Would those same strategies work in other classrooms? Can we use those same strategies when teaching students different concepts and skills?

Are there any concepts and skills that your entire team needs help with to teach well? Why is that? What makes that skill so challenging for students to master? What strategies are you using to teach those concepts and skills? Where can you find new ideas for teaching students those concepts and skills?

What do these patterns mean for you as a team of instructors? Can these patterns help you plan more effective intervention and extension experiences for students? Can these patterns help you pinpoint an area for continued study for your learning team? What next steps will you take to address those patterns?

Step 3: Plan for Intervention and Extension

Generally, students fall within one of three categories on assessments: (1) those needing additional time and attention, (2) those needing extra practice, or (3) those ready for extension beyond grade-level essentials. Plan one activity that can be used with each of those three groups.

	Students Identified for Reinforcement, Extra Practice, or Extension	**Planned Instructional Strategy**
Additional Time and Support List the students in your classes who you think need direct reteaching because they are making significant conceptual mistakes when answering assessment questions.		
Additional Practice List the students you think have mastered the concept covered in this assessment but who are making simple mistakes that can be corrected with extra practice instead of direct reteaching.		
Extensions List the students who you know have mastered the concept covered on this assessment and are ready to move beyond grade-level expectations.		

Source: Adapted from Bailey, K., & Jakicic, C. (2012). *Common formative assessment: A toolkit for Professional Learning Communities at Work. Bloomington, IN: Solution Tree Press.*

Tool: Targeting Tier 2 Interventions

Taking Action *reference: Essential Action 3.5—Analyze and Respond to Common Assessment Data, p. 138*

Instructions: Assessment expert Sarah Schuhl (as cited in Sonju, Kramer, Mattos, & Buffum, 2019) recommends that once teacher teams have given a common formative assessment, they break students into four groups: (1) far from proficient, (2) close to proficient, (3) proficient, and (4) advanced. Then, to begin targeting interventions, teachers should look for patterns in student responses in each of those four groups by answering the following four questions.

1. What common understandings does this group of students demonstrate?
2. What common errors is this group of students making?
3. What common misunderstandings does this group of students demonstrate?
4. What common misconceptions does this group of students demonstrate?

Use the table on page 2 of this tool to analyze the results of your next common assessment.

Tier 1 Teacher Team Essential Actions 1

Name of Assessment:

Response Patterns for Students Who Are *Far From Proficient*	Response Patterns for Students Who Are *Close to Proficient*	Response Patterns for Students Who Are *Proficient*	Response Patterns for Students Who Are *Advanced*
Our Plan for Intervening	Our Plan for Intervening	Our Plan for Extending	Our Plan for Extending
Students Participating	Students Participating	Students Participating	Students Participating

Source: Adapted from Sonju, B., Kramer, S. V., Mattos, M., & Buffum, A. (2019). Best practices at tier 2: Supplemental interventions for additional student support, secondary. Bloomington, IN: Solution Tree Press.

Sample: Targeting Tier 2 Interventions

Taking Action reference: Essential Action 3.5—Analyze and Respond to Common Assessment Data, p. 138

Name of Assessment: Rounding

Response Patterns for Students Who Are *Far From Proficient*	Response Patterns for Students Who Are *Close to Proficient*	Response Patterns for Students Who Are *Proficient*	Response Patterns for Students Who Are *Advanced*
• Rounds to the incorrect place value • Unable to explain answers • Writes several large numbers as the answer for item 2 • Chooses the largest number of cards; some explain why 4,512 > 4,516 for item 3	• Rounds the values correctly • Unable to explain answers using a picture or words—simply restates the numbers • Unable to use place value names when explaining rounding in item 3	• Able to round correctly • Rounding explanations only include a rule for rounding up or down (for example, it is a five, so round up)	• Able to round correctly • Rounding explanations include place value language and number lines
Our Plan for Intervening	**Our Plan for Intervening**	**Our Plan for Extending**	**Our Plan for Extending**
Joyce will work with this group of students. Her students significantly outperformed our students on the assessment, which means her strategy for teaching rounding was effective. She can reteach that lesson to our students easily.	Katelyn will work with this group of students. She will use open number lines and practice with three-digit numbers and place values. We hope students will get a good visual of why rounding happens by using open number lines.	Bill will work with this group of students. He will have them work in small groups to create word problems reinforcing their rounding rule. Then, groups will swap word problems and draw a picture solution to a partner group's problem.	Bill will also work with this group of students. He will introduce them to writing expanded number forms and ask them to create visuals representing the expanded forms of four-digit numbers. (Expanded form is another visual representation we haven't taught our students.)
Students Participating	**Students Participating**	**Students Participating**	**Students Participating**
• Joyce: Val, Caroline, Jon-Jon, Britton, Stella • Bill: Kavya, Sarah, Jacob • Katelyn: Donovan, Omar, Yosstin	• Joyce: Chris, Tristan, Ella, Maria • Bill: Jace, Will, Mariah, Lainee, Ricardo, Thomas, Om • Katelyn: Robert, George, Aubrey, Terrell, Meghna, Jessica		• Joyce: Owen, Rushil, Sabrina • Bill: Lucas, Rita, Rae, Mona • Katelyn: August, Lily

Source: Adapted from Sonju, B., Kramer, S. V., Mattos, M., & Buffum, A. (2019). Best practices at tier 2: Supplemental interventions for additional student support, secondary. Bloomington, IN: Solution Tree Press.

138 REPRODUCIBLE

Tier 1 Teacher Team
Essential Actions 1

Tool: Essential Standards Student Tracking Chart

Taking Action reference: Essential Action 3.5—Analyze and Respond to Common Assessment Data, p. 138

Student Name	Essential Standards									
	Standard or Outcome	Target 1	Target 2	Target 3	Target 4	Standard or Outcome	Target 1	Target 2	Target 3	Target 4

Source: Mattos, M., Buffum, A., Malone, J., Cruz, L. F., Dimich, N., & Schuhl, S. (2025). Taking action: A handbook for RTI at Work (2nd ed.). Bloomington, IN: Solution Tree Press, p. 151.

The Big Book of Tools for RTI at Work © 2025 Solution Tree Press • SolutionTree.com
Visit **go.SolutionTree.com/RTIatWork/BBTRTI** and enter the unique access code found on the book's inside front cover to access this reproducible.

Tool: Reflecting on Our Cycle of Instruction

Taking Action *reference: Essential Action 3.5—Analyze and Respond to Common Assessment Data, p. 138*

Instructions: Now that you have worked through a cycle of instruction, it is time to reflect on your learning. Use the following questions to guide your thinking.

Questions for Reflection

What was the essential outcome or skill you were teaching your students during this inquiry cycle?

What was the most effective instructional strategy you used to teach this essential outcome or skill? How do you know it was effective? Will you revise this strategy when teaching this skill in future years? How? Why would those revisions make sense?

What were students' common misconceptions and mistakes when trying to master this essential outcome or skill? Why do you think that those misconceptions and mistakes were so common? How did you address them?

What have you learned that will inform your practice moving forward? Did you discover some prerequisites that must be carefully taught before students can master this outcome or skill? Did you find some logical extensions that students can move to after learning this outcome or skill? Have you discovered an instructional strategy you might use when teaching other essential skills?

Resources Designed to
Support Tier 1 Schoolwide Essential Actions

Tool: Ensuring Access to Essential Grade-Level Curriculum

Taking Action *reference: Essential Action 4.1—Ensure Access to Essential Grade-Level Curriculum, p. 154*

Instructions: Review all guiding coalition responsibilities. Designate a team member (or two) to form and lead a committee of stakeholders for discussing each responsibility, assessing the current reality, and gathering and presenting recommendations. Designate a time frame and deadline for each committee. Reach consensus on decisions and action steps, with the understanding that all decisions and actions must be revisited and re-evaluated for effectiveness over time.

Guiding Coalition Responsibilities	Guiding Coalition Lead	Current Reality	Committee Input	Time Frame for Committee Work	Decisions and Action Steps
1. Identify essential standards.					
2. Dedicate specific times in the master schedule for teaching essential standards.					
3. Eliminate below-grade-level learning tracks.					
4. Guarantee all students receive essential grade-level curriculum as part of their Tier 1 core instruction.					
5. Identify and provide interventions for students needing Tier 1 support in grade-level curriculum.					

Source: Mattos, M., Buffum, A., Malone, J., Cruz, L. F., Dimich, N., & Schuhl, S. (2025). Taking action: A handbook for RTI at Work (2nd ed.). Bloomington, IN: Solution Tree Press, p. 165.

Tool: Developing a Master Schedule for Three Tiers of Instruction

Taking Action reference: Essential Action 4.1—Ensure Access to Essential Grade-Level Curriculum, p. 154

Instructions: A school's guiding coalition—or a specific subset of this team—can use the following process to build a master schedule that supports three tiers of instruction as described in *Taking Action: A Handbook for RTI at Work, Second Edition* (Mattos et al., 2025).

Schedule Building Step	Explanation	Examples
Step 1 Determine the amount of time needed daily for essential learning.	The master schedule should specifically indicate the time needed to teach the essentials of each curriculum effectively. At the elementary level, this means scheduling specific blocks of time for each subject area. At the secondary level, this means ensuring a minimum pathway to graduation is established and clear. This pathway should prepare students for the opportunity to apply to a four-year university.	**Elementary:** A school decides that students need seventy minutes of mathematics and ninety minutes of English language arts instruction daily, as well as thirty minutes of science and social studies instruction on alternating days, to realistically achieve essential learning. This is specifically blocked on the schedule for each teacher. **Secondary:** A school decides that students need the following credits for graduation aligned with their state's university entrance requirements. • Three mathematics credits: algebra II minimum • Four English language arts credits • Three science credits: includes biology and chemistry • Four social studies credits: includes economics, world history, U.S. history, civics • Two physical education or health credits • One half credit personal finance • One half credit employability skills • Eight elective credits
Step 2 Determine the structure for Tier 2 intervention.	The master schedule should specifically provide time for Tier 2 interventions and extensions, ensuring access for all students. To accomplish this task, a decision must be made on method, frequency, and duration of intervention. Options for methods may include small-group rotations (workshop approach), a designated schoolwide time, or a minimum time designated in each course. Schools should analyze their needs for Tier 2 instruction to inform how much time should be dedicated for this purpose.	**Elementary:** A school decides that each grade level will have a designated time for Tier 2 instruction referred to as *what I need* (WIN) time. This will occur daily and last for thirty minutes. This time will be common for each grade level to allow an all-hands-on-deck approach to providing students with support. All subjects are supported during this designated time. Another elementary school decides that Tier 2 instruction will be designated as one of the small-group rotations that occur during the English language arts and mathematics workshop times. The specific rotation time for Tier 2 is noted on the schedule and is coordinated to provide an all-hands-on-deck approach. This occurs daily for twenty minutes in English language arts and fifteen minutes in mathematics, aligning to small-group rotations. **Secondary:** A school decides to have a common schoolwide time for Tier 2 instruction called *what I need* (WIN) time. This occurs on Monday, Wednesday, and Friday each week for thirty minutes. All teachers are available during this time to support students.

Schedule Building Step	Explanation	Examples
		Another school decides to establish that each class designates thirty minutes of instruction per week to Tier 2 instruction. Each content area is designated a specific day of the week for this purpose to allow support to be coordinated from schoolwide resources if available.
Step 3 Determine the structure for Tier 3 interventions.	The master schedule should specifically indicate when students are available for Tier 3 intensive interventions without disrupting their Tier 1 instruction on essentials or their opportunity for Tier 2 instruction. The school should consider the best structure for this delivery. This may include a small-group rotation (workshop approach), a scheduled course, or a designated time during a course where essentials are not covered.	**Elementary:** A school decides that Tier 3 interventions, usually occurring thirty minutes daily, will occur during the school's English language arts small-group rotations. Students can still meet with the teacher in a Tier 1 group and be available for a Tier 2 group as small groups meet for fifteen minutes within a sixty-minute rotation block.
		Secondary: A school creates Tier 3 intervention courses that count as elective credit for students. These include a mathematics support course, a literacy support course, and an academic skills support course. These courses are provided in addition to the traditional pathway courses, not in place of them. For example, students who have demonstrated a need for intensive mathematics intervention as ninth-grade students are assigned mathematics support to address their universal skill needs in addition to their participation in algebra I.
Step 4 Map the schedule.	After considering the needs and structures for each of the three tiers of instruction, a schedule is mapped. When putting this puzzle together, the school is careful to ensure that time is specifically noted for Tier 1 instruction on essentials, Tier 2 interventions and extensions, and Tier 3 intensive support. In addition, the schedule is coordinated in such a way that students can participate in all three tiers as needed. In addition to looking at student availability, staff availability must also be considered.	**Elementary:** A school creates a schedule that has specific times listed for each subject area based on time needed to provide instruction on Tier 1 essentials. For Tier 2, the school creates WIN time for each grade level that occurs daily and lasts for thirty minutes. Additionally, the school determines that Tier 3 instruction occurs as a part of designated small-group rotation time in the English language arts block. The identified Tier 3 instruction times are common for each grade level but are scheduled across grades to not overlap. This allows specialists to have access to each grade level.
		Secondary: A school creates a seven-period day with about five periods, depending on the grade level, being dictated by the minimum course pathway to graduation. In addition, the school develops a thirty-minute advisory period each day. On Mondays and Fridays, this advisory period is used for instruction on schoolwide behavioral expectations, social-emotional learning, or college and career readiness skills. From Tuesday through Thursday, this time is reserved for Tier 2 instruction where teachers can support students. For Tier 3, courses are built into the master schedule to provide interventions. These courses are aligned to core area courses and cover prerequisites to support the universal skill needs of students and support their experience in their Tier 1 course.

Schedule Building Step	Explanation	Examples
Step 5 Get feedback and refine.	After a schedule is created, the school should solicit feedback from stakeholders to inform refinement. Stakeholders may see various conflicts or provide other insight that can be remedied before implementing the schedule.	A school, led by the guiding coalition, does the following. • Develops an initial schedule • Has representatives take the initial schedule to each collaborative team to provide an explanation and solicit feedback • Makes refinements based on feedback from teams • Presents the refined schedule at a faculty meeting for another round of feedback • Makes refinements based on faculty feedback • Meets with families or a representative group to explain the modified schedule, seeking input • Makes final adjustments
Step 6 Create and execute an implementation plan.	The school creates a plan for implementing the schedule. This plan should include rolling out the schedule, supporting the needs around the schedule, and monitoring for potential adjustments.	A school's guiding coalition creates a schedule for three tiers of instruction. This is refined through feedback. The guiding coalition then does the following. • Holds a meeting to explain the schedule to faculty and staff • Provides communication to families, including students, on the schedule's purpose and differences they may notice • Provides ongoing professional learning to faculty and staff based on their roles • Discusses the schedule's implementation at each month's meeting to provide additional support or clarification as needed

Reference

Mattos, M., Buffum, A., Malone, J., Cruz, L. F., Dimich, N., & Schuhl, S. (2025). *Taking action: A handbook for RTI at Work* (2nd ed.). Bloomington, IN: Solution Tree Press.

Template: Developing a Master Schedule for Three Tiers of Instruction

Taking Action *reference: Essential Action 4.1—Ensure Access to Essential Grade-Level Curriculum, p. 154*

Instructions: Use the following template while working with your scheduling team to create a schedule that allows students to receive all three tiers of instruction required in a system of interventions.

Schedule Building Step	Our Current Reality	Our Next Actions
Step 1 Determine the amount of time needed daily for essential learning.		
Step 2 Determine the structure for Tier 2 intervention.		
Step 3 Determine the structure for Tier 3 interventions.		
Step 4 Map the schedule.		
Step 5 Get feedback and refine.		
Step 6 Create and execute an implementation plan.		

The Big Book of Tools for RTI at Work © 2025 Solution Tree Press • SolutionTree.com
Visit **go.SolutionTree.com/RTIatWork/BBTRTI** and enter the unique access code found on the book's inside front cover to access this reproducible.

Tool: Eliciting Feedback on Our Master Schedule

Taking Action *reference: Essential Action 4.1—Ensure Access to Essential Grade-Level Curriculum, p. 154*

Instructions for respondents: As we develop a master schedule for next year, we would like your feedback about our current schedule's strengths and weaknesses. Please answer the following questions with your collaborative team.

Your Name:

Your Grade-Level or Collaborative Team:

Questions for Reflection

What parts of our master schedule worked well for your grade-level or collaborative team last year? How did those parts of our master schedule make it easier for your grade-level or collaborative team to facilitate meaningful instruction and interventions?

What parts of our master schedule did not work well for your grade-level or collaborative team last year? How did those parts of our master schedule make it more difficult for your grade-level or collaborative team to facilitate meaningful instruction and interventions?

What parts of our master schedule would your grade-level or collaborative team change? How would changing those parts of our master schedule make it easier for your grade-level or collaborative team to facilitate meaningful instruction and interventions?

What other input does our guiding coalition need to hear to develop a master schedule that facilitates meaningful instruction and interventions?

Source: Questions adapted from Springer, C. (2021, February 3). From theory to practice: A jigsaw approach to an elementary master schedule [Blog post]. Accessed at https://allthingsplc.info/from-theory-to-practice-a-jigsaw-approach-to-an-elementary-master-schedule/ on April 23, 2023.

Tool: Reflecting on Your Master Schedule

Taking Action *reference: Essential Action 4.1—Ensure Access to Essential Grade-Level Curriculum, p. 154*

Instructions: Working with members of your guiding coalition, answer the following reflection questions to evaluate the strengths and weaknesses in your current master schedule.

Questions for Reflection

How was our current master schedule created? What priorities did we set when creating it? How did those priorities positively and negatively affect learning in our building?

What do we need within our schedule to help our students succeed? Do we need more time in core classes? Do we need more intervention time? Do we need more time for some students to meet with specialists to address gaps in universal learning skills?

What barriers prevent us from creating a schedule that allows us to help more students learn at higher levels? Do we share specialists with another school, making it difficult to schedule time for our students to receive the help that they need? Do we have certain groups of students who must be in certain classes at certain times, preventing them from receiving instruction in grade-level essentials? Do we have cultural resistance regarding the importance of providing intervention time in our master schedule?

What are the non-negotiables in our master schedule? What core elements of our current schedule are essential and cannot be adjusted? Where do we have flexibility? What do we feel strongly enough about to ensure that it is reflected in our new master schedule?

What next steps do we have to take to move forward? Do we need permission from anyone to revise our master schedule? Do we need to consider coordinating shared specialists across schools? Do we need to build buy-in with faculty members? When will we get started?

Tier 1 Schoolwide Essential Actions

Source: Questions adapted from Stack, B. M., & Vander Els, J. G. (2018). Breaking with tradition: The shift to competency-based learning in PLCs at Work. Bloomington, IN: Solution Tree Press.

Checklists: Establishing Common Expectations, Targeting Instruction, and Reinforcing Positive Behaviors

Taking Action *reference: Essential Action 4.2—Identify and Teach Essential Academic and Social Behaviors, p. 166*

Establishing Common Expectations

Goal	Long-Term Vision	First Steps
Achieve collective responsibility.	Staff view the success of all students as part of their professional practices.	☐ Share successes across the grade levels. ☐ Analyze case studies as a staff. ☐ Vertically collaborate. ☐ Horizontally collaborate.
Craft a behavior matrix.	Staff reach consensus on those behaviors that are most significant to student and school success.	☐ Review data. ☐ Collect and validate anecdotal evidence. ☐ Identify three to five behavioral attributes concisely and appropriately. ☐ Define age-appropriate expectations for students and staff. ☐ Identify settings (environments) across the campus for which it is most important to articulate appropriate behaviors.
State positive expectations.	Craft statements that positively state the way in which students will appropriately behave in settings across the campus.	☐ Identify behaviors that *disrupt* learning. ☐ Articulate the optimally desired behaviors that will *support* learning. ☐ Write three to five specific, observable behavioral characteristics for each broad behavioral attribute in each identified setting.
Model the behavioral expectations.	Staff explicitly and intentionally model the behaviors that they expect students to exhibit.	☐ Identify specific ways in which staff can model the behaviors they expect to see from students. ☐ Identify specific times and settings during which staff can model the behaviors they expect to see from students. ☐ Develop a respectful way in which staff can hold one another accountable to effectively and positively model behaviors.

Targeting Instruction

Goal	Long-Term Vision	First Steps
Effectively manage classrooms with well-communicated and reinforced structures, routines, and procedures.	Staff collaborate about their techniques for establishing structured, predictable learning environments.	☐ Devote time before the school year to reviewing ways in which classrooms will be managed and organized. ☐ During the first few weeks of school, check in with colleagues on the success of their efforts to establish efficient learning environments. ☐ During the first few weeks of school, check with students on their understanding of the rules and routines of a positive learning environment.
Consistently model, reinforce, and monitor.	Staff, at all times, talk the talk and walk the walk, faithfully reinforcing and tracking both positive and negative behaviors.	☐ Follow the same behavioral expectations as students and be open to friendly reminders from colleagues. ☐ Utilize the same method for reinforcing and recognizing positive behavior. ☐ Led by the administration, the staff understand and follow the way in which instances of both positive and negative behavior will be documented and monitored.
Explicitly teach schoolwide behavioral expectations.	Staff regularly and explicitly teach and reteach the behaviors that all students are expected to exhibit.	☐ The school sets aside time during which all students and staff receive explicit instruction on behavioral expectations. ☐ The school communicates the matrix and expectations to all stakeholders (parents, office staff, custodial staff) and shares the plan with the central office. ☐ The behavioral team anticipates times of the year during which behavioral expectations will need to be reviewed.

Reinforcing Positive Behaviors

Goal	Long-Term Vision	First Steps
Catch students being good.	Staff consistently and specifically reinforce at least four times as many positive behaviors as negative behaviors.	☐ Ensure focus on and recognition of behaviors, not personalities. ☐ Specifically describe the reasons why positive behaviors are receiving recognition. ☐ Agree to use the same methods to reinforce or to recognize, or both, positive behaviors. ☐ Formally or informally monitor individual and collective efforts to ensure we are recognizing four positive behaviors for every one negative behavior.
Build relationships.	Staff systemically ensure that every student has a positive connection with at least one adult on campus.	☐ School administration identifies students who are involved in any form of extracurricular activities. ☐ Study and implement strategies for building positive communities of learning within every classroom. ☐ Students in the yellow and red zones are assigned (formally or informally) mentors with whom they have established a connection and with whom they will check in regularly.
Provide schoolwide celebrations.	Formally and informally, the school regularly celebrates and recognizes positive behaviors.	☐ Consider a drawing or other systemwide method to further recognize students whose positive behavior has been recognized. ☐ Brainstorm rewards that are low cost or no cost, preferably academic in nature, that will appeal to students and will serve as an incentive. ☐ Ensure that external means of motivating students are balanced by internal means. Over time, the goal is to move to more intrinsic and less extrinsic reinforcement, when students make good decisions for the satisfaction it instills instead of the reward it brings.

Source: Buffum, A., Mattos, M., & Malone, J. (2018). Taking action: A handbook for RTI at Work. Bloomington, IN: Solution Tree Press, pp. 149–151; Hierck, T., Coleman, C., & Weber, C. (2011). Pyramid of behavior interventions: Seven keys to a positive learning environment. Bloomington, IN: Solution Tree Press.

Tool: Reflecting on the Recipe for a Successful Learner

Taking Action *reference: Essential Action 4.2—Identify and Teach Essential Academic and Social Behaviors, p. 166*

Instructions: To start a conversation about the role skills and dispositions play in learners' successes, ask teachers to work individually to fill in the following three diagrams. Once teachers have completed their responses, have them work with members of their teacher teams and with those in different grade levels or subject areas to answer the reflection questions on page 2 of this tool.

In the blanks in the diagram to the right, write down percentages representing **the impact** you think knowledge, skills, and dispositions have on a learner's success. Remember that your percentages should total 100 percent.

Explain your percentages:

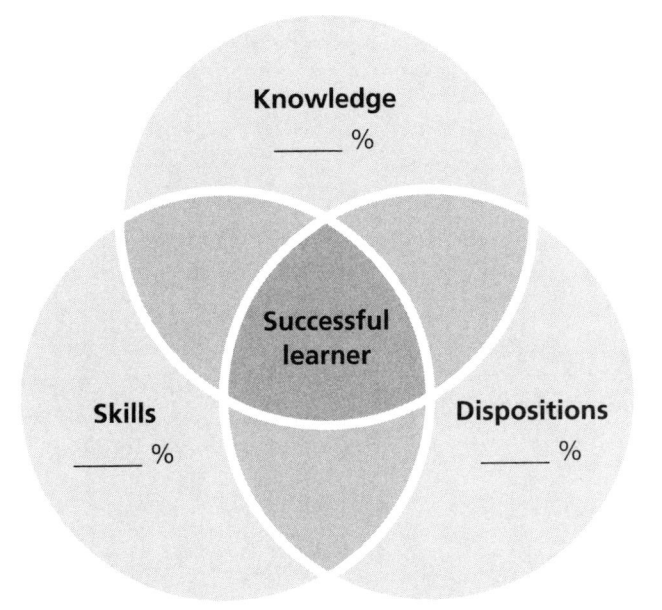

In the blanks in the diagram to the right, write down percentages representing the time you spend **delivering instruction** on knowledge, skills, and dispositions in your classroom or classrooms. Remember that your percentages should total 100 percent.

Explain your percentages:

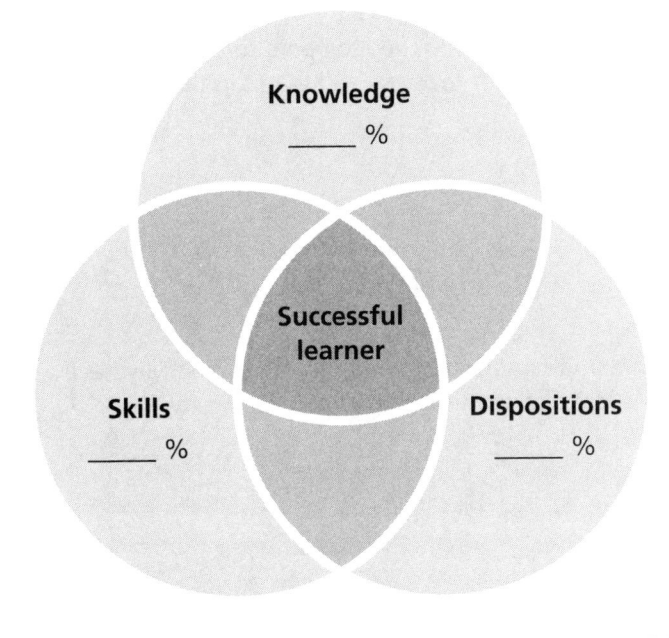

In the blanks in the diagram to the right, write down percentages representing the time you spend **providing interventions** in knowledge, skills, and dispositions in your classroom or classrooms. Remember that your percentages should total 100 percent.

Explain your percentages:

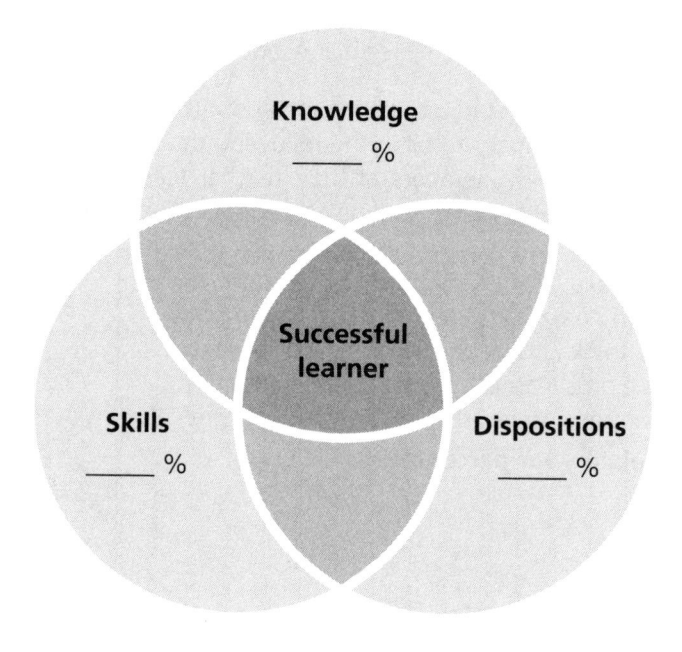

Questions for Reflection

What patterns did you notice in your percentages?

How did your percentages compare to those of other teachers and teacher teams? Should the percentages given by different teachers and teams in the same school be roughly the same? Why or why not?

What implications do the answers in this activity have for the students in our school? What action steps should we take after completing this activity?

Tool: Reviewing the Skills Necessary to Succeed in the Modern Workplace

Taking Action *reference: Essential Action 4.2—Identify and Teach Essential Academic and Social Behaviors, p. 166*

Instructions: Every four years, the World Economic Forum (WEF) lists the top ten skills necessary to succeed in the modern workplace. Following are the top ten lists published by the WEF in 2020 and 2023. Examine those lists with your school's guiding coalition, then work together to answer the reflection questions at the end of this tool.

Top Ten Skills Needed in the Workplace in 2025 (WEF, 2020)	Top Ten Skills Needed in the Workplace in 2025 (WEF, 2023)
1. Analytical thinking and innovation	1. Analytical thinking
2. Active learning and learning strategies	2. Creative thinking
3. Complex problem solving	3. Resilience, flexibility, and agility
4. Critical thinking and analysis	4. Motivation and self-awareness
5. Creativity, originality, and initiative	5. Curiosity and lifelong learning
6. Leadership and social influence	6. Technological literacy
7. Technology use, monitoring, and control	7. Dependability and attention to detail
8. Technology design and programming	8. Empathy and active listening
9. Resilience, stress tolerance, and flexibility	9. Leadership and social influence
10. Reasoning, problem solving, and ideation	10. Quality control

Questions for Reflection

What patterns do you see in the types of skills and dispositions identified as essential by the WEF (2020, 2023)? Are there any skills that appear in both lists? What skills don't appear in either list? Do the skills that appear in both lists share any commonalities?

How do the skills that appear in the top ten lists generated by the WEF (2020, 2023) compare to those in your required curricula? Is there any overlap between these skills and the skills detailed in your required curricula? Where do those overlapping skills appear in your required curricula?

page 1 of 2

Which of the top ten skills identified by the WEF (2020, 2023) are you currently teaching to students? Where is that instruction happening? Do all students have universal access to this instruction? If not, which students are and are not receiving this instruction?

How are we assessing mastery of the top ten skills the WEF (2020, 2023) identified? Do we have shared proficiency scales or rubrics? Can our teachers apply those uniformly?

How are we providing intervention or extension to students struggling with or excelling at the top ten skills identified by the WEF (2020, 2023)? What actions are we taking to ensure that all students learn the top ten skills at the highest levels? Who are the right people to lead interventions and extensions in the top ten skills?

How can we improve the work that we are doing to ensure that students master the top ten skills identified by the WEF (2020, 2023)? Do we need to identify a few skills to prioritize in our initial work? Who will identify those skills? Will we ask individual grade levels or subject areas to concentrate on individual skills? Will we choose one skill for our entire school to prioritize? What will our first step be, and when will we take it?

References

World Economic Forum. (2020). *The future of jobs report 2020*. Accessed at www3.weforum.org/docs/WEF_Future_of_Jobs_2020.pdf on December 13, 2023.

World Economic Forum. (2023, April 30). *The future of jobs report 2023*. Accessed at www.weforum.org/publications/the-future-of-jobs-report-2023 on March 15, 2024.

Checklist: Concentrating Instruction on Social and Academic Behaviors

Taking Action *reference: Essential Action 4.2—Identify and Teach Essential Academic and Social Behaviors, p. 166*

Instructions: In *Pyramid of Behavior Interventions: Seven Keys to a Positive Learning Environment,* authors Tom Hierck, Charlie Coleman, and Chris Weber (2011) introduce readers to three criteria that schools can use to determine whether they effectively concentrate instruction on social and academic behaviors. Guiding coalitions can use this checklist to rate their school's efforts against these criteria.

Rating Scale: 1—This work is not currently happening in our building, 2—We are developing or refining our work in this area, 3—This is an established practice in our building

Critical Action 1: Establishing common social and academic behavioral expectations				
Your Rating (Circle one.)			**Indicator**	**Notes**
1	2	3	School rules, codes of conduct, and mission statements have been condensed into a few easy-to-remember, positively phrased common words or phrases.	
1	2	3	Behavioral expectations are linked to academic expectations.	
1	2	3	Students, staff, and parents know the social and academic behavioral expectations.	
1	2	3	Everyone in the school uses the same common language when introducing and reinforcing social and academic behavioral expectations.	
1	2	3	Adults model social and academic behavioral expectations.	

Critical Action 2: Targeted instruction in social and academic behavioral expectations				
Your Rating (Circle one.)			**Indicator**	**Notes**
1	2	3	Schoolwide social and academic behavioral expectations are taught directly by all staff to all students and in context. **Sample:** *Appropriate lunchroom behavior is taught in the lunchroom.*	
1	2	3	Students are given opportunities to develop, practice, and demonstrate appropriate social and academic behaviors.	

Your Rating			Indicator	Notes
1	2	3	Common social and academic behavioral expectations are reviewed regularly, practiced often, and recognized and rewarded when displayed correctly.	
1	2	3	Social and behavioral skills are taught like academic skills: demonstrate, practice, review, and celebrate.	

Critical Action 3: Positive reinforcement of social and academic behavioral expectations					
Your Rating (Circle one.)			Indicator	Notes
1	2	3	Students are acknowledged for demonstrating mastery of social and academic behavioral expectations.	
1	2	3	Timely and specific feedback is provided to students on current mastery of social and academic behavioral expectations.	
1	2	3	The language used when giving feedback to students on current mastery of social and academic behavioral expectations is positive and promotes a growth mindset.	
1	2	3	Social and academic behaviors that we wish to see more commonly displayed are intentionally and systematically (in the same manner, at the same frequency, and for the same reasons) reinforced by all staff.	

Questions for Reflection

What patterns do you see in your checklist responses?

How will those patterns affect our efforts to teach our students the social and academic behaviors we want them to demonstrate?

How should we strengthen our efforts to help our students master the social and academic behaviors that we want them to demonstrate?

Reference

Hierck, T., Coleman, C., & Weber, C. (2011). *Pyramid of behavior interventions: Seven keys to a positive learning environment*. Bloomington, IN: Solution Tree Press.

Student Tool: What Do Successful People Do Differently?

Instructions: Successful students develop positive habits. Those habits include showing up on time, persevering, and progressing steadily toward success. Use the following rating scales to evaluate yourself against these criteria, then set a goal to improve your habits in one of these areas.

1. Review each criterion listed in the **Success Criteria** column of the following table.
2. Shade in a rating box representing your current work with this success criterion.
   - Shading 1 means I struggle with this.
   - Shading 5 means I do this well.
3. Record any additional details about your rating in the **Your Notes** column. For example, it is worth noting if you struggle with a success criterion in some classes but not others.

Student Name:						
Success Criteria	**Your Self-Assessment**					**Your Notes**
Show Up Successful people know it is only possible to improve by being fully present. As a result, they have good attendance.	1	2	3	4	5	
Prepare, Practice, and Persevere Successful people study, polish their skills when struggling, and push through struggles instead of giving up.	1	2	3	4	5	
Give Your Best Each Day Successful people recognize that effort matters. As a result, they lean into their work every day.	1	2	3	4	5	
Shut Down Failure Self-Talk Successful people know that their words shape their beliefs. As a result, they avoid using phrases like "I can't do this" or "It's too hard."	1	2	3	4	5	
Keep Improving in Comparison to Yourself Successful people make consistent, steady improvements. As a result, they constantly identify next steps to improve themselves.	1	2	3	4	5	

Questions for Reflection

What are your strengths when it comes to the characteristics of successful people?

What success criteria do you struggle with?

What is a goal that can help improve your habits in an area where you struggle? Start your plan with the phrase "Over the next nine weeks, I will work to _____."

Source: Success criteria from Mendler, A. N. (2021). Motivating students who don't care: Proven strategies to engage all learners (2nd ed.). Bloomington, IN: Solution Tree Press.

Tool: Assessment Purpose Map

Taking Action *reference: Essential Action 4.3—Create a Balanced Assessment Approach, p. 174*

Instructions: To develop an assessment purpose map, guiding coalitions, intervention teams, or teacher teams work together to compile a comprehensive list of all available assessments. For instance, a teacher team might include specific state assessments, district benchmarks, and team-created common formative assessments. Then, the team articulates each assessment's purpose and frequency. Finally, the team details how the data derived from each assessment is used. Once they have created an assessment purpose map, teams can use it to identify gaps or redundancies in their assessment plan and build a shared understanding of why each assessment is given.

Assessment	Assessment Purpose	Assessment Frequency	How Are We Using Data From This Assessment?
Sample: Reading Universal Screener	**Sample:** Identify where students are performing in relation to grade level by each assessed reading skill.	**Sample:** Three times per year: fall, winter, spring	**Sample:** This assessment is used, when triangulated with other site data, to determine who may benefit from intensive interventions or consistent extensions. Follow-up assessments or qualitative data are compiled in conjunction with screener data by the site intervention team. This assessment is also used to determine, generally, if the curriculum and instruction are meeting grade-level growth and achievement goals.

Tier 1 Schoolwide Essential Actions

page 1 of 2

Assessment	Assessment Purpose	Assessment Frequency	How Are We Using Data From This Assessment?

Tool: Assessment Stoplight Analysis

Taking Action *reference: Essential Action 4.3—Create a Balanced Assessment Approach, p. 174*

Instructions: Guiding coalitions, intervention teams, or collaborative teacher teams can use this tool for comprehensive data analysis upon receiving results from state assessments or district benchmarks. It's important to note that this analysis isn't intended for individual student decision making but rather to highlight trends across cohorts of students. Analyze state assessments or district benchmarks and fill in the first four rows of the following table together with your team. Then, populate the **Green Light**, **Yellow Light**, and **Red Light** columns at the end of this table with actionable steps to address your findings. To maintain focus, limit yourself to one or two action steps per box.

Assessment Being Analyzed:		
Assessment Stoplight Analysis		
Overall, the assessment shows we are currently successful at: *(Ensure you analyze data holistically and in a disaggregated manner.)*		
Actions currently in place that lead to that success are:		
Overall, the assessment shows we are not currently successful at: *(Ensure you analyze data holistically and in a disaggregated manner.)*		
Actions currently in place that may be hindering success are:		
Green Light The data from this assessment or assessments tell us to continue the following.	**Yellow Light** The data from this assessment or assessments tell us we need more information on the following.	**Red Light** The data from this assessment or assessments tell us to stop the following.

Tool: Assessment Reflection by Type

Taking Action *reference*: Essential Action 4.3—Create a Balanced Assessment Approach, p. 174

Instructions: Guiding coalitions can use the following chart to build their shared understanding of each assessment type used within their school. Begin by reviewing the types and purposes of common assessments detailed in the first and second columns. Then, assign an overall rating for your school's use of each assessment type and provide a rationale for your rating in the third and fourth columns. Finally, answer the overall reflection questions at the end of the table to establish a set of actionable next steps.

Assessment Type	Purpose	Rating	Rationale
Large-Scale Data These assessments are usually externally mandated assessments delivered once per year. These include state or provincial assessments, Advanced Placement exams, and so on.	Sites use these data to determine overall effectiveness, trends over time, and where there are any needs.	Currently, our site is using these data effectively: ☐ Strongly agree ☐ Agree ☐ Neutral ☐ Disagree ☐ Strongly disagree	
Benchmark Data These assessments are usually chosen by a system as a curriculum and instruction monitoring tool.	Sites use these data to track progress toward school goals and screen for intervention needs (Tier 3).	Currently, our site is using these data effectively: ☐ Strongly agree ☐ Agree ☐ Neutral ☐ Disagree ☐ Strongly disagree	
End-of-Unit Assessments Teachers and teams use these assessments to determine proficiency on standards following a unit of study.	Teachers and teams use these data to impact their practice, determine students in need of additional support, and identify students who would benefit from extension.	Currently, our site is using these data effectively: ☐ Strongly agree ☐ Agree ☐ Neutral ☐ Disagree ☐ Strongly disagree	
Common Formative Assessments Teachers and teams use these assessments to determine proficiency as a check during a cycle of learning.	Teachers and teams use these data to impact their practice, determine students in need of additional support, and identify students who would benefit from extension.	Currently, our site is using these data effectively: ☐ Strongly agree ☐ Agree ☐ Neutral ☐ Disagree ☐ Strongly disagree	

Ongoing Formative Assessment These assessments are used by teachers on a more regular basis than other assessments.	Teachers use these data to impact their practice, determine students in need of additional support, and identify students who would benefit from extension.	Currently, our site is using these data effectively: ☐ Strongly agree ☐ Agree ☐ Neutral ☐ Disagree ☐ Strongly disagree	

Questions for Reflection

Which assessments do we use most frequently?

Why do we believe these are used most frequently?

Which assessments do we use least frequently?

Why do we believe these are used the least frequently?

What will we do because of this reflection?

Source: Adapted from Mattos, M., Buffum, A., Malone, J., Cruz, L. F., Dimich, N., & Schuhl, S. (2025). Taking action: A handbook for RTI at Work (2nd ed.). Bloomington, IN: Solution Tree Press.

Tool: Grading Reflection and Planning

Taking Action *reference: Essential Action 4.4—Co-Create Schoolwide Grading Practices, p. 184*

Instructions: The following table identifies three areas of grading detailed in *Taking Action: A Handbook for RTI at Work, Second Edition* (Mattos et al., 2025) that guiding coalitions need to discuss when co-creating schoolwide grading practices. Start by reviewing each area detailed in the first column. Then, record evidence and plan the next steps for each area using the prompts in the second and third columns. After responding to all prompts, work together to create an action plan and establish a timeline for implementing grading improvements within your school.

Have we defined the purpose for grading? Is there a shared understanding of the purpose of site-wide grading that reflects learning as the priority?	Evidence that demonstrates this is in place:	Evidence that demonstrates this is not in place:
	What needs to be addressed?	What actions will we take to address these needs?
Have we used research-based evidence of effectiveness to determine shifts in grading practices? Are grades reported in a manner that shows proficiency in standards or targets?	Evidence that demonstrates this is in place:	Evidence that demonstrates this is not in place:
	What needs to be addressed?	What actions will we take to address these needs?
Have we identified the learning evidence to include in a student's grade? Is there a shared understanding of what evidence should be used to calculate final grades?	Evidence that demonstrates this is in place:	Evidence that demonstrates this is not in place:
	What needs to be addressed?	What actions will we take to address these needs?

Reference

Mattos, M., Buffum, A., Malone, J., Cruz, L. F., Dimich, N., & Schuhl, S. (2025). *Taking action: A handbook for RTI at Work* (2nd ed.). Bloomington, IN: Solution Tree Press.

Tool: Standards-Based Mindset Reflection and Planning

Taking Action *reference: Essential Action 4.4—Co-Create Schoolwide Grading Practices, p. 184*

Instructions: Author and consultant Tom Schimmer (2016) presents a standards-based mindset consisting of three integral components that collectively transform the grading paradigm. For schools co-creating grading practices, these components offer valuable insights to stimulate reflection and assess current practices. Both guiding coalitions and collaborative teams are encouraged to use the first column of the following table to review Schimmer's (2016) key components. Then, teams should record evidence and plan next steps for each area using the prompts in the second and third columns. After responding to all prompts, team members can work together to create an action plan for integrating a standards-based mindset into their grading practices.

Do we give students full credit for what they know? Don't combine old evidence of learning with new evidence. Instead, report on what a student currently knows.	Evidence this component is in place:	Evidence this component is not in place:
	What actions will we take to grow in this component?	How will we know when we have grown? (Evidence)
Have we redefined accountability? Don't use grades to punish irresponsibility. Instead, teach students to be responsible.	Evidence this component is in place:	Evidence this component is not in place:
	What actions will we take to grow in this component?	How will we know when we have grown? (Evidence)
Have we repurposed the role of homework? Don't use homework as an opportunity to generate a grade. Instead, use homework as a chance to practice, gather formative assessment information, and provide descriptive feedback.	Evidence this component is in place:	Evidence this component is not in place:
	What actions will we take to grow in this component?	How will we know when we have grown? (Evidence)

Reference

Schimmer, T. (2016). *Grading from the inside out: Bringing accuracy to student assessment through a standards-based mindset*. Bloomington, IN: Solution Tree Press.

Tool: Grading Practices Implementation

Taking Action *reference: Essential Action 4.4—Co-Create Schoolwide Grading Practices, p. 184*

Instructions: Site leaders, the guiding coalition, or a dedicated grading task force can utilize this tool as a road map for conducting a comprehensive grading review and facilitating the implementation of improved grading practices. To begin, review the grading practice component detailed in the first column of the following table. Then, evaluate your current status in the second column. Finally, generate a set of next steps to enhance your grading practices in the third column. Periodically revisit this document, revise your ratings, and adjust next steps as you progress through your grading improvement journey.

Grading Practice Component	Status	Next Steps
We have established a team to review grading practices and support improvements as needed.	☐ In place ☐ In progress ☐ Not yet started	
We understand that learning is our fundamental purpose.	☐ In place ☐ In progress ☐ Not yet started	
We understand that grading practices should reflect learning, and we have developed a purpose statement communicating that message.	☐ In place ☐ In progress ☐ Not yet started	
We have taken an inventory of our current grading practices. (Current reality)	☐ In place ☐ In progress ☐ Not yet started	

Grading Practice Component	Status	Next Steps
We have researched grading practices that are shown to be effective and supportive of student learning.	☐ In place ☐ In progress ☐ Not yet started	
We have developed a vision for grading practices. (Desired state)	☐ In place ☐ In progress ☐ Not yet started	
We have created an action plan to go from our current reality to our desired state. This includes how information will be shared, how learning will occur, and how ongoing support will be provided.	☐ In place ☐ In progress ☐ Not yet started	
We have determined a process to monitor implementation so we can learn and adjust.	☐ In place ☐ In progress ☐ Not yet started	
We have established short-term implementation goals so we can have celebrations on our journey.	☐ In place ☐ In progress ☐ Not yet started	

Source: Adapted from Mattos, M., Buffum, A., Malone, J., Cruz, L. F., Dimich, N., & Schuhl, S. (2025). Taking action: A handbook for RTI at Work (2nd ed.). Bloomington, IN: Solution Tree Press.

Tool: Preventions to Proactively Support Student Success

Taking Action *reference: Essential Action 4.5—Provide Preventions to Proactively Support Student Success, p. 192*

Instructions: As a team, brainstorm typical skills and needs for preventive support and strategies or tools for identifying students requiring that support. Review information on incoming students, assess as necessary, and identify those who require proactive preventions. Create a team plan of action, and forward recommendations to the guiding coalition for additional schoolwide support. Revisit prevention planning quarterly to ensure no student slips through the cracks.

Team: _____

Reliable Criteria	Strategy or Tool for Identifying Students and Their Needs	Students Needing Support	Skills or Needs Requiring Support	Team Actions	Recommendations to Guiding Coalition
Previous Struggles					
Gaps in Prerequisite Skills					
Predictable Developmental Needs					
Transitional Needs					

Source: Mattos, M., Buffum, A., Malone, J., Cruz, L. F., Dimich, N., & Schuhl, S. (2025). Taking action: A handbook for RTI at Work (2nd ed.). Bloomington, IN: Solution Tree Press, p. 196.

Tool Overview: Creating a Predictable-Is-Preventable Plan

Taking Action *reference: Essential Action 4.5—Provide Preventions to Proactively Support Student Success, p. 192*

Instructions for facilitator:

1. With your guiding coalition, identify students with predictable challenges that interfere with academics.
2. Describe the unique needs of students with the predictable challenges that you are addressing.
3. Develop specific action steps for *supporting the students* struggling with the predictable challenge that you are planning to address, *supporting the teachers* who work with students struggling with the predictable challenge that you are planning to address, and *supporting the parents* of students struggling with the predictable challenge that you are planning to address.
4. Identify faculty members responsible for designing, leading, and implementing each action step.
5. Establish a deadline for implementing and evaluating the effectiveness of each action step.

Tool: Creating a Predictable-Is-Preventable Plan

Taking Action *reference: Essential Action 4.5—Provide Preventions to Proactively Support Student Success, p. 192*

Our predictable-is-preventable plan for: _____

This plan details our school's specific actions whenever a new student arrives currently struggling with predictable challenges that impede their ability to master grade-level essentials.

Describe the unique needs and challenges of this group of students:					
Our strategies for **supporting students** struggling with this challenge		Our strategies for **supporting teachers** who work with students struggling with this challenge		Our plans for **supporting parents** of students struggling with this challenge	
Action Step	Led By	Action Step	Led By	Action Step	Led By

Questions for Reflection

What changes will we need to make to school schedules, structures, or expectations to effectively implement the action steps identified in this plan?

What additional resources will we need to effectively implement the action steps identified in this plan?

How will we evaluate this plan to determine whether our action steps positively impact the success of students who struggle with this predictable challenge?

Sample: Predictable-Is-Preventable Plan for Multilingual Students

Taking Action reference: Essential Action 4.5—Provide Preventions to Proactively Support Student Success, p. 192

This plan details our school's specific actions whenever a new student arrives currently struggling with predictable challenges that impede their ability to master grade-level essentials.

Describe the unique needs and challenges of this group of students:
We have found that our school's multilingual learners tend to have challenges that overlap with those of other marginalized communities.   1. May struggle to read and write in their native language.   2. May need help with the academic vocabulary of content-area classes.   3. May need help to understand the routines and patterns of U.S. schools.   4. May struggle to communicate with peers or find places where they feel like they belong in our school because of the language barrier.   5. May be struggling with food security or other issues associated with poverty at home.

Our strategies for **supporting students** struggling with this challenge		Our strategies for **supporting teachers** who work with students struggling with this challenge		Our plans for **supporting parents** of students struggling with this challenge	
Action Step	**Led By**	**Action Step**	**Led By**	**Action Step**	**Led By**
Develop and deliver translation training for students that includes the following. • Using https://translate.google.com for real-time translation of in-class instruction • Using Chrome to translate entire webpages • Translating Google Docs and Google Slides • Enabling translated captions on videos • Using on-screen keyboard settings to write in their native language	Ms. Burke	Develop and deliver translation training for teachers that covers the following. • Using https://translate.google.com for real-time translation of in-class instruction • Using Chrome to translate entire webpages • Translating Google Docs and Google Slides • Enabling translated captions on videos	Ms. Burke	Conduct a home survey with all parents within two weeks of enrollment. Determine the following. • Primary language spoken at home • Levels of previous education, including fluency in native language and English • Any unaddressed needs that will interfere with learning	Mr. Nowak
Develop a one-week multilingual orientation to be delivered during Tier 2 intervention time that includes the following. • English foundational phrases necessary for functioning in school • Introduction to school routines and procedures • Introduction to available resources for supporting multilingual students	Mr. Cruz	Ensure that teachers know the translation tricks taught to multilingual students so they can be on the lookout for them in the classroom.	Ms. Burke	Identify freely available resources that can help parents of multilingual students learn to speak English; communicate those resources to families.	Mr. Nowak

Establish Multilingual Buddies club that trains English-speaking students to be real-time support for multilingual students in academic core classes.	Ms. Coley	Ensure that teachers understand the role that preteaching academic vocabulary should play in supporting multilingual students.	Mr. Hennesey	Develop a "Tips and Tricks for Supporting Your Child in School" session tailored to multilingual students' unique needs. Deliver this session as necessary.	Mr. Nowak
Establish translation stations in common areas of the school with internet-connected computers to enable groups of students who speak different languages to work together.	Ms. Burke			Ensure parents know all the translation tricks taught to multilingual students when they arrive so they can be on the lookout for them at home.	Mr. Nowak

Questions for Reflection

What changes will we need to make to school schedules, structures, or expectations to effectively implement the action steps identified in this plan?

We will need to make the following changes to school schedules, structures, and expectations.

1. Someone will need to be free and ready to deliver the multilingual orientation during our Tier 2 intervention period every time we have a new multilingual student added to our roster. We need to build that flexibility into a faculty member's intervention schedule.
2. At the beginning of the year, we will need to set time aside for teacher translation training and for training in effective strategies for preteaching academic vocabulary to multilingual students.
3. We must find someone to run the Multilingual Buddies club. This should happen during our Tier 2 intervention period and give English-speaking multilingual buddies the time to meet and discuss the best ways to befriend and support new multilingual students as they arrive.

What additional resources will we need to effectively implement the action steps identified in this plan?

We will need flexible time during Tier 2 interventions for individuals to develop and deliver specific interventions for multilingual students. We will need a few additional computers for our translation stations. Other than that, this plan requires no additional resources.

How will we evaluate this plan to determine whether our action steps positively impact the success of students who struggle with this predictable challenge?

To evaluate the impact of our action steps, we will do the following.

1. Track student progress in their core classes.
2. Survey teachers about their fluency with translation tools and comfort level supporting multilingual students in the regular education classroom.
3. Survey multilingual students about their comfort level in core classes.

Tools for Building Tier 2 of Your Intervention Pyramid

One of the most important guiding principles of effective interventions is this: Target the cause of the problem, not the symptom. Students can fail the same test, but it does not mean they struggled for the same reason.

—Mike Mattos, Austin Buffum, Janet Malone, Luis F. Cruz, Nicole Dimich, & Sarah Schuhl

In the multitiered system of interventions, the primary purpose of Tier 2 is to ensure all students master the grade-level and course-specific essential skills, knowledge, and behaviors needed for success in the next grade or course. Many schools struggle at Tier 2 because they substitute purchasing intervention programs and hiring additional intervention staff in place of leveraging their collaborative teams and creating the processes proven to best ensure student learning. If a school has successfully utilized the tools in the previous two chapters, the staff should be organized and prepared to target Tier 2 interventions.

Specifically, the following are keys to effective Tier 2 interventions.

- Tier 2 interventions are not provided by individual teachers trying to intervene in their own classrooms—that is an outdated one-room-schoolhouse approach. Collaborative teacher teams take collective responsibility to lead interventions on their team-specific essential standards.

- An effective intervention identifies the specific standard, learning target, or behavior to be retaught; students assigned to a specific intervention should all have the same targeted need. Team common assessment data—targeted to specific team essential standards—should be the lifeblood of this process.

- There must be dedicated time in the master schedule to provide students additional time and support to master essential grade-level curriculum and behaviors.

- Students cannot miss Tier 1 instruction on new essential curriculum to receive this help.

- Tier 2 and Tier 3 support cannot be provided at the same time, as some students will need both.

- Tier 2 behavior interventions—the reteaching and targeted support for students to master essential behaviors—are schoolwide processes guided by the school leadership team.

The resources in this chapter facilitate the work done at Tier 2 in a system of interventions. They are divided into two separate sections: the resources in the first section are designed to support teacher teams and are tied to the recommendations in chapter 5 of *Taking Action: A Handbook for RTI at Work, Second Edition* (Mattos et al., 2025): "Tier 2 Teacher Team Essential Actions." The resources in the second section are designed to support school guiding coalitions. They are tied to the recommendations made in chapter 6 of *Taking Action* (Mattos et al., 2025): "Tier 2 Guiding Coalition Essential Actions."

Section 1: Resources Designed to Support Tier 2 Teacher Team Essential Actions

Visit **go.SolutionTree.com/RTIatWork/BBTRTI** to access online-only tools.

- **"Tool: Building Shared Knowledge About Tier 2 Interventions and Extensions"** (page 190)—In the RTI at Work process (Mattos et al., 2025), teacher teams accept primary responsibility for designing and leading supplemental interventions for academic essential standards. For this work to be successful, however, teams must possess a strong grasp of the fundamental principles underlying effective Tier 2 interventions and extensions. Use this tool and its corresponding **answer key** (page 192) to build that understanding within your teams.

  - *Taking Action* reference: Essential Action 5.1—Design and Lead Tier 2 Interventions for Essential Academic Standards, p. 203

- **"Tool: Team-Based Intervention Plan for Struggling Learners"** (page 194)—Students who struggle to master essential academic standards generally struggle for one of four reasons: (1) they have gaps in prerequisite learning that make mastering current outcomes difficult, (2) they are making common mistakes and need additional opportunities to practice, (3) they are struggling to complete the specific task assigned to them but may be able to demonstrate mastery another way, or (4) they exhibit work behaviors such as failing to complete homework or participate in class that are preventing them from learning. Use this tool to develop an intervention plan and to maintain an up-to-date list of students who need support in one of these four areas.

- *Taking Action* reference: Essential Action 5.1—Design and Lead Tier 2 Interventions for Essential Academic Standards, p. 203

- **"Tool: Tier 2 Intervention Tracking by Individual Teacher"** (online only)—While teacher teams implementing the RTI at Work process work collaboratively to plan supplemental interventions addressing the most common reasons that students struggle to master essential academic standards, it remains the job of individual teachers to identify students in need of intervention by both name and need. Teachers can use this tool during an instruction unit to record the students assigned to their classes who will need additional learning time and support.

  - *Taking Action* reference: Essential Action 5.1—Design and Lead Tier 2 Interventions for Essential Academic Standards, p. 203

- **"Tool: Targeting Tier 2 Interventions for an Individual Student"** (page 195)—Teacher teams new to designing and leading supplemental interventions often ask, "What do you do when you repeatedly provide essential academic standards interventions, and you still have a student who struggles with mastery?" If that is a pattern for your collaborative team, there is a good chance that the supplemental interventions you provide do not target the exact cause of a student's struggles. For example, providing additional practice opportunities to students who have yet to master immediate prerequisite skills will not result in new learning. Use this tool to develop a targeted intervention plan for an individual student who is not responding to your supplemental interventions.

  - *Taking Action* reference: Essential Action 5.1—Design and Lead Tier 2 Interventions for Essential Academic Standards, p. 203

- **"Checklist: Differentiation Strategies"** (page 197)—Designing and leading supplemental interventions for essential academic standards requires teachers to have a firm grasp of the possible strategies to differentiate learning experiences for struggling students. Use this checklist to build your knowledge of how teachers can differentiate instruction and identify strategies you can implement during your supplemental intervention periods.

  - *Taking Action* reference: Essential Action 5.1—Design and Lead Tier 2 Interventions for Essential Academic Standards, p. 203

- **"Tool: Re-Engagement Strategies That Work"** (online only)—To make supplemental interventions for essential academic standards effective, teachers must use instructional strategies different from those used during initial instruction. More importantly, they need to use instructional strategies with a proven record of helping students learn at higher levels. Review the strategies detailed in this tool and decide which would be easy to implement into your Tier 2 intervention work. These strategies were identified as having the greatest average effect on student achievement by Robert J. Marzano, Debra J. Pickering, and Jane E. Pollock (2001) in *Classroom Instruction That Works: Research-Based Strategies for Increasing Student Achievement* and affirmed in both *The New Art and Science of Teaching* (Marzano, 2017) and *The New Classroom Instruction That Works* (Goodwin & Rouleau, 2022).

- *Taking Action* reference: Essential Action 5.1—Design and Lead Tier 2 Interventions for Essential Academic Standards, p. 203

■ **"Tool: Tier 2 AI Prompts for Classroom Teachers"** (page 199)—Collaborative teams can face significant challenges when designing and leading supplemental interventions for academic essential standards. These challenges often involve finding innovative ways to introduce essentials and creating customized content for struggling students. Artificial intelligence tools—such as ChatGPT (https://chat.openai.com), Gemini (https://gemini.google.com), and MagicSchool (https://magicschool.ai)—can effectively address both obstacles. Explore this tool to discover ways that artificial intelligence can help you provide additional support to your struggling learners.

- *Taking Action* reference: Essential Action 5.1—Design and Lead Tier 2 Interventions for Essential Academic Standards, p. 203

■ **"Tool: Developing a Parent Permission Slip for Student Use of ChatGPT in High School Classrooms"** (online only)—High school teachers face a significant challenge when providing supplemental interventions for academic essentials due to the diverse range of student needs at any given moment. The task of tailoring support for a cohort of over one hundred students can be overwhelming, if not seemingly insurmountable. However, high school students can be empowered to seek out their own support by using emerging artificial intelligence tools like ChatGPT (https://chat.openai.com) or Gemini (https://gemini.google.com) as collaborative thought partners. Educators interested in teaching high school students to harness the potential of artificial intelligence tools as aids on their learning journey should craft a permission slip informing parents of their intentions and providing them with the chance to opt their students out of this opportunity. This tool, collaboratively developed with the support of ChatGPT (OpenAI, 2023), can serve as a template for schools in the process of creating their own permission slips for students' classroom use of artificial intelligence tools.

- *Taking Action* reference: Essential Action 5.1—Design and Lead Tier 2 Interventions for Essential Academic Standards, p. 203

- **"Student Tool: Tier 2 AI Prompts for High School Students"** (online only)—Given that AI tools are set to transform the way that people work and learn, it is essential to equip high school students with the skills necessary to utilize those tools as collaborative learning partners. In the short term, doing so ensures that every student has access to timely assistance in mastering grade-level essentials. In the long term, doing so enables every student to realize the full potential in the available artificial intelligence tools. Use this collection of prompts to introduce students to the range of support that AI chatbots like ChatGPT (https://chat.openai.com) or Gemini (https://gemini.google.com) can provide to learners.
    - *Taking Action* reference: Essential Action 5.1—Design and Lead Tier 2 Interventions for Essential Academic Standards, p. 203

- **"Tool: Prerequisite Planning Document"** (page 201)—Teacher teams can prevent students from needing supplemental interventions by screening students in the immediate prerequisite skills necessary for mastering academic essential standards. By thinking carefully about and then prescreening for necessary prerequisites, teams can identify and address gaps that will keep students from successfully mastering essential academic standards before instruction in those essentials even begins. Use this planning tool to develop plans for identifying and preteaching prerequisite vocabulary, knowledge, and skills for your next unit of study.
    - *Taking Action* reference: Essential Action 5.2—Identify and Target Immediate Prerequisite Skills, p. 211

- **"Tool: Preparing a Prerequisite Pretest"** (page 204)—Teams can also screen for immediate prerequisite skill mastery by delivering short prerequisite pretests one or two weeks before a new unit of study. They will then use the information gathered from these pretests to target students with preventive instruction designed to ensure that they have mastered the knowledge and skills necessary to learn essential academic standards. Use this tool and its **overview** (page 203) to identify declarative and procedural prerequisites for an upcoming academic essential standard and write a pretest to identify students who would benefit from supplemental instruction in prerequisite skills.
    - *Taking Action* reference: Essential Action 5.2—Identify and Target Immediate Prerequisite Skills, p. 211

- **"Tool: Analyzing Prerequisite Pretest Results"** (page 206)—Once a team has given students a prerequisite pretest, members must analyze the results and develop a plan for addressing learning gaps that will prevent students from mastering essential academic standards during initial instruction.

Analyzing pretest results includes recording the specific questions that students answered incorrectly and examining response patterns across classrooms. Use this tool to analyze results with your collaborative team after giving a prerequisite pretest for an upcoming unit of study.

- *Taking Action* reference: Essential Action 5.2—Identify and Target Immediate Prerequisite Skills, p. 211

- **"Tool: Supplemental Intervention Practice Reflection Template"** (page 208)—Teacher teams that successfully develop effective supplemental interventions for essential academic standards are committed to acting on the collected data regarding their intervention practices. That ability to act depends on developing collective awareness of the strengths and weaknesses of the strategies a team is experimenting with. To better document what your team knows about your supplemental intervention strategies, complete this reflection template for each practice you believe in.

  - *Taking Action* reference: Essential Action 5.3—Monitor the Progress of Students Receiving Tier 2 Academic Interventions, p. 219

- **"Tool: Rating the Effectiveness of Interventions on Your Learning Team"** (page 210)—It is key for readers of *The Big Book of Tools for RTI at Work* to understand that there is no one "right" tool to use to accomplish the individual essential actions detailed in *Taking Action: A Handbook for RTI at Work, Second Edition* (Mattos et al., 2025). The key is twofold: find a tool that (1) starts the right conversations on your team and (2) is formatted in a way that you find helpful. To prove that point, we have included a second tool to evaluate the efficacy of supplemental intervention strategies. Much like "Tool: Supplemental Intervention Practice Reflection Template" (page 208), this tool guides teams through questions designed to prompt thinking about an individual intervention strategy. This tool also includes a rating scale that teams can use to rank intervention strategies. Review these two tools and select one your teacher team can use when evaluating your supplemental intervention practices.

  - *Taking Action* reference: Essential Action 5.3—Monitor the Progress of Students Receiving Tier 2 Academic Interventions, p. 219

- **"Tool: Individual Student Intervention Report"** (page 211)—In *Learning by Doing*, DuFour and colleagues (2024) argue that schools should create a "timely, mandatory process for staff members to identify students for interventions" (p. 205). Use this template to create a detailed report for each student who is still struggling to master grade-level essentials after receiving first-best instruction and initial attempts at reteaching.

- *Taking Action* reference: Essential Action 5.3—Monitor the Progress of Students Receiving Tier 2 Academic Interventions, p. 219

■ **"Tool: The Struggle to Prioritize Planning for Extensions"** (online only)—Teachers know they need to take specific actions to intervene for students who struggle to master essential academic standards, and they are intentional about planning supplemental interventions. However, they often struggle to be just as intentional about planning for extensions. If this is true in your school, use this reflection tool to think through the role that planning for extensions plays in the work of your teacher team.

- *Taking Action* reference: Essential Action 5.4—Extend Student Learning, p. 223

■ **"Tool: Building Your Learning Team's Knowledge About Extensions"** (page 213)—Teacher teams that excel at providing extensions to students working beyond mastery expectations of essential academic standards possess a solid foundational understanding of some of the most common strategies used to extend learning: asking students to demonstrate mastery at levels beyond grade-level proficiency, giving students opportunities to study nonessential curriculum, teaching students above-grade-level curriculum, and introducing students to real-life essential outcome examples in action (DuFour et al., 2024; Roberts, 2019). Review those strategies and reflect on your team's current extension practices using this tool.

- *Taking Action* reference: Essential Action 5.4—Extend Student Learning, p. 223

■ **"Tool: Weekly Extension Planning Template"** (page 214)—The unfortunate truth is that conversations about extension (the fourth PLC critical question; DuFour et al., 2024) are rarely prioritized by learning teams during their weekly collaborative meetings. As a result, students who fall into this question 4 group quickly become at risk because their unique learning needs are overlooked or dismissed by teams who are pressed for time (Roberts, 2019; Weichel, McCann, & Williams, 2018). To avoid this trap, start each collaborative team meeting using this simple template to record the essential outcomes you will teach in the upcoming week and your initial plans for providing extensions.

- *Taking Action* reference: Essential Action 5.4—Extend Student Learning, p. 223

■ **"Tool Overview: Creating a Tiered Task Card to Extend Student Learning"** (page 215)—One of the easiest ways to create extensions for question 4 students is creating a tiered task card that details a series of four leveled tasks that accomplish two goals: they (1) are connected to your grade-level essentials and (2) increase in cognitive complexity. The task card allows students who are ready for an extension to interact with essentials at levels beyond grade-level proficiency expectations. Use this overview, **student tool** (page 216), and corresponding **samples** (page 217) to develop a tiered task card for an upcoming unit of study.

- *Taking Action* reference: Essential Action 5.4—Extend Student Learning, p. 223

▪ **"Tool: Using AI Chatbots to Develop Extension Tasks"** (page 219)—Teacher teams frequently emphasize interventions over extensions when planning at Tier 2 in the RTI at Work process. While this approach may seem logical due to the urgency of supporting students who haven't yet mastered grade-level essentials, it can inadvertently put the highest-achieving students at risk by not providing them with adequate challenges. The AI chatbot prompts outlined in this tool can help classroom teachers develop meaningful extensions for their question 4 students.

- *Taking Action* reference: Essential Action 5.4—Extend Student Learning, p. 223

Section 2: Resources Designed to Support Tier 2 Schoolwide Essential Actions

Visit **go.SolutionTree.com/RTIatWork/BBTRTI** to access online-only tools.

▪ **"Tool: Questions to Consider When Creating a Schedule for Supplemental Interventions"** (page 221)—Repurposing minutes in the school day to create a schedule that allows for supplemental interventions is technically easy, requiring nothing more than "subtracting minutes from some periods, adding the minutes up, and inserting an extra period into the daily schedule" (Buffum, Mattos, & Malone, 2018, p. 190). The real challenge is ensuring that the time, energy, and effort associated with planning and delivering supplemental interventions do not become overwhelming. Addressing this challenge depends on carefully managing logistic details like assigning students and staff to interventions, developing a plan for transitioning students to interventions, and efficiently monitoring student progress because of interventions. Guiding coalitions can use this tool to address the most common logistic challenges schools face when creating a schedule for supplemental interventions.

- *Taking Action* reference: Essential Action 6.1—Schedule Time for Tier 2 Interventions and Extensions, p. 232

- **"Tool: Avoiding the Common Pitfalls of Supplemental Intervention Periods"** (online only)—In *Taking Action: A Handbook for RTI at Work, Second Edition*, Mike Mattos and colleagues (2025) outline four common pitfalls that lead to the failure of supplemental intervention periods: (1) turning supplemental intervention periods into fun and games for some students, (2) taking electives or specials away from students to provide supplemental interventions, (3) failing to ensure that placement in supplemental intervention periods is flexible, and (4) thinking that supplemental intervention periods are a cure-all for struggling students. Use this tool to determine whether your school has fallen into these common intervention traps.
  - *Taking Action* reference: Essential Action 6.1—Schedule Time for Tier 2 Interventions and Extensions, p. 232

- **"Tool: Evaluating Your Plan for Providing Supplemental Interventions"** (page 224)—Mattos and colleagues (2025) also share four essential criteria that schools should consider when creating a schedule that ensures student access to both Tier 1 instruction and Tier 2 interventions. Use this tool to evaluate your school's current plan for providing supplemental interventions against those criteria.
  - *Taking Action* reference: Essential Action 6.1—Schedule Time for Tier 2 Interventions and Extensions, p. 232

- **"Tool: Staff Survey on the Efficacy of a Supplemental Intervention Period"** (page 226)—Finally, Mattos and colleagues (2025) suggest that schools should survey their faculties about the efficacy of their supplemental intervention periods. Doing so could motivate staff to invest instructional minutes into supplemental intervention sessions. They argue, "School faculty find it easier to commit to trying a new schedule if they know there will be opportunities to tweak the process when it's not working well" (Mattos et al., 2025, p. 237). Use this survey to gather information from your faculty about the efficacy of your supplemental intervention period.
  - *Taking Action* reference: Essential Action 6.1—Schedule Time for Tier 2 Interventions and Extensions, p. 232

- **"Tool: Developing Schoolwide Criteria for Identifying Students in Need of Tier 2 Behavioral Support"** (page 228)—Teacher teams implementing the RTI at Work process use the results of team-developed common formative assessments to identify students needing Tier 2 academic support for learning. Schools implementing the RTI at Work process must be just as deliberate about developing shared definitions of mastery and criteria for evaluating their students' social behaviors, academic dispositions, and health and home circumstances. Otherwise, it is impossible to guarantee students will receive targeted Tier 2 interventions for these challenges in a timely manner. Guiding coalitions can use this tool and its corresponding **protocol** (page 230) to develop schoolwide criteria for identifying students needing Tier 2 behavioral support.

- *Taking Action* reference: Essential Action 6.2—Establish a Process to Identify Students Who Require Tier 2 Behavior Interventions, p. 242

- **"Tool: Evaluating Your Systematic Response to Student Interventions"** (page 233)—Schools that create a systematic response to interventions follow five clear steps: (1) they identify students who need help, (2) determine the right intervention to meet students' learning needs, (3) monitor student progress to determine whether interventions are working, (4) revise their plans if a student is not responding to an intervention, and (5) extend learning once a student has mastered essential curriculum (Mattos et al., 2025). Guiding coalitions can use this tool and its **overview** (page 232) to learn more about these steps and evaluate their current response to interventions.

  - *Taking Action* reference: Essential Action 6.2—Establish a Process to Identify Students Who Require Tier 2 Behavior Interventions, p. 242

- **"Tool: Staff Recommendation Form for Students Needing Behavioral Support"** (page 236)—Targeting interventions depends on identifying the root causes of student struggles before taking action. While team-developed common formative assessments are valuable tools for identifying students needing academic interventions, students struggling with behaviors, health concerns, attendance, or challenges at home are often identified through teacher observation. As a result, the original architects of the RTI at Work process, Mattos and colleagues (2018), argue that schools interested in developing an effective system of intervention create a "schoolwide staff recommendation process to identify students who need behavior interventions" (p. 242). This tool is a recommendation form that schools can use to identify students needing behavioral support.

  - *Taking Action* reference: Essential Action 6.2—Establish a Process to Identify Students Who Require Tier 2 Behavior Interventions, p. 242

- **"Tool: Reviewing Your Plan for Providing Supplemental Interventions for Students Struggling With Social Behaviors, Academic Behaviors, and Health and Home Challenges"** (page 238)—As Mattos and colleagues (2025) explain:

  > Just as one would not expect every student to learn essential *academic* standards by the end of initial instruction, a school must not assume every student will consistently demonstrate

essential behaviors merely because they were taught at the beginning of the year. (p. 247)

Mattos and colleagues (2025) detail a series of social behaviors, academic behaviors, and health and home challenges that a guiding coalition must plan and implement interventions for. Use this tool to reflect on your school's current efforts to support students struggling to master these essentials.

- *Taking Action* reference: Essential Action 6.3—Plan and Implement Tier 2 Interventions for Essential Social and Academic Behaviors, p. 247

- **"Tool: Planning Interventions for Students With Attendance Issues"** (page 243)—For some students, attendance—not academic ability—is the primary barrier to mastering grade-level essential standards. After all, learning new concepts and skills is difficult when you are not present for instruction. Guiding coalitions must develop targeted interventions for students with emerging attendance issues (Mattos et al., 2025). Schools with strong systems of interventions often develop smaller teams of professionals with expertise in attendance issues—counselors, administrators, attendance secretaries, and school social workers—that accept lead responsibility for delivering these interventions to students (Mattos et al., 2025). Those teams can use this table to track and document interventions for students struggling with attendance.

  - *Taking Action* reference: Essential Action 6.3—Plan and Implement Tier 2 Interventions for Essential Social and Academic Behaviors, p. 247

- **"Tool: Tracking the Reasons Students Struggle With Work Completion"** (online only)—Work completion is the primary barrier to mastering grade-level essentials for other students. After all, the tasks teachers assign are intentionally designed to give students opportunities to practice with essential academic standards. While it's easy to identify students struggling with work completion, remember that not all students struggle to complete assignments for the same reasons. That means planning and implementing supplemental interventions for work completion must begin by gathering information on the specific challenges preventing individual students from completing assignments— a process that this tool and its **overview** (online only) facilitate.

  - *Taking Action* reference: Essential Action 6.3—Plan and Implement Tier 2 Interventions for Essential Social and Academic Behaviors, p. 247

- **"Tool: Analyzing the Reasons Students Struggle With Work Completion— Data Table"** (online only): Once teachers have used "Tool: Tracking the Reasons Students Struggle With Work Completion" (online only) to collect data on the specific reasons why students are failing to complete assignments, your leadership team must analyze that data to plan targeted interventions for those students. Use this tool to complete that data analysis in your next meeting.

- *Taking Action* reference: Essential Action 6.3—Plan and Implement Tier 2 Interventions for Essential Social and Academic Behaviors, p. 247

- **"Student Tool: Self-Reflection Template for Students Struggling With Work Completion"** (online only)—One intervention strategy to use when students struggle with work completion is to ask students to identify why they fail to finish assignments. Involving students directly in analyzing their work completion struggles empowers them to become active partners in the intervention process—a step that develops responsibility in learners and can ease the demands on classroom teachers and other practitioners who are leading interventions for essential social and academic behaviors. Use this self-reflection template to start conversations with middle or high school students about incomplete or missing assignments.

  - *Taking Action* reference: Essential Action 6.3—Plan and Implement Tier 2 Interventions for Essential Social and Academic Behaviors, p. 247

- **"Student Tool: Student Survey on Missing or Late Work"** (page 246)— A similar strategy that middle and high school teachers can use when planning and implementing supplemental interventions for students who struggle with work completion is to survey students with the most missing assignments. Doing so can help teachers find the specific reason an individual student struggles with work completion—an essential first step toward designing an effective intervention. Use this survey to gather information from the students in your classroom who are failing to complete assigned work.

  - *Taking Action* reference: Essential Action 6.3—Plan and Implement Tier 2 Interventions for Essential Social and Academic Behaviors, p. 247

- **"Tool: Quarterly Work Behaviors Student Self-Assessment"** (online only)— Schools that are planning and implementing supplemental interventions for essential social and academic behaviors can also engage students in regularly self-assessing the specific work behaviors that lead to academic success. Doing so reminds students that success depends on something more than academic ability and creates opportunities for teachers and parents to regularly talk with students about essential social and academic behaviors. This tool can help start those conversations in your building.

  - *Taking Action* reference: Essential Action 6.3—Plan and Implement Tier 2 Interventions for Essential Social and Academic Behaviors, p. 247

- **"Student Tool: Learning Profile Survey—Secondary"** (page 248) and **"Student Tool: Learning Profile Survey—Primary"** (page 250): Planning and implementing supplemental interventions for essential social and academic behaviors involves acknowledging that students' affects and learning environments are unique and can directly impact their ability to succeed in the classroom. Learning profile surveys delivered at the beginning of each school year can help schools gather the information necessary to address these unique needs successfully. Teachers of secondary students can ask their students to complete these surveys as a part of in-class activities, while teachers of primary students can ask parents to complete these surveys as a part of beginning-of-the-year orientations, open houses, or parent-teacher conferences.

- *Taking Action* reference: Essential Action 6.3—Plan and Implement Tier 2 Interventions for Essential Social and Academic Behaviors, p. 247

■ **"Tool: RTI at Work Pro-Solve Intervention Targeting Process—Tier 1 and Tier 2"** (page 252): Planning and implementing supplemental interventions for individual students with the most significant academic and behavioral needs begins by answering a series of five questions: (1) What is the concern that we have for this student?, (2) What is the cause of the concern for this student?, (3) What is our desired outcome for this student?, (4) What steps should we take to achieve our desired outcome for this student?, and (5) Who is going to take lead responsibility to ensure that each intervention is implemented for this student? (Mattos et al., 2025). The school will need problem-solving processes *and* protocols—what Mattos and colleagues (2025) call a *pro-solve* process. Use this tool to develop a targeted Tier 1 or Tier 2 intervention plan for struggling students.

- *Taking Action* reference: Essential Action 6.4—Coordinate Interventions for Students Needing Academic *and* Behavior Supports, p. 256

■ **"Tool: Defining Lead Responsibilities for Academic and Behavioral Interventions"** (page 253)—Coordinating interventions for students needing academic and behavioral support can only begin after a school has identified specific faculty members who will take lead responsibility for ensuring intervention implementation and monitoring progress (Mattos et al., 2025). Mattos and colleagues (2025) explain, "At some point, the buck must stop with specific staff members who take the lead for each intervention for this student" (p. 258). Use this table to learn more about the types of academic and behavioral interventions a building should offer and to create lists of faculty members with the expertise necessary to deliver each intervention.

- *Taking Action* reference: Essential Action 6.4—Coordinate Interventions for Students Needing Academic *and* Behavior Supports, p. 256

Conclusion

Tier 2 interventions in a multitiered system of supports are designed to ensure that all students master essential skills, knowledge, and behaviors needed for success in the next grade level or course. Collaborative teacher teams take collective responsibility for designing and delivering Tier 2 skill interventions on essential academic standards by using common formative assessment data. Why? Because they have the right professional knowledge and expertise to lead this work. Who is better to provide initial reteaching on grade-level essential standards than the teachers who collaboratively identified those essentials and developed a guaranteed and viable curriculum at Tier 1 in the RTI at Work process? While collaborative teacher teams design and deliver Tier 2 interventions on essential academic standards, guiding coalitions lead efforts to schedule supplemental interventions, evaluate the efficacy of Tier 2 interventions, and establish criteria for identifying students in need of Tier 2 behavioral support (that is, support for behavioral, attendance, and home challenges).

Whether they are designed to reteach essential academic standards or the skills and behaviors needed for success in the next grade level, Tier 2 interventions are targeted and specific. Collaborative teams use common misconceptions, misunderstandings, mistakes, or a combination of these to build intervention groups, knowing that reteaching is easier when all students are struggling to master an academic essential for the same reason. Professionals providing interventions in academic skills and dispositions work just as systematically to identify the specific behaviors students are struggling with before designing plans for reteaching. When done well, Tier 2 interventions are effective because they address the exact cause of a student's initial struggles to learn grade-level essentials. In addition, they are immediate interventions that are preventing future gaps in understanding.

The tools in this chapter are designed to help readers effectively implement Tier 2 interventions. By emphasizing collaborative efforts, targeted interventions, and data-driven decision making, schools can better support all students in mastering essential knowledge, skills, and behaviors for academic success before falling far enough behind to need the intensive interventions that Tier 3 offers in a multitiered system of supports.

Resources Designed to

Support Tier 2 Teacher Team Essential Actions

Tool: Building Shared Knowledge About Tier 2 Interventions and Extensions

Taking Action *reference: Essential Action 5.1—Design and Lead Tier 2 Interventions for Essential Academic Standards, p. 203*

Instructions: To surface what you already know about the role teacher teams play in designing and leading supplemental interventions for academic essentials, work with your team to decide whether the following statements are true or false. Then, check your answers against those provided in "Answer Key: Building Shared Knowledge About Tier 2 Interventions and Extensions" (page 192) and correct your answers if necessary.

Statement	Your Answer	Correct Answer	Your Rationale
Teams should provide intervention and extension for every outcome in their required curriculum.	☐ True ☐ False	☐ True ☐ False	
Classroom teachers always provide interventions for struggling students.	☐ True ☐ False	☐ True ☐ False	
Teachers cannot move forward in their curriculum until all students have mastered the standards they are currently studying.	☐ True ☐ False	☐ True ☐ False	
The best intervention strategy is good initial instruction.	☐ True ☐ False	☐ True ☐ False	

Teams with successful interventions always start instruction by administering pretests of grade-level essentials.	☐ True ☐ False	☐ True ☐ False	
Sorting students into targeted intervention groups is the most important action teams take when analyzing common formative assessment results.	☐ True ☐ False	☐ True ☐ False	
Teams should use state testing results early in the school year to identify students who need intervention, extension, or both.	☐ True ☐ False	☐ True ☐ False	
The most important interventions that we provide to students address the outcomes we are required to teach by our state standards.	☐ True ☐ False	☐ True ☐ False	
I can name the four most common strategies for extending learning.	☐ True ☐ False	☐ True ☐ False	
I can name the four most common reasons why students struggle to master grade-level essentials.	☐ True ☐ False	☐ True ☐ False	

Answer Key: Building Shared Knowledge About Tier 2 Interventions and Extensions

Taking Action *reference: Essential Action 5.1—Design and Lead Tier 2 Interventions for Essential Academic Standards, p. 203*

Instructions: Review the answers and rationale provided in the second and third columns of the following table. Compare them to the answers that your team generated on the previous page. What answers did you get right? What answers did you get wrong? What answers surprised you, had you wondering, or left you relieved? What changes do you need to make to your intervention efforts?

Statement	Correct Answer	Explanation
Teams should provide intervention and extension for every outcome in their required curriculum.	☐ True ☑ False	Because the total number of standards for most courses is overwhelming, it is both unrealistic and unreasonable to expect teachers and teams to provide intervention and extension for every outcome. Instead, teams focus their Tier 2 intervention and extension efforts on the essentials in their required curriculum. If time allows for additional interventions and extensions, teams can begin targeting nonessentials, but ensuring that students receive additional time and support to master essentials is the top priority.
Classroom teachers always provide interventions for struggling students.	☐ True ☑ False	It is true that classroom teachers accept primary responsibility for providing interventions in grade-level academic standards, but students struggle in school for reasons that go beyond academics. In a system of interventions, the school's guiding coalition accepts primary responsibility for interventions in social behaviors, health and home issues that prevent a student from succeeding, and learners' dispositions.
Teachers cannot move forward in their curriculum until all students have mastered the standards they are currently studying.	☐ True ☑ False	While it is true that all students must master grade-level essential standards before the end of the school year, that does not mean teams can't move forward in their instruction until all students have mastered those essentials. Instead, teams should keep a careful record of students who have yet to master current essentials, continue discussions about additional intervention strategies worth trying, and set aside time for continued reteaching of those essentials.
The best intervention strategy is good initial instruction.	☑ True ☐ False	There is not enough time or personnel available to provide intervention to large numbers of students. Instead, teams should invest their time and energy in finding the most effective strategies for teaching their essentials, therefore preventing students from needing intervention.
Teams with successful interventions always start instruction by administering pretests of grade-level essentials.	☐ True ☑ False	Pretests of grade-level essentials *could* be a valuable tool, if teachers and teams are willing to carefully analyze data to identify specific outcomes that individual students have mastered and plan differentiated instruction for those students. The problem is that teachers rarely do this work because it can be incredibly time consuming. Instead, teams should design and deliver *pretests of prerequisite skills*—things students need to know before working with grade-level essentials—and use the information gathered to preteach those prerequisites to students before starting instruction in a grade-level essential.

Sorting students into targeted intervention groups is the most important action teams take when analyzing common formative assessment results.	☐ True ☑ False	While it is true that teams must sort students into targeted intervention groups, that work is rarely difficult for teams. In fact, teachers can probably build those groups without much effort at all. Instead, looking for common patterns in student work samples is most important when analyzing common formative assessment results. What can students in each intervention group already do? What common mistakes are they making? What common misunderstandings do they have? Spotting those patterns can help teams effectively target their Tier 2 intervention efforts.
Teams should use state testing results early in the school year to identify students who need intervention, extension, or both.	☐ True ☑ False	Tier 2 interventions provide students with extra time and support to master the essentials that are currently being taught in class. That information cannot be gleaned from state testing results. Instead, it is gleaned from team-created common formative assessments given during a cycle of instruction.
The most important interventions that we provide to students address the outcomes we are required to teach by state standards.	☐ True ☑ False	The most important interventions are those that address specific reasons why students are struggling in school—and sometimes, students aren't struggling for academic reasons. Instead, they are struggling with essential skills, dispositions, or social behaviors. Providing students who are missing essential skills, dispositions, or behaviors with academic interventions won't address the root causes of their classroom struggles.
I can name the four most common strategies for extending learning.	☑ True ☐ False	Teachers can extend learning by doing the following. • Introduce students to above-grade-level curriculum. • Ask students to work beyond grade-level expectations. • Introduce students to nonessential outcomes in the required grade-level curriculum. • Ask students to explore how grade-level curriculum impacts the world beyond the classroom.
I can name the four most common reasons why students struggle to master grade-level essentials.	☑ True ☐ False	The following are the four most common reasons why students struggle to master essentials. 1. They have gaps in prerequisite knowledge that teachers must address before students can master the grade-level essential. 2. They need additional practice opportunities with the grade-level essential. 3. They need an alternative way to demonstrate mastery of the grade-level essential. 4. Their work behaviors—participation, work completion, and effort—are preventing them from mastering the grade-level essential.

Tool: Team-Based Intervention Plan for Struggling Learners

Taking Action *reference: Essential Action 5.1—Design and Lead Tier 2 Interventions for Essential Academic Standards, p. 203*

Instructions: Record the essential outcomes that you are currently teaching. Then, indicate the type of intervention that you are planning and outline your intervention plan in the provided space. Finally, list the students in each classroom who need this intervention. Remember that students struggle to master essential outcomes for different reasons. You will need to create a separate intervention plan for each of the reasons that the students of your learning team are struggling.

Essential Outcomes We Are Currently Teaching:

Type of Intervention We Are Planning

- ☐ **Support with prerequisite learning** for students with gaps in foundational knowledge and skills that are preventing them from mastering the essential outcomes that we are currently teaching
- ☐ **Additional practice** for students who are making common mistakes that are likely to be easily corrected with a few opportunities to work with the essential outcomes again
- ☐ **Alternative demonstrations of mastery** for students who are struggling with a specific task and who might be able to demonstrate mastery of an essential outcome in a different way
- ☐ **Support for work behaviors** for students who are struggling to master an essential outcome because they haven't yet developed the habits demonstrated by successful learners (for example, coming to class prepared, participating in classroom discussions, or completing homework)

Our Intervention Plan:

List the students in each class who are currently in need of this intervention.

Teacher:	Teacher:	Teacher:	Teacher:

Source: Ferriter, W. M. (2020). The big book of tools for collaborative teams in a PLC at Work. Bloomington, IN: Solution Tree Press, p. 162.

Tool: Targeting Tier 2 Interventions for an Individual Student

Taking Action reference: Essential Action 5.1—Design and Lead Tier 2 Interventions for Essential Academic Standards, p. 203

Instructions: Use the following template to develop a targeted intervention plan for a student who is not responding to your supplemental interventions.

Name of Student:
Essential Standard or Standards Student Is Struggling to Master:

Questions for Reflection	Your Responses
Why do you think this student is struggling to master this essential standard?	This student: ☐ Needs more time to master the standard ☐ Isn't motivated to work on the standard ☐ Doesn't understand how the standard was taught ☐ Doesn't have the foundational prerequisite skills from prior years related to mastery of the standard ☐ Doesn't have the immediate prerequisite skills to master the standard ☐ Other:
What evidence supports your conclusions about why this student struggles to master this essential standard? • What specific evidence from assessments (pretests, universal screeners, and common formative assessments) can you use to support your conclusions? • What specific evidence from classroom observations can you use to support your conclusions? • What specific evidence from previous performances can you use to support your conclusions?	

page 1 of 2

What next steps will you take to support this student?	
• Will you reteach this concept to this student using a different instructional practice? • Will you assign this student to a specific intervention group and provide additional support during a schoolwide intervention period? • Will you reteach prerequisite skills to this student and then reassess, looking for mastery on the grade-level essential you are teaching? • Will you modify how this student can demonstrate mastery, considering their struggles with foundational skills in reading, written expression, basic numeracy, or the primary language of instruction?	
Which other students are struggling to master this essential standard for the same reasons? • Would they benefit from the same interventions?	
When will you take action? • Does this intervention have to occur before you move forward in your instructional sequence? • Do you need to coordinate with your collaborative team before you can deliver an intervention to this student? • Do you need to do additional research before you can provide effective interventions to this student?	

Checklist: Differentiation Strategies

Taking Action *reference: Essential Action 5.1—Design and Lead Tier 2 Interventions for Essential Academic Standards, p. 203*

Instructions: Teachers *differentiate instruction* by considering their students' unique needs and interests when developing instructional materials. Differentiation usually involves making modifications to the following (Strickland, 2007; Tomlinson, 2017).

- The **methods** that students use to access content
- The **process** students use to practice with essential outcomes
- The **products** that students create to demonstrate mastery of essential outcomes

Reflect on the work that your learning team is doing with differentiation by placing a check mark next to strategies in the following checklist that you are already integrating into your instruction and a star next to strategies you are ready to tackle. Cross out strategies that are beyond your team's current ability.

Method	Process	Product
☐ **Leveraging student interests:** Incorporate topics that interest students within the subject matter to increase engagement and motivation.	☐ **Flexible grouping:** Create groups based on students' learning needs, interests, or styles that can change as their learning progresses.	☐ **Varied assessment options:** Allow students to show what they know through different formats, such as presentations, written reports, art projects, or digital creations.
☐ **Use of varied texts and resources:** Provide materials at varying reading levels and formats (such as videos, texts, podcasts, and graphic novels) to match individual learning preferences and reading abilities.	☐ **Scaffolded instructions:** Provide step-by-step guidance for complex tasks, gradually reducing support as students gain independence.	☐ **Rubrics with clear criteria:** Provide rubrics that detail varying levels of understanding or skill, allowing for varied end products that demonstrate learning.
☐ **Learning stations or centers:** Create stations that students rotate through, each offering a different activity or approach to the content.	☐ **Differentiated homework:** Assign homework based on individual student needs, strengths, and areas for growth, making out-of-class learning more personal and effective.	☐ **Reflection opportunities:** Incorporate reflection as a product of learning, enabling students to demonstrate their process of learning and self-assessment.
☐ **Visual aids and infographics:** Use visual summaries of information for complex or content-heavy topics.	☐ **Tiered assignments:** Offer varied assignment levels to match students' readiness levels, ensuring all students can access the material at their own level.	☐ **Portfolio assessment:** Allow students to compile a portfolio of their work throughout the course to show their learning progression.
☐ **Adaptive technology tools:** Implement software or devices designed to support learning disabilities, such as speech-to-text programs or text-to-speech readers.		

Method	Process	Product
☐ **Dual-language resources:** Offer materials in students' native languages alongside English to support multilingual learners. ☐ **Self-paced modules:** Offer modules that students can work through at their own pace, with checkpoints for understanding.	☐ **Graphic organizers:** Provide visual aids like Venn diagrams or flowcharts to help students organize their thoughts and understandings. ☐ **Simulation and games:** Use educational simulations and games to make learning interactive and engaging, reinforcing concepts through play.	☐ **Student-created test questions:** Have students create test questions related to the unit of study, demonstrating their understanding of key concepts. ☐ **Choice boards:** Use choice boards or menus that allow students to choose from a variety of learning activities that reflect their preferred learning method or interests. ☐ **Peer teaching projects:** Prepare and deliver a lesson or tutorial on a subject area, teaching classmates about a specific topic.

Source: Adapted from Strickland, C. (2007). Tools for high-quality differentiated instruction: An ASCD action tool. *Arlington, VA: ASCD; Tomlinson, C. A. (2017).* How to differentiate instruction in academically diverse classrooms *(3rd ed.). Arlington, VA: ASCD.*

Questions for Reflection

Name one differentiation strategy that you are already implementing. Where are you using that strategy? How effective is that strategy? Is it easy for teachers to implement? Do students enjoy it? Can teachers easily replicate the strategy in other units?

Name one differentiation strategy that you would consider implementing immediately. Why does it make sense to start working with that strategy right now? What unit or lesson would you use this strategy with? What steps are necessary before you can integrate this strategy into your work with students?

References

Strickland, C. (2007). *Tools for high-quality differentiated instruction: An ASCD action tool.* Arlington, VA: ASCD.

Tomlinson, C. A. (2017). *How to differentiate instruction in academically diverse classrooms* (3rd ed.). Arlington, VA: ASCD.

Tool: Tier 2 AI Prompts for Classroom Teachers

Taking Action *reference: Essential Action 5.1—Design and Lead Tier 2 Interventions for Essential Academic Standards, p. 203*

Instructions: Collaborative teacher teams should ensure that all students master grade-level academic essentials. That means you must design and lead supplemental interventions whenever students are struggling. Use the following prompts with an AI chatbot like ChatGPT (https://chat.openai.com) or Gemini (https://gemini.google.com) to help you with this work.

AI chatbots can help you identify common mistakes students might be making.	AI chatbots can generate alternative demonstrations of mastery.
• I am a *[grade level and subject area]* teacher. I have students struggling to *[grade-level concept or skill]*. Can you tell me the most common mistakes they will make? **Sample:** *I am a middle school pottery teacher. I have students struggling to glaze pottery. Can you tell me the most common mistakes they will make?*	• Can you give me ten different ways *[grade level and subject area]* students can demonstrate mastery of *[grade-level concept or skill]* without making a written product or summary? **Sample:** *Can you give me ten different ways third-grade students can demonstrate mastery of rounding three-digit numbers without making a written product or summary?*
AI chatbots can offer unique strategies for reteaching a concept.	**AI chatbots can generate, level, and translate reading passages.**
• I am a *[grade level and subject area]* teacher. I need to teach my students *[grade-level concept or skill]*. Can you give me five original ideas for teaching this concept to my students? **Sample:** *I am a third-grade teacher. I need to teach my students to multiply. Can you give me five original ideas for teaching this concept to my students?*	• Can you write a high-interest, five-paragraph reading passage for *[grade level and subject area]* students on *[grade-level concept or skill]*? • Can you rewrite that passage on the *[grade level]* reading level? • Can you translate this passage into *[language]*? • Can you summarize the most important points of this passage in five bullets written at the *[grade level]* reading level?
AI chatbots can provide new ways to explain ideas to struggling students.	**AI chatbots can create mnemonic devices.**
• I am a *[grade level and subject area]* student. Can you explain *[grade-level concept or skill]* to me like a beginner? **Sample:** *I am a third-grade student learning science. Can you explain implosion to me like I am a beginner?* **Note:** Pretending to be a student in this prompt will ensure that ChatGPT returns an explanation in language your students are likely to understand.	• Can you create a mnemonic device that *[grade level and subject area]* students can use to remember *[grade-level concept or skill]*? **Sample:** *Can you create a mnemonic device that civics students can use to remember the steps that a bill must take to become a law?*

page 1 of 2

AI chatbots work for behaviors too.
- Can you give me three activities for teaching *[behavioral expectation]* like *[examples of behavioral expectation]* to *[grade level]* students?

Sample: Can you give me three activities for teaching proper work behaviors like organization, coming to class prepared, and participating in class to middle school students?

AI chatbots can write songs.
- Can you create a song that *[grade level and subject area]* students can use to remember *[grade-level concept or skill]*?

Sample: Can you create a song that high school students can use to remember what happened at the Potsdam Conference?

AI chatbots can create review games for students to play.
- Can you create a game that *[grade level and subject area]* students can play to review *[grade-level concept or skill]*?

Sample: Can you create a game that kindergarten students can play to review their letter sounds?

AI chatbots can create body movements.
- Can you create a body movement that *[grade level and subject area]* students can use to remember *[grade-level concept or skill]*?

Sample: Can you create a body movement that seventh-grade students can use to remember the rules of the caste system?

Tool: Prerequisite Planning Document

Taking Action *reference: Essential Action 5.2—Identify and Target Immediate Prerequisite Skills, p. 211*

Instructions: Use this planning document with your collaborative team to first identify and then develop plans for preteaching prerequisite vocabulary, knowledge, and skills for your next unit of study.

Essential Outcome We Are Planning For:

page 1 of 2

The Big Book of Tools for RTI at Work © 2025 Solution Tree Press • SolutionTree.com
Visit **go.SolutionTree.com/RTIatWork/BBTRTI** to download this free reproducible.

Questions for Reflection

How will we screen our students to assess current mastery levels with these prerequisites?

What resources will we use to preteach these prerequisites to students who have not mastered them?

When will we preteach these prerequisites to students who have not mastered them?

Who will lead this work?

Tool Overview: Preparing a Prerequisite Pretest

Taking Action *reference: Essential Action 5.2—Identify and Target Immediate Prerequisite Skills, p. 211*

In *Taking Action: A Handbook for RTI at Work, Second Edition*, authors Mattos and colleagues (2025) suggest that teams systematically screen students for immediate prerequisite skill mastery before starting a new instruction unit. Doing so allows teams to proactively address knowledge and skill gaps that will prevent students from successfully mastering grade-level academic essentials. Teams can screen for immediate prerequisite skill mastery by delivering short prerequisite pretests one to two weeks before a new unit of study and then using the information gathered from these pretests to target students with preventive instruction designed to ensure they have mastered the knowledge and skills necessary to learn essential academic standards.

To prepare a prerequisite pretest, your team should do the following.

1. **Identify the grade-level essentials you are expected to teach:** Targeted instruction in prerequisite skills starts once a team has a clear, shared understanding of the grade-level essentials they are expected to teach.

2. **Identify declarative and procedural prerequisites:** Mattos and colleagues (2025) recommend that teams identify the declarative and procedural prerequisites required to master grade-level essentials.
   - *Declarative prerequisites* include the concepts, ideas, facts, and vocabulary that students must already know to master grade-level essentials.
   - *Procedural prerequisites* include the skills that a student must already be able to do to master grade-level essentials.

3. **Write three to five questions designed to test student mastery of declarative and procedural prerequisites:** Prerequisite pretests should be intentionally short. Teachers should be able to deliver them quickly. If a prerequisite pretest takes too long to deliver, analyze, or respond to, teachers will begin to question the value of pretesting for prerequisites.

4. **Tie each question to a specific prerequisite:** Like all good assessments, questions on a prerequisite pretest should assess one isolated concept or skill. By deliberately connecting each question to an individual prerequisite, teams facilitate their response to the data they collect. Targeted interventions are only possible when teachers are clear about the exact gaps that individual students are bringing with them to the classroom.

5. **Generate an expected response and identify common mistakes students are likely to make:** When teams discuss the answers they expect students to give to—and the mistakes students are likely to make on—prerequisite pretest questions, they build a shared understanding of what mastery looks like in action. That shared understanding of mastery is essential to high-functioning collaborative teams.

Use "Tool: Preparing a Prerequisite Pretest" on page 204 to complete this work with your collaborative team.

Reference

Mattos, M., Buffum, A., Malone, J., Cruz, L. F., Dimich, N., & Schuhl, S. (2025). *Taking action: A handbook for RTI at Work* (2nd ed.). Bloomington, IN: Solution Tree Press.

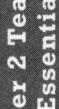

Tool: Preparing a Prerequisite Pretest

Taking Action *reference: Essential Action 5.2—Identify and Target Immediate Prerequisite Skills, p. 211*

Instructions: Use the following template to design a short, five-question pretest to assess mastery of prerequisite skills and knowledge that a student must have learned to master your grade-level essentials.

Grade-Level Essential Standard or Standards We Teach:	
Identifying Declarative Prerequisites: List any concepts, ideas, or vocabulary that a student **must already know** to master this grade-level essential standard.	**Identifying Procedural Prerequisites:** List any skills that a student **must already be able to do** to master this grade-level essential standard.

Prerequisite Pretest Questions

Generate five questions to use as a prerequisite pretest. Tie each question to a specific declarative or procedural prerequisite skill to facilitate efforts to address gaps in prerequisite knowledge.

Question	Prerequisites This Question Assesses	Expected Student Response	Common Mistakes Students Struggling With Prerequisite Knowledge Will Likely Make

page 1 of 2

Question	Prerequisites This Question Assesses	Expected Student Response	Common Mistakes Students Struggling With Prerequisite Knowledge Will Likely Make

Questions for Reflection

When will we give our prerequisite pretest?

How will we deliver our prerequisite pretest?

How will we analyze the results of our prerequisite pretest?

When will we intervene for students who struggle on our prerequisite pretest?

Tool: Analyzing Prerequisite Pretest Results

Taking Action *reference: Essential Action 5.2—Identify and Target Immediate Prerequisite Skills, p. 211*

Instructions: After giving a prerequisite pretest, analyze your data using the tracking chart and reflection questions this tool provides. Use the following process.

1. Record the prerequisite learning each question on your pretest assesses in the appropriate box at the end of the tracking chart.
2. Record the names of students who fail your prerequisite pretest in the **Student Name** column.
3. If a student has answered a question incorrectly, place an *X* in the column beneath that question number.
4. If a student has answered a question correctly, leave the column beneath that question number blank.
5. Use the **Additional Notes** column to record observations about a student's performance on your pretest.

Student Name	Question Number					Additional Notes
	1	2	3	4	5	
Prerequisite Learning Covered in Question:						

Questions for Reflection

What patterns can you spot in the data you collected from students who failed your prerequisites pretest? Which questions are proving to be the most difficult for students? Are students having an equally hard time with questions covering knowledge and skill prerequisites, or is one type of prerequisite more difficult than the other? Are there any commonalities between students who are struggling with your prerequisite pretest?

How do the patterns in the data you collected from students who failed your prerequisites pretest compare to those collected by your collaborative partners? Are students across classrooms struggling with the same questions? Did students in some classrooms experience greater struggles with some questions? What are some possible explanations for results that differ across classrooms?

How will you respond to these prerequisite pretest results? Are you going to preteach concepts during small-group instruction? Will you regroup students and deliver instruction during your schoolwide intervention period? Are some teachers better suited to provide prerequisites reteaching for this unit than others?

Tool: Supplemental Intervention Practice Reflection Template

Taking Action *reference: Essential Action 5.3—Monitor the Progress of Students Receiving Tier 2 Academic Interventions, p. 219*

Instructions: To better document what your team knows about your supplemental intervention strategies, work with your collaborative team to complete this reflection template for each practice you believe in.

Learning Team:
Intervention Practice:
Questions for Reflection **What evidence do we have that this intervention practice has a measurable impact on student learning?** Are scores on our common assessments going up? Have we noticed that students successfully apply new knowledge or skills independently since we began using this practice? Is this practice equally effective for every student, or does it seem to benefit some groups more than others? How do we know? How does that change the way we feel about this practice?   **How approachable is this intervention practice?** Is it a teaching strategy that everyone on our team can implement with fidelity and consistency, or is it a strategy that might be difficult for new teachers or teachers new to our team to master? Are we sure this is an intervention practice we won't abandon because it is too hard to implement?

What are the unique strengths of this intervention practice? Is it connected to school or district goals? Is it easy to translate to different content areas or contexts? Is it well suited for our student population? Why should we believe in this practice? What value does it bring to our students, teachers, and team? Are there any unique limitations to this practice? What makes it hard to embrace?

What one change would make this intervention practice more approachable and easier to implement? What one change would make it more motivating for our students? What one change would make this intervention practice more appropriate for struggling learners? What about high achievers and multilingual learners?

What unanswered questions do we still have about this intervention practice? Are there any practical steps we can take to answer these questions? What next steps can we take with this intervention practice? Will we continue to tinker with it or shelve it? Why?

Source: Adapted from Ferriter, W. M., Graham, P., & Wight, M. (2013). Making teamwork meaningful: Leading progress-driven collaboration in a PLC at Work. *Bloomington, IN: Solution Tree Press.*

Tool: Rating the Effectiveness of Interventions on Your Learning Team

Taking Action reference: Essential Action 5.3—Monitor the Progress of Students Receiving Tier 2 Academic Interventions, p. 219

Instructions: Complete one tracking template for each of the intervention practices that your learning team experiments with. In a few short sentences, describe this intervention. What essential knowledge and skills was it designed to address? Then answer the questions in each column in order to fully outline the effectiveness of the intervention, the materials you used, and ways to use this intervention in the future. Finally, assign a rating to the intervention using the provided scale.

Intervention Practice:

Evidence of Effectiveness	Required Materials	Future Revisions and Applications
How do you know that this intervention was effective? What evidence have you collected to show that the intervention has impacted student learning in a positive way? Did the intervention work better for some students than others? Why?	What resources were necessary to ensure effective implementation of this intervention? Include physical materials, lessons, and any additional faculty members who helped with this intervention practice.	What changes can you make to improve this intervention practice? How easily could you adapt this intervention practice to address other essential knowledge and skill gaps?

Rate This Intervention Practice

1	2	3	4	5
This intervention was ineffective or difficult to implement. It isn't useful to our team and should be abandoned.	Despite showing signs of some promise, there are too many implementation challenges to make this intervention worthwhile.	This intervention has promise—but it is going to need significant revisions to remain part of our team's intervention plans.	This intervention was highly effective, and with a few simple revisions, it will be easy to implement. We should continue to polish and improve it.	This intervention was highly effective and easy to implement just as it is. We should find ways to adapt it to new situations.

Source: Ferriter, W. M. (2020). The big book of tools for collaborative teams in a PLC at Work. Bloomington, IN: Solution Tree Press, p. 164. Adapted from Graham, P., & Ferriter, W. M. (2010). Building a Professional Learning Community at Work: A guide to the first year. Bloomington, IN: Solution Tree Press.

Tool: Individual Student Intervention Report

Taking Action *reference: Essential Action 5.3—Monitor the Progress of Students Receiving Tier 2 Academic Interventions, p. 219*

Instructions: Use this template to create a detailed report for all students who are still struggling to master essential standards in your current unit of study after receiving first-best instruction and initial attempts at reteaching. Start by recording the essential standards that they are still struggling to master and the specific type of support that they need in order to be successful. Finally, document your attempts at intervention, using a new row for each attempt.

Student Name:

Which essential standards is this student still struggling to master?

What type of support does this student need in order to be successful with these essential standards?
*Check all that apply. Address each checkmark in the following **Notes** section.*
- ☐ This student needs support with prerequisite learning.
- ☐ This student needs additional practice opportunities.
- ☐ This student needs alternative ways to demonstrate mastery.
- ☐ This student needs to develop positive work behaviors (completing tasks, planning long-term projects, coming to class prepared, being organized).
- ☐ This student needs support with attendance or social skills.
- ☐ Other:

Notes
Include any details that can help target interventions for this student. What specific prerequisite skills is this student missing? What work behaviors or social skills is this student struggling with? What lessons was this student absent for? What alternative methods for demonstrating mastery work best for this student?

Record of Interventions

Create an entry in the following section for each of the interventions provided to this student.

Date	Description of the Intervention Attempt *Did you reteach a prerequisite skill? Did you address a specific work behavior or social skill? Did you provide an extra practice task? Which one?*	Notes *How effective was this attempt at intervention? How do you know? What will you try next? Who can help you provide additional support to this student?*

Source: Ferriter, W. M. (2020). The big book of tools for collaborative teams in a PLC at Work. *Bloomington, IN: Solution Tree Press, pp. 166–167.*

Tool: Building Your Learning Team's Knowledge About Extensions

Taking Action *reference: Essential Action 5.4—Extend Student Learning, p. 223*

Instructions: Use this tool to build knowledge about the four most common extension strategies. Then, use the questions that follow to reflect on your team's current extension practices.

Common Extension Strategies

Asking students to demonstrate mastery at levels beyond grade-level proficiency In most cases, curricula for different content areas have been carefully spiraled, exposing students to similar concepts at increasing levels of complexity from year to year. Collaborative teams use these curricular spirals to create proficiency scales and rubrics that define multiple levels of mastery for each essential outcome. Then, they use these scales and rubrics to extend learning by asking question 4 students to demonstrate mastery at levels that go beyond grade-level proficiency.	**Giving students opportunities to study nonessential curriculum** When working together to answer the first critical question of learning in a PLC (What do we want our students to learn?), collaborative teams divide the outcomes in their required curriculum into two simple categories: (1) need to knows and (2) nice to knows. Need to knows become the grade-level essentials that teams work together to ensure that every student learns. Nice to knows are nonessential outcomes that question 4 students can be exposed to as part of extension tasks.
Teaching students above-grade-level curriculum Learning in most content areas is progressional. The concepts and skills that students are introduced to this year are designed to prepare them for success in the same content area next year. As a result, effective teachers spend time studying what it is that students *have already learned* and what it is that students *are going to learn next*. High-performing learning teams use this knowledge of learning progressions in their curriculum to create extension tasks, giving question 4 students chances to wrestle with above-grade-level concepts and skills.	**Introducing students to real-life examples of essential outcomes in action** Students of all ages have an inherent need to see value in the content and skills that they are being asked to master. Engagement, then, is dependent on ensuring that students have a clear sense of why their learning matters. Collaborative teams use this need for relevance to create extensions by introducing question 4 students to real-life examples of essential outcomes in action or by asking question 4 students to use the knowledge that they have learned to solve real-life problems.

Questions for Reflection

Which of these common extension strategies does your team use most frequently? Why?

Which of these common extension strategies does your team use least often? Why?

Which of these common extension strategies feels the most doable to you? Why?

What steps can your team take right now to integrate more meaningful opportunities for extension into the work that you are doing with students?

Source: Ferriter, W. M. (2020). The big book of tools for collaborative teams in a PLC at Work. *Bloomington, IN: Solution Tree Press, p. 206. Adapted from DuFour, R., DuFour, R., Eaker, R., Many, T. W., & Mattos, M. (2016).* Learning by doing: A handbook for Professional Learning Communities at Work *(3rd ed.). Bloomington, IN: Solution Tree Press; Roberts, M. (2019).* Enriching the learning: Meaningful extensions for proficient students in a PLC at Work. *Bloomington, IN: Solution Tree Press.*

Tool: Weekly Extension Planning Template

Taking Action *reference: Essential Action 5.4—Extend Student Learning, p. 223*

Instructions: Complete this extension planning template at the beginning of each collaborative meeting to clarify your plans for addressing the needs of the question 4 students your learning team serves.

Learning Team: _____ **Date:** _____

Essential Outcomes We Are Teaching This Week	Best Strategy for Extending These Outcomes (Check one.)
	☐ Demonstrating mastery at levels beyond grade-level proficiency ☐ Studying nonessential curriculum ☐ Studying above-grade-level curriculum ☐ Studying a real-life example of these outcomes in action
Our Initial Plan for Extending These Outcomes:	

Source: Ferriter, W. M. (2020). The big book of tools for collaborative teams in a PLC at Work. Bloomington, IN: Solution Tree Press, p. 197.

Tool Overview: Creating a Tiered Task Card to Extend Student Learning

Taking Action *reference: Essential Action 5.4—Extend Student Learning, p. 223*

Instructions: To create a tiered task card to extend student learning, review the following key, which outlines Norman L. Webb's (2002) Depth of Knowledge (DOK) levels. Then, use those descriptions to create four leveled tasks connected to your current grade-level essentials. Record those tasks in "Student Tool: Creating a Tiered Task Card to Extend Student Learning" (page 216). When you finish, you will have a tiered task card to engage students ready for extensions.

Depth of Knowledge Key

DOK Level 1	DOK Level 2	DOK Level 3	DOK Level 4
Recall and Reproduction	**Skills and Concepts**	**Strategic Thinking**	**Extended Thinking**
DOK 1 tasks involve the simple recall of information. Answers to DOK 1 tasks are either right or wrong. No reasoning is required to complete these tasks. Instead, students gather facts and information or apply simple formulas.	DOK 2 tasks involve applying knowledge. Students explain, describe, categorize, or interpret acquired information. DOK 2 tasks always require students to decide how to approach the problem.	DOK 3 tasks involve higher levels of reasoning than the two previous task types. Students develop logical arguments based on evidence, draw conclusions based on data, or provide justifications and reasoning to defend their positions.	DOK 4 tasks involve the highest level of cognitive demand. Students make connections within or between content areas, evaluate several possible solutions, or explain alternative perspectives from multiple sources. DOK 4 tasks may also ask students to apply what they have learned to real-life contexts.
Sample task: *Can you list the four primary pathogens that cause human diseases?*	**Sample task:** *What are the similarities and differences between the two main types of pathogens that cause human diseases: viruses and bacteria?*	**Sample task:** *Rank the four main types of pathogens that cause human diseases in order from "most dangerous" to "least dangerous." Defend your rankings with reasoning.*	**Sample task:** *Find an example of a disease outbreak in the world. Research the reasons for the outbreak and offer recommendations about how the outbreak should have been treated.*

Reference

Webb, N. L. (2002, March 28). *Depth-of-Knowledge levels for four content areas.* Accessed at http://ossucurr.pbworks.com/w/file/fetch/49691156/Norm%20web%20dok%20by%20subject%20area.pdf on December 13, 2023.

Student Tool: Creating a Tiered Task Card to Extend Student Learning

Tiered task card for: _____
(Name of our current unit of study)

> **Instructions for students:** When you have demonstrated mastery of our grade-level essentials through your classroom assessments or work products, you are ready for extension tasks that push your thinking beyond grade-level mastery. This card includes the extension activities for our current unit of study. To complete it, follow these steps.
>
> 1. Unless your teacher gives you different instructions, start with the activity labeled DOK Level 1.
> 2. When you have completed the first activity, move to the task labeled DOK Level 2, DOK Level 3, and DOK Level 4.
> 3. You may choose any work product from the list at the end of the task card to demonstrate mastery of each task.
> 4. Your teacher will use your completed work to replace scores on classroom assignments that you place out of because you are working beyond grade-level expectations *or* as reworks for any assignments with scores you are trying to raise.

Tasks to Complete

DOK Level 1	DOK Level 2	DOK Level 3	DOK Level 4
Recall and Reproduction	**Skills and Concepts**	**Strategic Thinking**	**Extended Thinking**
Task:	Task:	Task:	Task:

You may choose to demonstrate what you know in any of the following ways.

Write a paragraph	Create a set of Google slides	Record a video	Make a podcast or audio recording
Develop a Venn diagram	Make a graphic organizer	Create a cartoon	Have a debate with a friend

The Big Book of Tools for RTI at Work © 2025 Solution Tree Press • SolutionTree.com
Visit **go.SolutionTree.com/RTIatWork/BBTRTI** to download this free reproducible.

Sample: Tiered Task Card—Middle Grades Science: Fossils

Taking Action *reference: Essential Action 5.4—Extend Student Learning, p. 223*

We have been studying fossils in class over the past two weeks. Specifically, we have been looking at the following.
- The difference between the main types of fossils
- What index fossils are and why they are important
- How scientists use fossils to understand the development of life on Earth better

A major fossil discovery was made in Northern Canada in early 2020.

Read more about that discovery here: https://bit.ly/3SG0Gw6

Then, see if you can complete each of the following tasks.

Tasks to Complete

DOK Level 1	DOK Level 2	DOK Level 3	DOK Level 4
Recall and Reproduction	**Skills and Concepts**	**Strategic Thinking**	**Extended Thinking**
Task: Can you summarize the fossil discovery made in Northern Canada?	**Task:** Can you name the type of fossil discovered in Northern Canada? Defend your decision with reasoning. Remember, we have been studying mold fossils, cast fossils, petrified fossils, preserved fossils, carbonized fossils, and trace fossils.	**Task:** How would you rate the fossil discovery made in Northern Canada? Use a scale from 1 to 5—where one represents not very important and five represents most important fossil discovery ever. Defend your ranking with reasoning.	**Task:** Find an example of another significant fossil discovery in the last one hundred years. Then, explain why that fossil discovery was even more important than the discovery made in Northern Canada.

You may choose to demonstrate what you know in any of the following ways.

Write a paragraph	Create a set of Google slides	Record a video	Make a podcast or audio recording
Develop a Venn diagram	Make a graphic organizer	Create a cartoon	Have a debate with a friend

Sample: Tiered Task Card—Middle Grades Mathematics: Slope

Taking Action *reference: Essential Action 5.4—Extend Student Learning, p. 223*

We have studied slope and how it relates to relationships in class over the past two weeks. Specifically, we have been looking at the following.

- How to identify the slope given a graph, table, and equation
- What the slope means in the context of the input-output relationship
- How direction is essential to consider when finding the slope of a line

Slope Dude has been our source of information when talking about slope. Here is a video from Slope Dude himself.

Watch Slope Dude explain the slope of a line: www.youtube.com/watch?v=ZcSrJPiQvHQ

Then, see if you can complete each of the following tasks.

Tasks to Complete

DOK Level 1	DOK Level 2	DOK Level 3	DOK Level 4
Recall and Reproduction	**Skills and Concepts**	**Strategic Thinking**	**Extended Thinking**
Task: List the four different types of slopes that Slope Dude mentions in his video.	**Task:** Opposite slopes are not the same. Provide a rationale for why a slope of (−1) and a slope of 1 are not the same using your understanding of the four different types of slopes.	**Task:** Create a real-life scenario incorporating each slope ratio between the input (x) and output (y). Remember that the x value must remain the same for undefined relationships while the y value changes.	**Task:** Slope Dude created a metaphor to help mathematicians understand slope, using phrases like "puff, puff positive" and "the side of a mountain." Please create your own analogy to describe the different types of slopes and present it in a fashion that will help mathematicians understand slopes.

You may choose to demonstrate what you know in any of the following ways.

Make a Slope Dude diagram	Create a set of Google slides	Record a video	Make a podcast or audio recording
Develop a Venn diagram	Make a graphic organizer	Create an activity (short quiz)	Have a debate with a friend

Tool: Using AI Chatbots to Develop Extension Tasks

Taking Action *reference: Essential Action 5.4—Extend Student Learning, p. 223*

Instructions: Ensuring high levels of learning for all students means we must develop extension tasks to challenge students who have already mastered grade-level essentials. Ask an AI chatbot like ChatGPT (https://chat.openai.com) or Gemini (https://gemini.google.com) the following prompts to help you with this work.

AI chatbots can create tasks at different Depth of Knowledge (DOK) levels. • Can you generate four tasks leveled by DOK that *[grade level and subject area]* students learning about *[grade-level concept or skill]* can complete? **Sample:** *Can you generate four tasks leveled by DOK that AP biology students learning about Mendelian genetics can complete?* **Pro tip:** You can also ask ChatGPT to generate materials lists or directions for each task that it generates for you.	**AI chatbots can generate metaphors for concepts.** • Can you give me three metaphors that can help *[grade level and subject area]* students understand *[grade-level concept or skill]*? **Sample:** *Can you give me three metaphors that can help sixth-grade students understand feudalism?* **Pro tip:** Once you have your metaphors, you can ask groups of students to rank them from *most accurate* to *least accurate* or *most valuable* to *least valuable*. You can also ask groups to "beat the bot" by coming up with a better metaphor than the ones generated by ChatGPT.
AI chatbots can generate badging tasks. • Can you give me a list of five badges *[grade level and subject area]* students can earn while learning about *[grade-level concept or skill]*? • Can you write a set of directions that students can follow to earn each of these badges? Please use bullets and student-friendly language. **Sample:** *Can you give me a list of five badges fourth-grade students can earn while learning about the structure and function of internal and external parts of plants and animals?* **Pro tip:** Want to see what a badging task for extension can look like? Visit https://b.link/biotasks to see the final product using the previous sample prompt.	**AI chatbots can generate role, audience, format, topic (RAFT) activities.** • Can you create four RAFT activities for *[grade level and subject area]* students learning about *[grade-level concept or skill]*? I want the roles to be: *[sample roles]*. **Sample:** *Can you create four RAFT activities for eighth-grade science students learning about the spread of infectious diseases? I want the roles to be: medical professional, politician, business owner, and person who caught the disease.* **Pro tip:** You can also give AI chatbots specific product types or formats that you want your students to create while working on RAFT activities (for example, infographics, songs, posters, or cartoons). Doing so allows you to reinforce products that you are already teaching or include products that you know your students enjoy making.
AI chatbots can spark debates. • I am a *[grade level]* teacher. I am teaching *[insert grade-level concept]* and I want to engage my students in a debate. Can you tell me what aspects of this concept are controversial? **Sample:** *I am a third-grade teacher. I am teaching ecosystems and I want to engage my students in a debate. Can you tell me what aspects of this concept are controversial?* **Pro tip:** Consider using Flip (https://info.flip.com) to create an online discussion forum for your students to argue the pros and cons of the controversial ideas that AI chatbots generate for you.	**AI chatbots can help you connect your curriculum to the real world.** • Can you give me a bulleted list of examples of where I might see *[concept students are studying]* in current events? **Sample:** *Can you give me a bulleted list of examples of where I might see the science concept of substance density in current events?* **Pro tip:** Students are drawn to current events because it helps them feel knowledgeable in family discussions. Finding current events connected to your essentials is one of the best ways to create extension tasks.

Resources Designed to
Support Tier 2 Schoolwide Essential Actions

Tool: Questions to Consider When Creating a Schedule for Supplemental Interventions

Taking Action reference: *Essential Action 6.1—Schedule Time for Tier 2 Interventions and Extensions*, p. 232

Instructions: Guiding coalitions can use this tool to address the most common logistic challenges schools face when creating a schedule for supplemental interventions.

Questions to Consider	Our Responses	Next Steps to Move This Work Forward	Who Will Lead This Work?	Deadline for Completion
When will we offer supplemental interventions? • Will we provide supplemental interventions every day? • How long will our supplemental intervention periods last? • At what point during the day will we hold our supplemental intervention sessions?				
How will we determine what supplemental interventions to offer? • What are the areas of greatest need in our building? • Will we intervene around social behaviors, academic behaviors, and health and home challenges?				

Tier 2 Schoolwide Essential Actions

Questions to Consider	Our Responses	Next Steps to Move This Work Forward	Who Will Lead This Work?	Deadline for Completion
How will students be assigned to supplemental intervention sessions? • Will teachers share students for interventions? • How will we handle students who need supplemental interventions in multiple areas? • How will intervention assignments be communicated to students? • How will intervention assignments be communicated to other interested parties in the school? • What will we do for students who don't need extra help?				
How will staff be assigned during supplemental intervention periods? • Do we have any faculty members with special expertise or certifications that we can assign to specific interventions? • Are there any contractual requirements we must consider when assigning staff to supplemental intervention periods? • How can we use uncertified staff to support students and teachers during our supplemental intervention periods?				

How will we monitor student progress during supplemental intervention periods? • Will classroom teachers reassess learners after attending a supplemental intervention period? • Will we use rubrics or checklists to monitor student progress during supplemental intervention periods?		
How will we gather feedback from faculty members on our plan for providing supplemental interventions? • What information would we need from faculty members to evaluate our plan for providing supplemental interventions? • How often will we ask for feedback? • How will we communicate findings after collecting feedback?		
Our guiding coalition will reconvene on _____ to review this plan for addressing the logistic challenges of our supplemental intervention period.		

Source: Questions adapted from Mattos, M., Buffum, A., Malone, J., Cruz, L. F., Dimich, N., & Schuhl, S. (2025). Taking action: A handbook for RTI at Work (2nd ed.). Bloomington, IN: Solution Tree Press.

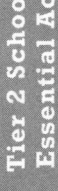

Tier 2 Schoolwide Essential Actions 2

Tool: Evaluating Your Plan for Providing Supplemental Interventions

Taking Action reference: Essential Action 6.1—Schedule Time for Tier 2 Interventions and Extensions, p. 232

Instructions: In *Taking Action: A Handbook for RTI at Work, Second Edition*, Mattos and colleagues (2025) outline a set of four essential criteria schools should consider when creating a schedule that ensures students access to both Tier 1 instruction and Tier 2 interventions. Use this tool to evaluate your school's current plan for providing supplemental interventions against those criteria.

Tier 2 Schoolwide Essential Actions

Criteria to Consider When Evaluating a Plan for Providing Supplemental Interventions	Our Plan for Providing Supplemental Interventions	Alignment With the Essential Characteristics of an Effective Supplemental Intervention Plan	Plan Changes We Should Consider for Providing Supplemental Interventions
Supplemental intervention sessions should be offered with appropriate frequency. • Supplemental intervention sessions are offered at least twice a week and more often if needed. • Supplemental intervention sessions are offered as often as necessary, but no more.	*How frequent are our current supplemental intervention sessions?*	☐ Our school's efforts are closely aligned with this characteristic of an effective supplemental intervention plan. ☐ Our school's efforts are somewhat aligned with this characteristic of an effective supplemental intervention plan. ☐ Our school's efforts are not aligned with this characteristic of an effective supplemental intervention plan.	
Supplemental intervention sessions are of appropriate duration. • Supplemental intervention sessions are about thirty minutes long. • Supplemental intervention sessions give teachers enough time to provide targeted instruction on one specific learning goal. • Enough time has been built into our schedule for student transitions to supplemental intervention sessions.	*What is the current duration of our supplemental intervention sessions?*	☐ Our school's efforts are closely aligned with this characteristic of an effective supplemental intervention plan. ☐ Our school's efforts are somewhat aligned with this characteristic of an effective supplemental intervention plan. ☐ Our school's efforts are not aligned with this characteristic of an effective supplemental intervention plan.	

The Big Book of Tools for RTI at Work © 2025 Solution Tree Press • SolutionTree.com
Visit **go.SolutionTree.com/RTIatWork/BBTRTI** and enter the unique access code found on the book's inside front cover to access this reproducible.

Supplemental intervention sessions should be available to all students. • We offer supplemental intervention sessions during the instructional day instead of before or after school. • Students are required—rather than invited—to attend supplemental intervention sessions. • Teachers and other highly trained professionals are contractually available to teach students during supplemental intervention sessions.	*When are our current supplemental intervention sessions offered?*	☐ Our school's efforts are closely aligned with this characteristic of an effective supplemental intervention plan. ☐ Our school's efforts are somewhat aligned with this characteristic of an effective supplemental intervention plan. ☐ Our school's efforts are not aligned with this characteristic of an effective supplemental intervention plan.
Supplemental intervention sessions should never introduce new essential curriculum. • Students attending supplemental intervention sessions never miss out on beginning new essential curriculum. • Core teachers use supplemental intervention time to reteach essential standards or to teach nonessential curricula.	*What kind of instruction do we deliver during our supplemental intervention sessions?*	☐ Our school's efforts are closely aligned with this characteristic of an effective supplemental intervention plan. ☐ Our school's efforts are somewhat aligned with this characteristic of an effective supplemental intervention plan. ☐ Our school's efforts are not aligned with this characteristic of an effective supplemental intervention plan.

Reference

Mattos, M., Buffum, A., Malone, J., Cruz, L. F., Dimich, N., & Schuhl, S. (2025). *Taking action: A handbook for RTI at Work* (2nd ed.). Bloomington, IN: Solution Tree Press.

Tool: Staff Survey on the Efficacy of a Supplemental Intervention Period

Taking Action *reference: Essential Action 6.1—Schedule Time for Tier 2 Interventions and Extensions, p. 232*

Instructions: Over the last few months, we have committed instructional minutes to a supplemental intervention period for teachers to provide Tier 2 interventions. We know this means you have less time for direct instruction, so we want to ensure that our supplemental intervention period works well. Please take time during your next collaborative team meeting to complete this survey. Our guiding coalition will use your responses to make any necessary changes to our supplemental intervention period.

Note: While you can complete this survey anonymously, we hope you will include your name or the name of your collaborative team. Doing so will allow us to follow up with you if we have clarifying questions about your responses.

Name of Faculty Member or Collaborative Team Responding to This Survey: _____

Question 1: On a scale from 1 to 5, **how important** is it for our school to create time within our daily schedule for supplemental interventions around grade-level essentials?						
Not Important	1	2	3	4	5	**Very Important**

Explain Your Rating:

Question 2: On a scale from 1 to 5, **how effective** has our current plan been for providing supplemental interventions around grade-level interventions?						
Not Effective	1	2	3	4	5	**Very Effective**

Explain Your Rating:

Questions for Reflection

What has been the greatest challenge that adding a supplemental intervention period to our schedule has created for you as an individual teacher or a collaborative team member?

What has been the greatest benefit that adding a supplemental intervention period to our schedule has provided you as an individual teacher or a collaborative team member?

What changes should we consider making to our supplemental intervention plan? How will those changes result in higher levels of student learning? How will those changes make providing supplemental interventions around grade-level essentials easier for classroom teachers?

What additional thoughts would you like to share with our guiding coalition as they review our school's plan for devoting time during our master schedule for supplemental interventions around grade-level essential standards?

Tool: Developing Schoolwide Criteria for Identifying Students in Need of Tier 2 Behavioral Support

Taking Action reference: Essential Action 6.2—Establish a Process to Identify Students Who Require Tier 2 Behavior Interventions, p. 242

Guiding coalitions can use "Protocol: Developing Schoolwide Criteria for Identifying Students in Need of Tier 2 Behavioral Support" on page 230 to create a set of criteria to identify students needing behavioral support.

Common Reasons Students Struggle With Learning	Definition of Mastery	Identification Criteria	Tier 2 Intervention Plan
Following School and Classroom Rules			
Getting Along With Adults			
Getting Along With Peers			
Student Motivation			

Work Completion			
Organization			
Attendance			
Health Concerns			
Home Concerns			
Other:			

Protocol: Developing Schoolwide Criteria for Identifying Students in Need of Tier 2 Behavioral Support

Taking Action *reference: Essential Action 6.2—Establish a Process to Identify Students Who Require Tier 2 Behavior Interventions, p. 242*

Instructions: A school's guiding coalition can use the following protocol to guide discussions as members complete the "Tool: Developing Schoolwide Criteria for Identifying Students in Need of Tier 2 Behavioral Support" table on page 228. This process aims to establish clear criteria to identify students who need additional time and support to master grade-level essential social behaviors, academic dispositions, and health and home circumstances.

Step 1: Conduct an Initial Review

Review the common social behaviors, academic dispositions, and health and home circumstances that can cause students to struggle with learning detailed in the first column. Here are questions to consider.

- If you were to add any behavioral issues to this list because they are prevalent in your building, what would they be?
- If you were to choose three behavioral issues to focus your school's time and attention on, what would they be?
- If you were to remove three behavioral issues from this list because they are not prevalent in your building, what would they be?
- Which behavioral issues would be the easiest to develop Tier 2 interventions for?
- Which behavioral interventions would have the most significant impact on student success in your building?

Once your guiding coalition has completed step 1, work together to develop a shared definition of mastery, a set of clear identification criteria, and a Tier 2 intervention plan for each of the *behavioral* issues that are the most prevalent in your building.

Step 2: Create Shared Definitions of Mastery

Develop a shared definition of mastery for each of the *behavioral* issues identified in step 1. This definition should include three or four bullet points describing what grade-level mastery of the social behavior, academic disposition, or health and home circumstance looks like in action. Here are questions to consider.

- What do you expect students to know and be able to do with this behavioral issue?
- What would students do if they mastered this grade-level social behavior, academic disposition, or health and home circumstance?
- How often would you expect students to demonstrate mastery of this grade-level social behavior, academic disposition, or health and home circumstance?

Step 3: Create Shared Identification Criteria

For each of the *behavioral* issues identified in step 1, develop a set of criteria that teachers can use to identify students needing additional time and support for learning this grade-level social behavior, academic disposition, or health and home circumstance. Your criteria should be easy to apply consistently for all teachers. Here are questions to consider.

- How frequently would a student have to struggle with the skills defined in your shared definition of mastery before receiving Tier 2 intervention support?
- How severe would a student's struggles with the skills need to be before receiving Tier 2 intervention support?

- What observations would a teacher need to make before assigning a student to Tier 2 intervention support for this grade-level social behavior, academic disposition, or health and home circumstance?

Step 4: Create a Tier 2 Intervention Plan

Finally, develop a specific plan for providing struggling students with additional time and support to learn each of the *behavioral* issues identified in step 1. Here are questions to consider.

- Who will deliver this Tier 2 intervention for social behaviors, academic dispositions, or health and home circumstances?
- When will this Tier 2 intervention for social behaviors, academic dispositions, or health and home circumstances happen?
- Did we intentionally teach our students about this social behavior, academic disposition, or health and home circumstance? If not, would initial Tier 1 instruction be a more effective first step for our school?
- Who are the experts in our faculty that can help us to generate Tier 2 strategies to address these social behaviors, academic dispositions, or health and home circumstances?
- How will we know if our intervention efforts were effective?

Tool Overview: Evaluating Your Systematic Response to Student Interventions

Taking Action reference: Essential Action 6.2—Establish a Process to Identify Students Who Require Tier 2 Behavior Interventions, p. 242

In *Taking Action: A Handbook for RTI at Work, Second Edition*, Mattos and colleagues (2025) detail five steps taken by schools that have created a systematic response to student interventions.

1. **Identify students who need help:** The most important step in a systematic response to intervention is identifying students who need help. This step must be completed perfectly because until a struggling student has been identified, a school can't provide additional time and support for learning.

2. **Determine the right intervention to meet students' learning needs:** A fundamental truth in all schools is that students needing additional learning time and support don't all struggle for the same reasons. Some may struggle because they have gaps in the prerequisite knowledge necessary to master new grade-level essentials, while others may struggle because they have yet to master the essential skills and dispositions of a learner. That means schools must ensure that intervention efforts align with each struggling learner's identified needs.

3. **Monitor each student's progress to determine whether interventions are working:** The goal of schools committed to the RTI at Work process isn't simply to provide struggling students with interventions. Instead, the goal is to ensure that students learn at grade level or higher each year. To create a systematic response to intervention, we must carefully monitor the effectiveness of the interventions we offer to individual students.

4. **Revise if a student is not responding to an intervention:** Regardless of how carefully a school identifies students who need additional help and determines the proper intervention to meet each student's unique learning needs, there will be times when students receiving interventions fail to make progress. Schools with a systematic response to intervention use evidence of progress to identify students who are not responding to intervention and revise the support the school is providing.

5. **Extend once a student has mastered essential curriculum:** Many schools wrongly equate systematic interventions only with struggling students. Instead, schools with a systematic response to interventions work just as diligently to develop and deliver extensions to students working beyond grade-level expectations.

Guiding coalitions can use "Tool: Evaluating Your Systematic Response to Student Interventions" on page 233 to evaluate their current efforts in these five areas.

Reference

Mattos, M., Buffum, A., Malone, J., Cruz, L. F., Dimich, N., & Schuhl, S. (2025). *Taking action: A handbook for RTI at Work* (2nd ed.). Bloomington, IN: Solution Tree Press.

Tool: Evaluating Your Systematic Response to Student Interventions

Taking Action *reference: Essential Action 6.2—Establish a Process to Identify Students Who Require Tier 2 Behavior Interventions, p. 242*

According to the original architects of the RTI at Work process (Mattos et al., 2025), schools take five steps to create a systematic response to intervention. Those steps are:

1. Identify students who need help.
2. Determine the right intervention to meet students' learning needs.
3. Monitor each student's progress to determine whether the intervention is working.
4. Revise if the student is not responding to the intervention.
5. Extend once the student has mastered essential curriculum. (Mattos et al., 2025, pp. 242–243)

Use this checklist to rate your school's current efforts to create a systematic response to intervention.

Rating Scale: 1—We haven't tackled this yet, 2—We are developing or refining our work in this area, 3—This is an established practice in our school

Step 1: Identify students who need help.		
Your Rating (Circle one.)	**Key Indicator**	**Next Steps**
1 2 3	Our school has a clear process for administering universal screeners to new students to identify academic and behavioral concerns requiring intervention.	
1 2 3	Our school uses existing knowledge of returning students to place them into interventions at the beginning of the school year.	
1 2 3	Our school has a clear process that allows faculty members to recommend students for additional academic or behavioral support.	
1 2 3	Our teacher teams administer short universal screeners on prerequisite skills for new students to quickly identify academic needs that may interfere with their ability to master grade-level essentials.	
1 2 3	Our teacher teams have the professional capacity to use common formative assessment data to identify students who need additional time and support for learning grade-level essential standards.	

			Step 2: Determine the right intervention to meet students' learning needs.	
1	2	3	Our classroom teachers and other school professionals regularly converse to determine the root cause of a student's struggles.	
1	2	3	Our school has developed specific interventions to address various academic and behavioral needs.	
1	2	3	Our school has created a schedule that allows students to receive intensive support in the universal skills of learning without missing grade-level essential instruction.	
1	2	3	Our teacher teams prioritize a student's multiple learning needs before determining the right intervention to offer first.	
1	2	3	Our collaborative teams provide students with academic interventions around current grade-level essentials.	
1	2	3	Our collaborative teams provide students with initial interventions in academic skills, dispositions, and behaviors.	
			Step 3: Monitor each student's progress to determine if the intervention is working.	
1	2	3	Our school has a well-established system for documenting students' progress when receiving interventions in grade-level essentials.	
1	2	3	Our school has a well-established system for documenting students' progress when receiving interventions in academic skills and dispositions.	
1	2	3	Our school has a well-established system for documenting students' progress when receiving interventions in social behaviors and attendance.	
1	2	3	Our students receiving interventions are regularly removed from them because they have made sufficient progress.	
1	2	3	Our school stops offering interventions when evidence suggests that our strategy is not working.	

			Step 4: Revise if the student is not responding to the intervention.	
1	2	3	Our students needing additional time and support move easily between interventions when evidence suggests that a change is needed.	
1	2	3	Our school's composition of intervention groups is fluid, allowing students to move into and out of specific interventions on an as-needed basis.	
1	2	3	Our school regularly identifies and experiments with new academic and behavioral interventions.	
1	2	3	Our faculty never gives up on a student needing additional time and support for learning. Instead, when a student struggles while receiving an intervention, we look for new strategies to try.	
			Step 5: Extend once the student has mastered the essential curriculum.	
1	2	3	Our school's faculty members understand that extension is an intervention designed to help students learn at higher levels.	
1	2	3	Our school is as deliberate about planning extensions for students working beyond grade-level expectations as we are about planning interventions for students struggling to meet grade-level expectations.	
1	2	3	Our students who have met grade-level expectations are involved in rigorous, challenging instruction around academic essentials.	
1	2	3	Our collaborative teams understand the four strategies for extending learning. 1. Asking students to demonstrate mastery beyond grade-level expectations 2. Teaching students above grade-level curriculum 3. Giving students opportunities to study nonessential curriculum 4. Introducing students to examples of essential outcomes in current events	

Reference

Mattos, M., Buffum, A., Malone, J., Cruz, L. F., Dimich, N., & Schuhl, S. (2025). *Taking action: A handbook for RTI at Work* (2nd ed.). Bloomington, IN: Solution Tree Press.

Tool: Staff Recommendation Form for Students Needing Behavioral Support

Taking Action *reference: Essential Action 6.2—Establish a Process to Identify Students Who Require Tier 2 Behavior Interventions, p. 242*

Instructions: Do students struggle to succeed in your class because behaviors, health concerns, attendance, or challenges at home prevent them from learning (Mattos et al., 2025)? Complete the following recommendation form and submit it to your grade-level leadership or intervention team representative.

Student Name:	Grade Level:

What do you suspect is preventing this student from learning?

(Choose one root cause from the following list.)

- ☐ **Essential social behaviors:** Respectful behavior toward peers and adults, ability to cooperate with others
- ☐ **Essential academic behaviors:** Remaining on task, showing motivation and effort, completing assignments, staying organized
- ☐ **Proper attendance:** Coming to school regularly, coming to class on time
- ☐ **Health concerns:** Chronic illnesses (asthma, diabetes, and so on) or temporary illnesses (influenza, broken bones, and so on) interfere with learning, sleep issues, food scarcity
- ☐ **Home concerns:** Anxiety, depression, parent divorce, parent job loss, death in the family
- ☐ **Other:** _____

Summarize this student's academic and social strengths:

What does this student do well in your class? Do they demonstrate the same strengths in other courses? How have those strengths moved this student forward as a learner?

Summarize your concerns for this student:

Be as detailed as possible. What observations have led you to this recommendation? How long has this problem been interfering with this student's learning? What support do you think this student needs to succeed in school?

Questions for Reflection	Your Response
What data support your argument that this student has the academic ability to succeed in your classroom? Examples: • Assessment results that indicate the ability to master grade-level essentials • Performance during previous school years, semesters, and quarters • Performance in other grade-level classes	
What data support your argument that this student needs a behavioral intervention? Examples: • Number of discipline referrals in the last quarter • Number of missing assignments in the last unit • Number of absences in the last month • Number of moments when learning was interrupted in the last two weeks	
What (if any) interventions has this student already received? Examples: • Referrals to school administrators • Referrals to school counselors • Parent contacts • Explicit teaching of expected behaviors • Teacher consultation with the special education team	

Current Academic Performance

Student's Current Grade in Class	Student's Scores on the Last Three Common Formative Assessments	Student's Scores on the Last Benchmark or Standardized Test

Teacher or Collaborative Team Submitting Referral:

Reference

Mattos, M., Buffum, A., Malone, J., Cruz, L. F., Dimich, N., & Schuhl, S. (2025). *Taking action: A handbook for RTI at Work* (2nd ed.). Bloomington, IN: Solution Tree Press.

Tool: Reviewing Your Plan for Providing Supplemental Interventions for Students Struggling With Social Behaviors, Academic Behaviors, and Health and Home Challenges

Taking Action *reference: Essential Action 6.3—Plan and Implement Tier 2 Interventions for Essential Social and Academic Behaviors, p. 247*

Instructions:

1. Review the list of essential social behaviors, academic behaviors, and health and home challenges in the first column of the following table.
2. Check each behavior that your school has planned and implemented an intervention for.
3. In the **Current Interventions for Essential Behaviors** column, list each intervention you have that supports students struggling with social behaviors, academic behaviors, and health and home challenges.
4. In the **Evidence That Our Current Interventions Are Effective** column, list data you have collected that confirm your efforts to support students struggling with social and academic behaviors and health and home challenges produce results.
5. In the **Next Steps** column, detail potential actions that can strengthen your school's work to intervene around social behaviors, academic behaviors, and health and home challenges.

After detailing your current efforts to support students with social behaviors, academic behaviors, and health and home challenges, use the reflection questions at the bottom of the tool to begin improving your school's intervention efforts.

Essential Social Behaviors	Current Interventions for Essential Social Behaviors	Evidence That Our Current Interventions Are Effective	Next Steps
Our school has systematic interventions for the following social behaviors. (Check all that apply.) ☐ Staying on task ☐ Using appropriate language ☐ Keeping hands and other body parts to themselves ☐ Self-monitoring impulsive behaviors ☐ Making friends ☐ Coming to class and school on time ☐ Appropriately responding to conflicts with others ☐ Speaking in front of others			

Tier 2 Schoolwide Essential Actions ②

Essential Academic Behaviors

Current Interventions for Essential Social Behaviors	Evidence That Our Current Interventions Are Effective	Next Steps
Our school has systematic interventions for the following academic behaviors. (Check all that apply.) ☐ Completing assignments ☐ Demonstrating sufficient effort ☐ Keeping work organized ☐ Retrieving materials on demand		

Health and Home Challenges			
Our school has systematic interventions for the following health and home challenges. (Check all that apply.) ☐ Participating in class or school due to health complications ☐ Focusing on school due to problems at home	**Current Interventions for Essential Social Behaviors**	**Evidence That Our Current Interventions Are Effective**	**Next Steps**

Final Review of Your Interventions for Essential Social Behaviors, Academic Behaviors, and Health and Home Challenges

Rate your interventions for essential social behaviors, academic behaviors, and health and home challenges. Remember that effective interventions are timely, directive, targeted to specific needs, systematic, research based, and administered by trained professionals.						
Our work with essential social behaviors needs significant improvement.	1	2	3	4	5	Our work with essential social behaviors is effective and efficient.
Our work with essential academic behaviors needs significant improvement.	1	2	3	4	5	Our work with essential academic behaviors is effective and efficient.
Our work with health and home challenges needs significant improvement.	1	2	3	4	5	Our work with health and home challenges is effective and efficient.

Questions for Reflection

Which of the three categories of supplemental behavior interventions (social behaviors, academic behaviors, and health and home challenges) do you feel the *best* prepared to plan and implement? Which will be the hardest for you to plan and implement? Why?

Review the unchecked bullets in the categories of supplemental behavior interventions (social behaviors, academic behaviors, and health and home challenges) mentioned previously. Rank those unchecked bullets from *most important* to *least important* for us to address. Does the information you recorded for current interventions and next steps reflect the priorities you just identified? Explain your reasoning.

Who will lead efforts in your building to strengthen your interventions around essential social behaviors, academic behaviors, and health and home challenges? Why is this the right person to lead these efforts?

Tool: Planning Interventions for Students With Attendance Issues

Taking Action *reference: Essential Action 6.3—Plan and Implement Tier 2 Interventions for Essential Social and Academic Behaviors, p. 247*

Instructions for school attendance team: Use the following table to document your intervention efforts for students with attendance patterns preventing them from succeeding in school.

1. In the **Name of Student** column, list any student with emerging attendance problems that are likely to interfere with their ability to master grade-level academic essentials.
2. In the **Recent Attendance Patterns** column, record bulleted statements detailing this student's current attendance data. How many days or class periods has this student missed? Are they missing specific days or class periods consistently? What other patterns can you spot in this student's absences?
3. In the **Reason for Attendance Struggles** column, indicate why this student struggles to get to school. Common reasons include family issues (for example, parents who struggle to get students to school), chronic illnesses that prevent regular attendance, and students who are aware of the importance of regular attendance and still choose not to come to school.
4. In the **Our Intervention Plan** column, detail your team's next steps to address this student's attendance issues. Will you coach or counsel their parents? Does there need to be a follow-up with the school nurse or other medical professionals? Should administrators visit this student and detail the consequences of continued absences? Is there a way to incentivize or reward regular attendance?
5. In the **Team Member Responsible** column, identify the staff member who will lead this intervention. Be sure to assign members with the right professional expertise to address each student's unique attendance needs. For example, suppose family issues are the primary cause of a student's attendance struggles. In that case, the school counselor or social worker is likely the right person to lead interventions for this student.
6. In the **Date of Next Attendance Review** column, list when your attendance team will revisit this student to review whether your intervention efforts are working.

Tier 2 Schoolwide Essential Actions 2

Name of Student	Recent Attendance Patterns	Reason for Attendance Struggles	Our Intervention Plan	Team Member Responsible	Date of Next Attendance Review
		☐ Family issue ☐ Chronic illness ☐ Student choice ☐ Other: _____			
		☐ Family issue ☐ Chronic illness ☐ Student choice ☐ Other: _____			
		☐ Family issue ☐ Chronic illness ☐ Student choice ☐ Other: _____			
		☐ Family issue ☐ Chronic illness ☐ Student choice ☐ Other: _____			

Name of Student	Recent Attendance Patterns	Reason for Attendance Struggles	Our Intervention Plan	Team Member Responsible	Date of Next Attendance Review
		☐ Family issue ☐ Chronic illness ☐ Student choice ☐ Other: _____			
		☐ Family issue ☐ Chronic illness ☐ Student choice ☐ Other: _____			
		☐ Family issue ☐ Chronic illness ☐ Student choice ☐ Other: _____			
		☐ Family issue ☐ Chronic illness ☐ Student choice ☐ Other: _____			

The Big Book of Tools for RTI at Work © 2025 Solution Tree Press • SolutionTree.com

Visit **go.SolutionTree.com/RTIatWork/BBTRTI** and enter the unique access code found on the book's inside front cover to access this reproducible.

Student Tool: Student Survey on Missing or Late Work

Student name: _____

Instructions: I have noticed that you need help to keep up with the work assigned. Because every assignment is essential to ensure learning at the highest levels, I want to help you improve at completing the work in my classroom. Please take a few minutes to answer these survey questions to provide feedback about why work completion is challenging. Then, we can meet and develop a plan to help you succeed.

Statement to Consider	Your Response	Tell Me More About This
I'm struggling to complete work in all my classes.	☐ Yes ☐ No ☐ Other	
I have been able to get my work done in other classes or grade levels.	☐ Yes ☐ No ☐ Other	
I believe that I can succeed in school.	☐ Yes ☐ No ☐ Other	
I use my class time to get started on assignments.	☐ Yes ☐ No ☐ Other	
I have a system for tracking both assignments and due dates.	☐ Yes ☐ No ☐ Other	
I know how I can get support and ask questions here at school.	☐ Yes ☐ No ☐ Other	
I am comfortable asking questions when I am confused or have fallen behind.	☐ Yes ☐ No ☐ Other	
I am so far behind that I don't know how to get caught up.	☐ Yes ☐ No ☐ Other	

I have gotten into a rut lately and am struggling to get out.	☐ Yes ☐ No ☐ Other	
Sometimes, I don't complete a task because I don't know how.	☐ Yes ☐ No ☐ Other	
Sometimes, I don't complete a task because I have lots of other responsibilities at home.	☐ Yes ☐ No ☐ Other	
If I'm honest, I just haven't felt like doing my work over the past few weeks.	☐ Yes ☐ No ☐ Other	

Questions for Reflection

What kind of help do you most need to get caught up on your missing work?

What else do you want your teachers to know about your struggles to complete your work?

Source: Original idea for student survey comes from colemanmom4 [@colemanmom4]. (2022, June 8). Curious as to how many educators have investigated why students turn in work late? Are students confident about the content? Do they know how to get started? Are they afraid to ask for help so they delay? Or are they just lazy? Would a student survey help? [Post]. X. *Accessed at https://twitter.com/colemanmom4/status/1534489804343234560 on December 12, 2023.*

Student Tool: Learning Profile Survey—Secondary

Instructions for students: To help me support you this year, I would like to better understand who you are as a learner. You can help me with that by filling out this learning profile survey. **I promise to keep this information private** and only use it to develop lessons customized to your interests, circumstances, and needs.

Confidential Learning Profile Survey For: _____

Initial Questions to Consider

Question	Your Response	Any Additional Details You Can Share
How much time do you have available for completing homework?	☐ I have a lot of time. ☐ I have some time. ☐ I have very little time.	
How much support do you get from adults (parents, older siblings, and other relatives) while completing schoolwork at home?	☐ I have a lot of support. ☐ I have some support. ☐ I have very little support.	
Which phrase best describes how you felt about school last year?	☐ I loved it. ☐ It was fine. ☐ I hated it.	
Which phrase best describes how you feel about this school year?	☐ I can't wait to get started. ☐ It will be fine. ☐ I'm dreading it.	
Which phrase best describes you as a learner?	☐ I'm a great learner. ☐ I'm good at learning some things but not others. ☐ I struggle a lot.	

If I gave you a choice, would you choose to:	☐ Work alone ☐ Work in small groups ☐ Work with the whole class	
If I gave you a choice, would you choose to:	☐ Read about a topic ☐ Watch a video about a topic ☐ Listen to a teacher explain a topic	
If I gave you a choice, would you choose to:	☐ Write a paragraph to show what I know ☐ Create a video to show what I know ☐ Make a poster to show what I know ☐ Other: _____	

Questions for Reflection

What was the **hardest part** of learning for you last school year?

What did **you like best** about learning last school year?

What do you hope to see **more** of when it comes to learning this school year?

What do you hope to see **less** of when it comes to learning this school year?

What do I need to know to help you be **more successful** this school year?

Student Tool: Learning Profile Survey—Primary

Instructions for parents: To help me better support your child this year, I would like to better understand who they are as a learner. You can help me with that by filling out this learning profile survey. **I promise to keep this information private** and only use it to develop lessons customized to your child's interests, circumstances, and needs.

Confidential Learning Profile Survey For: _____

Initial Questions to Consider

Question	Your Response	Any Additional Details You Can Share
How much time does your child have available for completing homework?	☐ My child has a lot of time to complete homework. ☐ My child has some time to complete homework. ☐ My child has very little time to complete homework.	
How much support does your child get from adults (parents, older siblings, other relatives) while completing schoolwork at home?	☐ My child gets lots of support. ☐ My child gets some support. ☐ My child gets a little support.	
Which phrase best describes how your child felt about school last year?	☐ They loved it. ☐ It was fine for them. ☐ They hated it.	
Which phrase best describes how your child feels about school this year?	☐ They can't wait to get started. ☐ It will be fine for them. ☐ They are dreading it.	
Which phrase best describes your child as a learner?	☐ They learn easily. ☐ They learn some things easily but struggle with others. ☐ They struggle a lot.	

If I gave your child a choice, would they choose to:	☐ Work alone ☐ Work in small groups ☐ Work with the whole class	
If I gave your child a choice, would they choose to:	☐ Read about a topic ☐ Watch a video about a topic ☐ Listen to a teacher explain a topic	
If I gave your child a choice, would they choose to:	☐ Write a sentence to show what they know ☐ Create a video to show what they know ☐ Draw a picture to show what they know ☐ Other: _____	

Questions for Reflection

What was the **hardest part** of learning for your child last school year?

What did your **child like best** about learning last school year?

What do you hope to see **more** of when it comes to learning this school year?

What do you hope to see **less** of when it comes to learning this school year?

What do I need to know to help your child to be **more successful** this school year?

The Big Book of Tools for RTI at Work © 2025 Solution Tree Press • SolutionTree.com
Visit **go.SolutionTree.com/RTIatWork/BBTRTI** and enter the unique access code found on the book's inside front cover to access this reproducible.

Tool: RTI at Work Pro-Solve Intervention Targeting Process—Tier 1 and Tier 2

Taking Action reference: Essential Action 6.4—*Coordinate Interventions for Students Needing Academic and Behavior Supports*, p. 256

Student: _____ Meeting date: _____

Participant: _____

	Targeted Outcomes	1. Concern	2. Cause	3. Desired Outcomes	4. Intervention Steps	5. Who Takes Responsibility
Led by Teacher Teams	Essential standards					
	Immediate prerequisite skills					
	English language					
Led by Schoolwide Teams	Academic behaviors					
	Social behaviors					
	Health and home					

Next meeting date: _____

Source: Mattos, M., Buffum, A., Malone, J., Cruz, L. F., Dimich, N., & Schuhl, S. (2025). Taking action: A handbook for RTI at Work (2nd ed.). Bloomington, IN: Solution Tree Press, p. 209; Buffum, A., Mattos, M., Weber, C., & Hierck, T. (2015). Uniting academic and behavior interventions: Solving the skill or will dilemma. Bloomington, IN: Solution Tree Press.

Tool: Defining Lead Responsibilities for Academic and Behavioral Interventions

Taking Action reference: Essential Action 6.4—Coordinate Interventions for Students Needing Academic and Behavior Supports, p. 256

Instructions: Using the following table, review the three types of supplemental academic and behavioral interventions that must be in place in every building. Then, list specific faculty members who will accept lead responsibility for ensuring those interventions are developed, delivered to students, and evaluated.

Points to Remember While Planning

1. Faculty members with the right qualifications to ensure success should lead each intervention.
2. Accepting lead responsibility for an intervention does not mean accepting sole responsibility. It is likely that the faculty member who accepts lead responsibility will build a team of colleagues to help them develop, deliver, and evaluate academic and behavioral interventions.
3. Some academic and behavioral interventions can be led by classified staff members because they do not require special training or certifications to administer.

Academic and Behavioral Intervention Needed	Faculty Members Accepting Lead Responsibility for This Intervention	Additional Notes Will only one faculty member lead this work? Will these faculty members need any additional training or resources? Are there central office staffers who can provide support to this team of faculty members?
Interventions for Academic Behaviors These are designed for students requiring assistance with academic behaviors like completing assignments, organizing their notebooks, coming to class with all necessary materials, managing their time, studying for tests and quizzes, and focusing during work time. **Staff members to consider:** • Support staff like teacher's assistants, secretaries, and custodians • Classroom teachers • Principals and assistant principals		

page 1 of 2

Interventions for Social Behaviors These are designed for students who need assistance with social behaviors like attending school, arriving to classes on time, showing respect to peers and adults, participating in group activities, behaving appropriately in all spaces, and using appropriate language for school. **Staff members to consider:** • Guidance counselors • Attendance secretaries • School social workers or psychologists • Principals and assistant principals • Classroom teachers with special training in programs like positive behavior interventions and supports (PBIS) or restorative justice		
Interventions for Health and Home These are designed for students who have health and home circumstances that affect student achievement. This can include students who: • Are hospitalized or who are receiving treatment for chronic conditions • Have manageable conditions like asthma or diabetes that can interfere with learning • Have experienced a death in the family, a recent divorce, or conflict with parents or guardians • Struggle with food security or homelessness **Staff members to consider:** • Guidance counselors • School social workers or psychologists • School nurses		

Tools for Building Tier 3 of Your Intervention Pyramid

Systematic, timely, and targeted identification of students in greatest need is the one area of RTI at Work with which schools must be able to identify, with near perfection, the students who are failing academically or behaviorally. If they don't, it may be too late to help.

—Mike Mattos, Austin Buffum, Janet Malone,
Luis F. Cruz, Nicole Dimich, & Sarah Schuhl

It is critical to stay focused on the ultimate goal of a school's system of interventions: to ensure that *all* students acquire the absolutely essential grade-level skills, knowledge, and behaviors needed for future success. To achieve this goal, all students must have access to grade-level essential curriculum and effective initial teaching (Tier 1), and some students will need additional time and support to master every essential standard by the end of the year (Tier 2). In addition to these outcomes, some students will enter a school lacking prerequisite skills that should have been mastered in previous grade levels. These students will need intensive supports to close their foundational gaps—this is the purpose of Tier 3.

The defining characteristics of Tier 3 are as follows (Mattos et al., 2025).

- Tier 3 is not regular education or special education—it is for any student who needs this level of help.

- Students needing Tier 3 support must improve at least two academic years of growth within their area or areas of need in a single calendar school year. If a student enters fifth grade reading at a third-grade level and then improves their reading skills by one grade level by the end of the school year, the student will still be two years below grade level. At this rate, the student will never catch up! The goal is to dramatically close gaps each school year.

- To achieve this growth rate, Tier 3 supports are built into a student's daily schedule.

- Like Tier 2, interventions are targeted by student and by standard. Students who need intensive mathematics reinforcement are not all missing the same foundational mathematics skills. Interventions are targeted based on individual needs, and students in the same intervention group should be working on the same foundational skill or skills.

- Tier 3 must be in addition to Tier 1 and Tier 2, not in place of them.

- Tier 3 interventions should be led by the most highly trained faculty members in a student's specific area or areas of need. Doesn't it make sense that students at your school with the greatest skill needs in reading should have their interventions guided by your best-trained reading staff? This means the regular education and special education educators should be working together to provide this support.

- Tier 3 is not a life sentence. When done well, student learning should accelerate, closing gaps and catching students up to grade level and beyond. This requires urgency, focus, an unwavering belief in the student's potential, and perseverance.

- Please note our vocabulary: we are *not* saying "Tier 3 kids." There is no such thing as a Tier 3 student. Instead, there are students who need Tier 3 support. These students should also be receiving access to grade-level essential curriculum at Tier 1, and they will most likely need extra help on grade-level essential curriculum at Tier 2. Labeling students by tier often reinforces tracking and ability grouping practices.

Tier 3 is guided by two schoolwide teams: (1) the guiding coalition and (2) the intervention team. Each team has a unique, specific purpose. The intervention team's primary purpose is to dig deeply into each student's specific needs that require Tier 3 support, determine the right intervention or interventions for each need, monitor if the interventions are working, and revise these supports as needed. In other words, the intervention team is the problem-solving team focused on *individual* student needs. The guiding coalition's job at Tier 3 is to allocate the time, people, and resources needed to support the intervention team's plan for each student.

The resources in this chapter facilitate Tier 3 work in a system of interventions. They are divided into two separate sections: The resources in the first section are designed to support guiding coalitions and are tied to the recommendations in chapter 7 of *Taking Action: A Handbook for RTI at Work, Second Edition* (Mattos et al., 2025): "Tier 3 Guiding Coalition Essential Actions." The resources in the second section are designed to support intervention teams. They are tied to the recommendations made in chapter 8 of *Taking Action* (Mattos et al., 2025): "Tier 3 Intervention Team Essential Actions."

Section 1: Resources Designed to Support Tier 3 Schoolwide Essential Actions

Visit **go.SolutionTree.com/RTIatWork/BBTRTI** to access online-only tools.

- **"Tool: Identifying Our Interventionists"** (page 269)—Students who require Tier 3 interventions should have regular access to highly trained professionals in their unique areas of need. These professionals may already be working in positions designed to provide specialized support to struggling students. They may also be professionals with unique qualifications, certifications, or experience currently working in more traditional roles in your building (Mattos et al., 2025). The key for guiding coalitions is fourfold: (1) identify the specific Tier 3 intervention needs in the building, (2) identify the faculty members with the right qualifications to work with each Tier 3 intervention group, (3) identify the specific dates and times that interventionists are available to work with students, and (4) identify the specific dates and times that interventionists can meet as a team. Use this tool to begin identifying the interventionists in your building.

  - *Taking Action* reference: Essential Action 7.1—Create a Dynamic, Problem-Solving Site Intervention Team, p. 265

- **"Tool: The Six Essential Functions of an Intervention Team"** (online only)—In buildings committed to ensuring that all students learn at the highest levels, the intervention team—comprising highly trained professionals ready to take action on behalf of students most at risk—must function at the highest levels. Members must be skilled at using data to identify gaps in the universal skills of learning, planning and prioritizing interventions for struggling students, and assessing the effectiveness of any intervention being implemented to support struggling learners. This tool—which details the six essential functions of an intervention team—can help intervention teams ensure they are tackling the right work together.

  - *Taking Action* reference: Essential Action 7.1—Create a Dynamic, Problem-Solving Site Intervention Team, p. 265

- **"Tool: End-of-Meeting Reflection for Intervention Teams"** (page 271)—The intervention team's work carries the highest stakes in any school implementing the RTI at Work process. After all, the students served by the intervention team have already fallen grade levels behind in mastering the universal skills of learning. Without urgent action, those students will suffer consequences that impact their ability to succeed in school and life. As a result, each intervention team meeting must be focused and intentional.

There is no room for wasted time. Site intervention teams can use this tool to evaluate the effectiveness of the time they are spending together.

- *Taking Action* reference: Essential Action 7.1—Create a Dynamic, Problem-Solving Site Intervention Team, p. 265

- **"Tool: Intervention Team Implementation Continuum"** (page 273)—Like any collaborative team, intervention teams develop their capacity one step at a time. Their early work focuses on knowledge building—developing a solid understanding of the essential functions and composition of effective intervention teams. Over time, they turn that knowledge into actions, such as choosing members with expertise to join the team, creating a meeting schedule that facilitates regular member participation, and communicating their purpose to the entire faculty. Mature teams then gather evidence of their work's efficacy and adjust when necessary to ensure that their time together is paying dividends for students. Use this continuum to evaluate your intervention team's current work.

  - *Taking Action* reference: Essential Action 7.1—Create a Dynamic, Problem-Solving Site Intervention Team, p. 265

- **"Tool: Observational Feedback for Intervention Teams"** (online only)—Working *hard* is not enough for intervention teams. Instead, intervention teams must spend their time *doing the right work*. To keep their teams focused on the right work, the Beaver Dam Unified School District in Beaver Dam, Wisconsin, regularly observes intervention teams. These observations ensure that teams implement the essential practices necessary to make their meetings productive. Use this tool—which is adapted from the work of the Beaver Dam Unified School District—to provide feedback to your intervention teams.

  - *Taking Action* reference: Essential Action 7.1—Create a Dynamic, Problem-Solving Site Intervention Team, p. 265

- **"Tool: Communicating the Purpose of the Intervention Team"** (page 276)—Schools new to the RTI at Work process often assume that the entire purpose of creating a tiered system of interventions is to identify students for special education services. Faculty members in schools like these often see the intervention team as the professional gatekeeper, determining who does and does not qualify for special education identification. To push back against this perception, it is essential to carefully communicate the intervention team's purpose to the entire faculty. Use this template as a starting point to craft a letter introducing your intervention team to your teachers.

  - *Taking Action* reference: Essential Action 7.1—Create a Dynamic, Problem-Solving Site Intervention Team, p. 265

- **"Tool: Universal Screening Planning Guide"** (page 277)—The first step that schools must take at Tier 3 in the RTI at Work process is to identify students who need intensive academic or behavioral support. This identification process is known as *universal screening*, and it should be conducted as early as possible. If schools have a clearly defined plan detailing the criteria and process for screening students at risk in the universal skills of learning, Tier 3 intervention efforts should begin no later than the first week of school (Mattos et al., 2025). Use this template and **protocol** (page 279) to develop a systematic plan for universal screening in your school.
  - *Taking Action* reference: Essential Action 7.2—Identify Students Needing Intensive Reinforcements, p. 271

- **"Tool: Universal Screening Tracking Template"** (page 280)—A companion to "Tool: Universal Screening Planning Guide" (page 277), this template can be used by faculty members administering universal screeners to keep a running record of students who meet a building's at-risk criteria for each of the universal skills of learning identified in *Taking Action: A Handbook for RTI at Work, Second Edition* (Mattos et al., 2025).
  - *Taking Action* reference: Essential Action 7.2—Identify Students Needing Intensive Reinforcements, p. 271

- **"Tool: Universal Screening Review Protocol"** (page 282)—Universal screening is often interpreted as giving nationally or provincially normed benchmark assessments to all students at the beginning of a school year to measure individual performance relative to other students across North America. While nationally or provincially normed benchmark assessments can serve as universal screeners, schools can also use state testing data, local assessments, or other local data (such as attendance patterns, discipline referrals, and teacher observations) to identify students who need intensive academic or behavioral support. This tool and accompanying **sample** (page 284) can help teams collect, organize, and analyze relevant data points while screening students for Tier 3 interventions.
  - *Taking Action* reference: Essential Action 7.2—Identify Students Needing Intensive Reinforcements, p. 271

- **"Tool: Surveying Teachers About Universal Screening"** (page 286)—In *Taking Action: A Handbook for RTI at Work, Second Edition*, Mattos and colleagues (2025) suggest that schools survey their faculty to gather information regarding what teachers know about universal screening and their level of commitment to using universal screeners to identify students needing Tier 3 support. They write, "If the survey shows either is lacking, it is essential to spend additional time strengthening these key outcomes"

(Mattos et al., 2025, p. 273). Guiding coalitions can use this survey to evaluate their faculty's readiness to use universal screening for targeting Tier 3 interventions.

- *Taking Action* reference: Essential Action 7.2—Identify Students Needing Intensive Reinforcements, p. 271

- **"Tool: Identifying Human Resources for Tier 3 Interventions"** (online only)—Facilitating interventions for students who have fallen two or more grade levels behind in the universal skills of learning requires specialized training that core classroom teachers rarely have. Therefore, each school site should take time to identify all staff with the professional expertise to support Tier 3 interventions. This tool uses a series of reflection questions outlined in *Taking Action: A Handbook for RTI at Work, Second Edition* (Mattos et al., 2025) and organizes them by each universal skill of learning, allowing a school site to work systematically to determine all possible staff members who can facilitate Tier 3 interventions. After answering these reflection questions, the intervention team can match student availability to staff member availability or modify schedules to ensure that the best-trained staff members deliver Tier 3 interventions.

  - *Taking Action* reference: Essential Action 7.3—Prioritize Resources Based on the Greatest Student Needs, p. 276

- **"Tool: Scenarios to Calibrate Tier 3 Decisions"** (page 287)—Like scoring performance on a classroom assignment using a rubric, determining the right course of action for a student struggling with the universal skills of learning can be subjective. Members of the guiding coalition and the intervention team look at the available data, interpret the data's meaning, and make the best decision possible. To do so, teams must calibrate their Tier 3 decisions by identifying clear decision criteria and applying them together in regular rehearsal conversations. Use the scenarios and **sample responses** (page 290) detailed in this tool to start those rehearsal conversations with your school leadership and intervention teams.

  - *Taking Action* reference: Essential Action 7.3—Prioritize Resources Based on the Greatest Student Needs, p. 276

- **"Tool: Planning for and Prioritizing Tier 3 Interventions"** (page 291)—School leadership and intervention teams must have a process to identify and fulfill Tier 3 intervention needs. Having that comprehensive process will reduce the need for prioritizing some interventions over others. However, intervention prioritization will still occur. This tool can first match interventionists to identified needs and then prioritize actions when intervention needs outweigh your school's available resources.

- *Taking Action* reference: Essential Action 7.3—Prioritize Resources Based on the Greatest Student Needs, p. 276

■ **"Tool: Developing a Tier 3 Referral Process Guide"** (online only)—*Taking Action: A Handbook for RTI at Work, Second Edition* (Mattos et al., 2025) suggests that guiding coalitions create a Tier 3 referral process handbook. Doing so clearly articulates the steps to develop intervention plans for students struggling with the universal skills of learning. A school's referral process handbook should include a rationale for the Tier 3 referral process and an outline of steps taken when a student is referred for those interventions. This tool and **template** (online only) detail a model referral process that schools can modify to fit their site's needs.

- *Taking Action* reference: Essential Action 7.4—Create a Systematic and Timely Process to Refer Students to the Site Intervention Team, p. 281

■ **"Tool: Teacher Referral Form"** (page 296)—As part of the RTI at Work process, staff members must have a method to refer students they are concerned about to the intervention team for consideration (Mattos et al., 2025). Teachers must provide documentation to support their concerns, but the referral process should be expedient to complete. Forgetting to require documentation from teachers means your intervention team will be overwhelmed by referrals. But creating a cumbersome referral process will deter staff members from referring students for extra support. Use this tool and **samples** (page 297) as a starting point for creating a referral form that your teachers can use to recommend a student to the intervention team.

- *Taking Action* reference: Essential Action 7.4—Create a Systematic and Timely Process to Refer Students to the Site Intervention Team, p. 281

■ **"Tool: Teacher Referral Processing Protocol"** (page 299)—An intervention team must process a teacher referral form for a student needing intensive support in the universal skills of learning. Processing the referral includes identifying the right member of the intervention team to accept lead responsibility for evaluating the referred student's intervention needs, gathering any additional data necessary for making a responsible intervention decision, discussing intervention plans with the entire intervention team, and communicating decisions to the referring teacher. Use this tool to walk your intervention team through those steps.

- *Taking Action* reference: Essential Action 7.4—Create a Systematic and Timely Process to Refer Students to the Site Intervention Team, p. 281

- **"Tool: Action Plan to Support a Referred Student"** (page 301)—While a school must have a process for teachers to refer students to the intervention team (Mattos et al., 2025), it is important to note that not every staff referral will result in an assignment to a Tier 3 intervention. Sometimes, a referred student may not meet the school's established criteria. Other times, a referred student's needs may be best addressed by the support available outside of a school's system of Tier 3 interventions. However, each referral should lead to additional support for the referring teacher and the struggling student. Use this tool and **sample** (page 303) to develop an action plan for providing additional support when your intervention team cannot prioritize a student for intensive intervention.
  - *Taking Action* reference: Essential Action 7.4—Create a Systematic and Timely Process to Refer Students to the Site Intervention Team, p. 281

- **"Tool: Intervention Evaluation and Alignment Chart"** (page 306)—As Mattos and colleagues (2025) explain in *Taking Action: A Handbook for RTI at Work, Second Edition*, "If a student is significantly behind in just one of these universal skills, they will struggle in virtually every grade level, course, and subject. And usually, students who are most at risk are behind in more than one area" (p. 16). What does that mean for guiding coalitions in the RTI at Work process? They must ensure that their Tier 3 interventions meet six essential criteria: they must be (1) targeted, (2) systematic, (3) research based, (4) administered by a trained professional, (5) timely, and (6) directive (Mattos et al., 2025). Use this tool, its **overview** (page 305), and its corresponding **protocol** (page 307) to determine how well your existing interventions measure up against those criteria.
  - *Taking Action* reference: Essential Action 7.5—Assess Intervention and Reinforcement Effectiveness, p. 284

- **"Tool: Guiding Coalition Review of Tier 3 Interventions"** (page 308)—The stakes are too high to merely hope that Tier 3 interventions will accelerate learning for students struggling to master the universal skills of learning. Instead, schools must regularly review their offered interventions by gathering evidence about the impact those interventions have on students as learners. Like collaborative teacher teams, guiding coalitions must refine, revise, and assess the impact their professional choices have on learners. This tool—an adapted version of work in the Beaver Dam Unified School District in Beaver Dam, Wisconsin—can help your guiding coalition review the effectiveness of the Tier 3 interventions your building offers.
  - *Taking Action* reference: Essential Action 7.5—Assess Intervention and Reinforcement Effectiveness, p. 284

Section 2: Resources Designed to Support Tier 3 Intervention Team Essential Actions

Visit **go.SolutionTree.com/RTIatWork/BBTRTI** to access online-only tools.

- **"Tool: Intervention Planning Tool for Site Interventionists"** (page 312)—Once student referrals for intensive interventions are received, reviewed, processed, and assigned to a specific interventionist, interventionists must develop a comprehensive plan that details the students assigned to the intervention; the frequency, duration, and intensity of the intervention; the strategies to be used; and the plan for monitoring student progress. This planning ensures the delivery of targeted, specific interventions. An interventionist can use this tool to create an intervention plan for a specific group of students they support.

  - *Taking Action* reference: Essential Action 8.1—Diagnose, Target, Prioritize, and Monitor Tier 3 Reinforcements, p. 294

- **"Tool: Writing Intervention Goals for Individual Students"** (online only)—A common mistake that schools make when developing and delivering intensive Tier 3 interventions to students who have fallen behind in the universal skills of learning is writing one universal goal for all students receiving an intervention instead of writing a specific goal for each student. While writing universal goals can save time, they also lose validity, making it difficult to determine whether an intervention is effective for each student. Remember, individual goals can likely be repurposed for additional students with similar intervention needs, so the challenge of writing individual goals becomes more manageable as intervention teams build more extensive collections of goals over time. This tool can help an interventionist develop a unique SMART goal and progress-monitoring plan for an individual student.

  - *Taking Action* reference: Essential Action 8.1—Diagnose, Target, Prioritize, and Monitor Tier 3 Reinforcements, p. 294

- **"Tool: Reviewing the Intervention Team Meeting Cycle"** (page 313)—An intervention team should schedule regular meetings throughout an intervention cycle to diagnose, treat, prioritize, and monitor its Tier 3 work. Those meetings are cyclical, designed to focus the team on asking and answering the right questions at the right time. The cycle starts with screening meetings, where the team reviews student referrals. Next, the team engages in planning meetings, prioritizing student needs, and creating intervention groups. Then, the team schedules monitoring meetings in which it reviews the effectiveness of interventions and makes in-cycle adjustments to student intervention plans. Finally, the team finishes an intervention cycle with reflection meetings, studying the efficacy of schoolwide intervention strategies. Use this tool to learn more about each intervention meeting type and evaluate the intervention team's work.

- *Taking Action* reference: Essential Action 8.1—Diagnose, Target, Prioritize, and Monitor Tier 3 Reinforcements, p. 294

- **"Tool: Scheduling Calendar for Intervention Team Meetings"** (online only)—The best way to ensure that intervention teams regularly engage in the four essential meeting types detailed in "Tool: Reviewing the Intervention Team Meeting Cycle" (page 313) is to schedule those meetings at the beginning of each intervention cycle. Doing so reminds intervention team members of the specific outcomes they should pursue in their meetings. It also allows the team to identify the members that must be in attendance if a meeting will achieve its desired results. Use this scheduling calendar to create a meeting plan for the next intervention cycle.

  - *Taking Action* reference: Essential Action 8.1—Diagnose, Target, Prioritize, and Monitor Tier 3 Reinforcements, p. 294

- **"Tool: Intervention Team Meeting Dashboard"** (page 316)—The most critical work that intervention teams engage in is regularly monitoring the progress of students receiving interventions. This work is essential because interventions must accelerate learning for students with significant gaps in the universal skills of learning. Teams must either modify or abandon an intervention if it is not closing those gaps. To conduct this monitoring, many intervention teams use a meeting dashboard where interventionists update the progress of students they support. By organizing progress-monitoring data in one dashboard, intervention teams set themselves up to make in-the-moment adjustments to student interventions. Use this template to create a meeting dashboard for your intervention team.

  - *Taking Action* reference: Essential Action 8.1—Diagnose, Target, Prioritize, and Monitor Tier 3 Reinforcements, p. 294

- **"Tool: Teacher and Interventionist Communication Template"** (page 318)—Tiered supports in the RTI at Work process are designed to support student success in universal instruction. Therefore, communication between those providing universal instruction and those providing interventions is critical. This tool offers a format for interventionists to share the focus of their efforts with the classroom teacher and up-to-date progress data on the intervention's goal. The teacher, reciprocally, can provide the interventionist with information on the skill's development in the classroom.

- *Taking Action* reference: Essential Action 8.1—Diagnose, Target, Prioritize, and Monitor Tier 3 Reinforcements, p. 294

- **"Tool: Teacher Report on Student Progress"** (page 320)—An intervention aims to develop students' identified lagging skills. More specifically, the goal is to see the development of these skills in the Tier 1 setting, transferring intervention learning to everyday instruction. Interventionists may see students progressing toward goals in the intervention setting. However, Tier 1 teacher input is needed to see what is transferring to universal instruction. This information informs intervention instruction. Approximately once per intervention cycle, the interventionist should receive input from the Tier 1 teacher or teachers. This tool facilitates quick and focused teacher-to-interventionist communication on classroom progress. Use it in place of—or in addition to—"Tool: Teacher and Interventionist Communication Template" found on page 318.

  - *Taking Action* reference: Essential Action 8.1—Diagnose, Target, Prioritize, and Monitor Tier 3 Reinforcements, p. 294

- **"Tool: Student Interview on Entrance to an Intervention"** (online only)—Students receiving Tier 3 interventions in the universal skills of learning often feel stigmatized, seeing themselves as less capable than their peers. These perceptions can limit the success of intervention efforts. Students who do not believe they can learn are less likely to lean in to the intensive instruction offered during intervention sessions. Interventionists can address student perceptions by conducting an interview when students first enter an intervention. These interviews communicate an intervention's purpose to students and elicit their support and investment. Use this tool to conduct an entrance interview with a student new to Tier 3 interventions in your building.

  - *Taking Action* reference: Essential Action 8.1—Diagnose, Target, Prioritize, and Monitor Tier 3 Reinforcements, p. 294

- **"Tool: Student Interview to Track Intervention Progress"** (online only)—Effective interventionists recognize that keeping students engaged throughout an entire intervention cycle is essential. To accomplish this, they regularly check in with their intervention groups, eliciting information from students about the work they are doing together. Not only can these moments of reflection leave students convinced that they are essential partners in the intervention process, but they can also provide interventionists with information to monitor their intervention strategies' effectiveness. Use this tool to conduct regular interviews with the students in your Tier 3 intervention group.

  - *Taking Action* reference: Essential Action 8.1—Diagnose, Target, Prioritize, and Monitor Tier 3 Reinforcements, p. 294

- **"Tool: Monitoring Student Progress After Exiting Interventions"** (online only)—While intervention teams should celebrate when students progress enough to exit Tier 3 interventions, it is essential to conduct regular check-ins with classroom teachers and students in the weeks following. Students may struggle once additional support has been taken out of their schedules, and teachers may struggle after losing regular contact with interventionists who are skilled in helping students master the universal skills of learning. Interventionists can use this tool to monitor student progress after they exit interventions.
  - *Taking Action* reference: Essential Action 8.1—Diagnose, Target, Prioritize, and Monitor Tier 3 Reinforcements, p. 294

- **"Tool: Considerations to Increase Intervention Effectiveness"** (page 321)—When an intervention team realizes an intervention is not producing desired results, members must immediately modify it. Doing so starts by reviewing the intervention's frequency, duration, and group size (Mattos et al., 2025). It also involves examining the intervention to ensure that it effectively targets identified student needs and is delivered by a trained interventionist (Mattos et al., 2025). Site intervention teams can use this tool to increase an intervention's effectiveness.
  - *Taking Action* reference: Essential Action 8.2—Ensure Proper Instructional Intensity, p. 298

- **"Tool: Communicating Intervention Plans to Parents"** (page 324)—Schools that implement the RTI at Work process understand that in addition to guaranteeing all students have access to grade-level essential instruction at Tier 1, it is their responsibility to take action at Tier 2 and Tier 3 by identifying, developing, implementing, and assessing interventions and extensions around grade-level essentials, academic skills and dispositions, and the universal skills of learning. The interventions provided are always customized to address individual students' unique needs. What schools don't do is expect parents to be the primary interventionists for their children. Instead, they accept responsibility for developing each learner's intervention plan and communicating it to parents. This template can be used to detail the intervention plan to the parents of students receiving additional time and support for learning.
  - *Taking Action* reference: Essential Action 8.3—Determine Whether Special Education Is Needed and Justifiable, p. 303

- **"Tool: Intervention Team Reflection Before a Special Education Referral"** (page 325)—Despite the intervention team's best efforts, some students receiving intensive interventions in the universal skills of learning will not make adequate progress toward meeting grade-level expectations. Some of these students may have disabilities, and additional special education services may be appropriate. However, the intervention team must ensure that the school's system practices are not the root cause of the student's struggles. If the team is confident in the services it has provided across all three tiers of instruction, then a referral for special education services may help the student receive learning support from the special education department.

- *Taking Action* reference: Essential Action 8.3—Determine Whether Special Education Is Needed and Justifiable, p. 303

Conclusion

Tier 3 interventions are designed to provide intensive support to the students most at risk in any building. Typically, students receiving Tier 3 interventions have fallen multiple years behind their grade-level peers in mastering the universal skills of learning: reading (decoding and comprehending grade-level text), writing effectively, applying number sense, comprehending the school's primary language, consistently demonstrating social and academic behaviors, and overcoming complications due to health and home (Mattos et al., 2025). Tier 3 interventions aim to achieve substantial growth within a single school year by closing significant gaps and allowing students to catch up to grade level and beyond. To achieve this, Tier 3 interventions must be integrated into a student's daily schedule, targeting specific individual needs.

The school guiding coalition and school intervention team take lead responsibility for designing and delivering Tier 3 interventions to students. The intervention team focuses on individual student needs, identifying appropriate interventions, monitoring student progress, and making necessary adjustments along the way. The guiding coalition provides the resources and support required for the intervention team's plans. It communicates the purpose of Tier 3 interventions to the school community, develops plans for screening students in the universal skills of learning, determines criteria for identifying students who qualify for Tier 3 interventions, and ensures that all students can receive Tier 3 interventions without missing new instruction in essential grade-level curriculum or additional time and support for learning grade-level essentials.

Tier 3 interventions play a critical role in closing educational gaps and ensuring that all students can succeed. By following the strategies and utilizing the resources outlined in this chapter, schools can create a systematic and effective approach to supporting students with the most intensive needs, accelerating their learning journeys.

Resources Designed to
Support Tier 3 Schoolwide Essential Actions

Tool: Identifying Our Interventionists

Taking Action *reference: Essential Action 7.1—Create a Dynamic, Problem-Solving Site Intervention Team, p. 265*

Instructions: Review each of the Tier 3 interventions detailed in the first column. Then, identify the faculty member or members with the right expertise to provide each intervention. Finally, identify times when each faculty member can work with students and meet with the intervention team.

Remember that while you may have specific faculty members in roles designed to support students with specific intervention needs (special education teachers, psychologists, nurses, counselors, and interventionists), you can also tap faculty members with specialized training in areas outside their current job assignment to support struggling students.

Tier 3 Intervention Support Needed in Our School	Faculty Members With the Qualifications or Experience Necessary to Provide This Intervention	Dates and Times That Interventionists Are Available to Work With Tier 3 Students	Dates and Times That Interventionists Are Available to Meet With One Another
Decoding and Comprehending Grade-Level Text			
Writing Effectively			
Applying Number Sense			
Comprehending the English Language (or the School's Primary Language)			

Consistently Demonstrating Social and Academic Behaviors *Examples:* Organization, work completion, cooperation, and showing respect to others			
Overcoming Complications Due to Health or Home *Examples:* Attendance issues, transience, and medical conditions that interfere with learning			

Questions for Reflection

What patterns do you notice in the faculty members qualified to work with your Tier 3 students? How will those patterns impact—positively or negatively—your efforts to provide meaningful interventions to every student?

What patterns do you notice in the dates and times that your interventionists are available to work with students? How will those patterns impact—positively or negatively—your efforts to provide meaningful interventions to every student?

What staffing or scheduling changes are needed to ensure that your Tier 3 students have frequent access to highly trained professionals in their area of need?

Tool: End-of-Meeting Reflection for Intervention Teams

Taking Action reference: Essential Action 7.1—Create a Dynamic, Problem-Solving Site Intervention Team, p. 265

Instructions: At the end of each meeting, the facilitator should ask the team reflection questions listed in the first column of the table at the end of the tool. Team members should score their work in today's meeting using the rating scale provided. The facilitator should record that score in the second column. After gaining consensus, a rationale for that rating can be listed in the third column. The meeting facilitator can use this information to make improvements for the next meeting.

Date of Meeting	
School	

Essential Functions of an Intervention Team		
Use relevant data to identify students needing schoolwide support in social-emotional learning, behaviors, or academics.	Determine specific interventions and establish goals for each student, prioritizing resources based on greatest needs.	Establish and utilize a student referral process, allowing staff to recommend students to the intervention team for consideration and support.
Regularly monitor intervention success at the student level using relevant data.	Make intervention adjustments (entrance, exit, and intensity) based on need during and after intervention cycles.	Assess the effectiveness of interventions offered. Learn from, celebrate the successes of, and adjust interventions based on those assessments.

Questions for Reflection	Rating	Rationale
Were the right people at today's meeting to fulfill our functions as an intervention team?	☐ No ☐ Somewhat ☐ Yes	
Was our meeting focused on the essential functions of an intervention team?	☐ No ☐ Somewhat ☐ Yes	
Did we have the necessary and relevant data available to make decisions?	☐ No ☐ Somewhat ☐ Yes	

Questions for Reflection	Rating	Rationale
Did we record what we discussed?	☐ No ☐ Somewhat ☐ Yes	
Did we end the meeting with an understanding of who is responsible for what actions? Was the timeline for those actions clear?	☐ No ☐ Somewhat ☐ Yes	
Did we notice any barriers to our team's effectiveness and efficiency?	☐ No ☐ Somewhat ☐ Yes	
Was this meeting an effective use of our time as we pursue our school's mission and vision?	☐ No ☐ Somewhat ☐ Yes	

Tool: Intervention Team Implementation Continuum

Taking Action reference: Essential Action 7.1—Create a Dynamic, Problem-Solving Site Intervention Team, p. 265

Instructions: Intervention teams can use this continuum to inform their next developmental steps. The team should read each indicator and select its current implementation level. Then, the team should list specific actions it can take to move to the next level of performance.

Indicator	Learning	Planning	Implementing	Refining
Our intervention team comprises specialists with the expertise needed for schoolwide interventions.	We are learning about the right composition of intervention teams and identifying potential members.	We are assembling the best people to serve on our intervention team.	We have assembled an intervention team and clearly understand the roles we will play to facilitate Tier 3 work.	We have assembled an intervention team, understand our roles, and are successfully fulfilling those roles.
	☐	☐	☐	☐
Next Steps:				
Our intervention team meets regularly with a clear focus for each meeting.	We are learning how often the intervention team should meet and the kind of work members tackle together.	We are developing a plan for the intervention team to meet regularly.	We are meeting regularly as an intervention team and are working on the focus of each meeting.	We have met regularly as an intervention team and have a clear focus for each meeting that works for us.
	☐	☐	☐	☐
Next Steps:				

Indicator	Learning →	Planning	Implementing	Refining
We have communicated the role of an intervention team to the rest of our faculty and staff.	We are learning about the purpose of the intervention team.	We are planning to share information about the intervention team with our staff.	We have communicated the purpose of the intervention team with all our staff.	We have communicated the purpose of the intervention team with all our staff and have convincing evidence that they understand our purpose.
	☐	☐	☐	☐
Next Steps:				
We focus our efforts on the six essential functions of an intervention team.	We are learning about the essential functions of an intervention team.	We are planning how our intervention team will focus on the essential functions.	We have organized our intervention team meetings to focus on the essential functions.	We have organized our intervention team meetings to focus on the essential functions and have convincing evidence that our focus leads to student results.
	☐	☐	☐	☐
Next Steps:				

Essential Functions of an Intervention Team		
Use relevant data to identify students needing schoolwide support in social-emotional learning, behaviors, or academics.	Determine specific interventions and establish goals for each student, prioritizing resources based on greatest needs.	Establish and utilize a student referral process, allowing staff to recommend students to the intervention team for consideration and support.
Regularly monitor intervention success at the student level using relevant data.	Make intervention adjustments (entrance, exit, and intensity) based on need during and after intervention cycles.	Assess the effectiveness of interventions offered. Learn from, celebrate the successes of, and adjust interventions based on those assessments.

Tier 3 Schoolwide Essential Actions

Tool: Communicating the Purpose of the Intervention Team

Taking Action *reference: Essential Action 7.1—Create a Dynamic, Problem-Solving Site Intervention Team, p. 265*

Instructions: This template is a starting point for your letter communicating your intervention team's purpose to your faculty. Remember that you are trying to outline your intervention team's purpose, actions, and benefits in your letter. Some schools also include the membership of the intervention team and the process for referring students to the intervention team in their introductory letters to teachers.

Dear Faculty and Staff,

I am proud to introduce the intervention team. The purpose of this communication is to let you know the purpose of this team, what the team focuses on, and how the team benefits our school. If you have questions, please reach out, and I will happily provide further information or clarity.

The purpose of establishing an intervention team is to ensure that the students in our school who are most at risk receive the support they need for success. Stated more simply, this team focuses its collective efforts on students struggling with the universal skills of learning. Staff with deep expertise in areas like reading, writing, numeracy, and academic and social behaviors assemble to help students master skills that go beyond the proficiency of individual teachers and collaborative teams.

Focusing only on students who are the most at risk, intervention teams spend their time on the following.

- Using relevant data to identify students needing support in social-emotional learning, behavior, and universal academic skills
- Determining the appropriate interventions for each identified student and planning to prioritize resources to deliver necessary interventions
- Monitoring interventions and adjusting them to best meet student needs
- Reviewing individual students referred by staff with concerns
- Evaluating intervention effectiveness to continually improve the process

This team is critical to our overall Response to Intervention at Work efforts.

In our system of interventions, classroom teachers and collaborative teams deliver first, best instruction each day. In addition, teachers and teams monitor student success in grade-level curriculum, providing additional time and support as needed. The intervention team takes lead responsibility for providing interventions that need schoolwide coordination from those with additional expertise in the universal skills of learning. This team will do its best to address student needs with the resources we have as part of an overall system designed to ensure high levels of learning for every student.

Thank you for being part of our educational community and working in the service of our students every day.

Sincerely,

SCHOOL PRINCIPAL

Tool: Universal Screening Planning Guide

Taking Action reference: *Essential Action 7.2—Identify Students Needing Intensive Reinforcements, p. 271*

Instructions: Use the following guide to screen students needing intervention.

Universal Skill	At-Risk Criteria	Screening Process	When	Who	Intensive Support Available
Reading					
Writing					
Number Sense					

Tier 3 Schoolwide Essential Actions 3

Universal Skill	At-Risk Criteria	Screening Process	When	Who	Intensive Support Available
English Language					
Social and Academic Behaviors					
Health and Home					

Source: Adapted from Mattos, M., Buffum, A., Malone, J., Cruz, L. F., Dimich, N., & Schuhl, S. (2025). Taking action: A handbook for RTI at Work (2nd ed.). Bloomington, IN: Solution Tree Press; Buffum, A., Mattos, M., & Weber, C. (2012). Simplifying response to intervention: Four essential guiding principles. Bloomington, IN: Solution Tree Press.

Protocol: Universal Screening Planning Guide

Taking Action *reference: Essential Action 7.2—Identify Students Needing Intensive Reinforcements, p. 271*

This activity is designed to assist a guiding coalition plan for universal screening by creating a process to identify students in need of intensive support *before* they fail. Because the purpose is to provide preventive support, it is best if this activity is completed prior to the start of the school year.

For each universal skill, answer a question for each column.

1. **At-risk criteria:** At each grade level, what criteria will be used to determine whether a student is in need of intensive support? For example, in reading, an elementary school may determine that any student entering first grade without the ability to properly recognize all twenty-six letters (uppercase and lowercase) is extremely at risk in reading and will be considered for immediate, intensive support. At a high school, any student whose reading ability is two or more years below grade level (grade-level equivalent) could be considered for immediate, intensive support.

2. **Screening process:** What screening assessment, process, or both will be used to identify students in need of intensive support? The guiding coalition should identify the most effective, efficient, and timely process to gather the at-risk criteria data on each student.

3. **When:** When will the screening process take place? Obviously, if the purpose of universal screening is to provide preventive support, then these data should be collected either prior to the start of the school year or as early in the school year as possible. Finally, as new students will enroll in the school throughout the year, it is important to consider how these students can be screened during the enrollment process.

4. **Who:** Who will administer the screening? As the guiding coalition has representation from every teacher team, as well as responsibility for coordinating school support staff, this team is best positioned to organize the resources necessary.

5. **Intensive support available:** What intensive intervention or interventions will be used to accelerate student learning and support the identified student? There is no point in universal screening if there is no plan to provide these students extra support in their area or areas of need.

One final consideration: For a school new to universal screening, it may be overwhelming to begin universal screening in all six universal skills, at all grade levels, immediately. In this case, we recommend that the guiding coalition identify the universal skill (reading, writing, number sense, English language, social and academic behaviors, health and home) that is currently the greatest area of need in its school. Start by focusing on this one. As the school builds skill and competence in this area, others can be added.

Source: Mattos, M., Buffum, A., Malone, J., Cruz, L. F., Dimich, N., & Schuhl, S. (2025). Taking action: A handbook for RTI at Work (2nd ed.). Bloomington, IN: Solution Tree Press, p. 275. Adapted from Buffum, A., Mattos, M., & Weber, C. (2012). Simplifying response to intervention: Four essential guiding principles. Bloomington, IN: Solution Tree Press.

Tool: Universal Screening Tracking Template

Taking Action reference: *Essential Action 7.2—Identify Students Needing Intensive Reinforcements, p. 271*

Instructions: While screening for intensive interventions, use this template to record individual students' names who meet the at-risk criteria detailed in your school's universal screening plan.

Grade Level:							
	Teacher:		**Teacher:**		**Teacher:**		**Teacher:**
Tier 3 Intervention Focus	Students needing this intervention focus:		Students needing this intervention focus:		Students needing this intervention focus:		Students needing this intervention focus:
Decoding and Comprehending Grade-Level Text							
Writing Effectively							
Applying Number Sense							

page 1 of 2

Comprehending the English Language (or the School's Primary Language)		
Consistently Demonstrating Social and Academic Behaviors *Examples:* Organization, work completion, cooperation, and showing respect to others		
Overcoming Complications Due to Health or Home *Examples:* Attendance issues, transience, and medical conditions that interfere with learning		

Tool: Universal Screening Review Protocol

Taking Action *reference: Essential Action 7.2—Identify Students Needing Intensive Reinforcements, p. 271*

Instructions: Guiding coalitions should complete one review protocol for each of the universal skills of learning, identifying specific data points that will be collected and analyzed to determine which students need intensive academic or behavioral interventions.

School or Site		School Year	
Date		Grade Level	

What is the goal of this screening?	☐ Determine intensive reading needs. ☐ Determine intensive writing needs. ☐ Determine intensive number sense needs. ☐ Determine intensive English language needs. ☐ Determine intensive social and academic behavior needs. ☐ Determine health and home needs.		
Data Points **Note:** This can include state assessments, local assessments, and other relevant local data.	**Data Point 1**	**Data Point 2**	**Data Point 3**
What assessments or local data will we use to identify students who may need intensive support? **Note:** At least three data points from relatively recent assessments or data sources should be used.			
What information will this assessment or local data tell us? **Sample:** *If reading is the goal of the screening, the assessment may tell us if the student needs support in foundational skills, vocabulary, comprehension, or a combination of areas.*			

What information on this assessment or local data will trigger the possible need for intensive support? **Sample:** *This may be a national percentile on an assessment, a certain number of absences in a term, a specific score on a school-administered pretest of prerequisite skills, or a certain number of discipline referrals.*			
Based on this assessment or local data, which students need intensive support? **Note:** Use the data rule from the previous question to compile this list of students.			
Based on the list of names from each data point, which students consistently need intensive support? **Note:** This question allows for data triangulation to inform intervention priorities. We should discuss—and possibly further assess—these students for intensive interventions.			
Next Steps Who will do what by when with the information collected on this form?			

Sample: Universal Screening Review Protocol

Taking Action *reference: Essential Action 7.2—Identify Students Needing Intensive Reinforcements, p. 271*

Instructions: Guiding coalitions should complete one review protocol for each of the universal skills of learning, identifying specific data points that will be collected and analyzed to determine which students need intensive academic or behavioral interventions.

School or Site	Sample School	School Year	2023–2024
Date	October 1	Grade Level	6

What is the goal of this screening?	☑ Determine intensive reading needs. ☐ Determine intensive writing needs. ☐ Determine intensive number sense needs. ☐ Determine intensive English language needs. ☐ Determine intensive social and academic behavior needs. ☐ Determine health and home needs.		
Data Points **Note:** This can include state assessments, local assessments, and other relevant local data.	**Data Point 1**	**Data Point 2**	**Data Point 3**
What assessments or local data will we use to identify students who may need intensive support? **Note:** At least three data points from relatively recent assessments or data sources should be used.	Local Benchmark: Reading May 2023	Local Benchmark: Reading September 2023	State Assessment: English language arts April 2023

What information will this assessment or local data tell us?
Sample: If reading is the goal of the screening, the assessment may tell us if the student needs support in foundational skills, vocabulary, comprehension, or a combination of areas.
	• Overall grade-level performance, national percentile, and Lexile level
	• Performance by domain in:
	  - Phonological awareness
	  - Phonics
	  - High-frequency words
	  - Vocabulary
	  - Comprehension in literary and informational text
		• Overall grade-level performance, national percentile, and Lexile level
		• Performance by domain in:
		  - Phonological awareness
		  - Phonics
		  - High-frequency words
		  - Vocabulary
		  - Comprehension in literary and informational text
			• Advanced, proficient, basic, or below basic performance
			• State percentile
			• Writing score
			• Reading score
			• English skills score

What information on this assessment or local data will trigger the possible need for intensive support? *Sample: This may be a national percentile on an assessment, a certain number of absences in a term, a specific score on a school-administered pretest of prerequisite skills, or a certain number of discipline referrals.*	• Students are two or more grade levels below overall • Students are more than two grade levels below in any specific domain • National percentile below 25th	• Students are two or more grade levels below overall • Students are more than two grade levels below in any specific domain • National percentile below 25th	• State percentile below 25th • Reading score basic or below basic
Based on this assessment or local data, which students need intensive support? **Note:** Use the data rule from the previous question to compile this list of students.	Reece P. Rushil D. Annalisa M. Hayley D. Thomas G. Jace V. Will S.	Javon B. Rushil D. Anna T. Luis S. Thomas G. Jace V. Riley C.	Javon B. Rushil D. Anna T. Dylan L. Thomas G. Jace V. Sha'Vonya M.
Based on the list of names from each data point, which students consistently need intensive support? **Note:** This question allows for data triangulation to inform intervention priorities. We should discuss—and possibly further assess—these students for intensive interventions.	Students with three data points of concern: Rushil D. Thomas G. Jace V. Students with two data points of concern: Javon B. Anna T.		
Next Steps Who will do what by when with the information collected on this form?	For the following students, the reading interventionist will analyze assessment data, schedule a meeting to conduct any further assessments that may assist us in providing the best intervention, and contact parents regarding concerns and next steps to support student learning. This will be conducted by next week's team meeting. Rushil D. Thomas G. Jace V. The school counselor will, for the following students, reach out to the classroom teacher to gather additional data. This will be brought back to next week's team meeting. Javon B. Anna T. At next week's team meeting, we will use this information to make intervention determinations and schedule them appropriately.		

Tool: Surveying Teachers About Universal Screening

Taking Action reference: Essential Action 7.2—Identify Students Needing Intensive Reinforcements, p. 271

Instructions: Schools that create an effective system of interventions for struggling students use universal screeners to identify students needing intensive interventions. Our guiding coalition is currently assessing our school's readiness to take this essential action. You can help by thoughtfully filling out this survey individually and returning it to your grade level's guiding coalition representative by _____.

Your name (optional): _____

Your grade level and subject area: _____

How much do you already know about the role universal screeners play in schools?						
The role universal screeners play in schools is a new topic for me.	1	2	3	4	5	I know a lot about the role universal screeners play in schools.

Statement to Consider	Your Response (Circle one.)		Your Reasoning
Universal screeners are nationally or provincially normed tests given to all students in reading and mathematics at the beginning of a school year.	True	False	
Schools should develop universal screeners for academic skills, dispositions, and behaviors.	True	False	
Schools should only place a student in Tier 3 interventions after gathering information about that student's current strengths and weaknesses over the first few weeks of the new school year.	True	False	
A short assessment developed by a collaborative team that assesses the prerequisite skills necessary to master grade-level essential standards can be used as a universal screener.	True	False	
We must identify, with near perfection, the students who are failing academically or behaviorally as quickly as possible.	True	False	
What questions, comments, or concerns do you want to share with our guiding coalition as we move forward with integrating universal screening into our school's intervention efforts?			

The Big Book of Tools for RTI at Work © 2025 Solution Tree Press • SolutionTree.com
Visit **go.SolutionTree.com/RTIatWork/BBTRTI** to download this free reproducible.

Tool: Scenarios to Calibrate Tier 3 Decisions

Taking Action *reference: Essential Action 7.3—Prioritize Resources Based on the Greatest Student Needs, p. 276*

Instructions: As a team, read each scenario and determine if consideration for Tier 3 intervention is appropriate based on the information provided. Record your response in the second column. In the third column, record your rationale for your response based on the information provided.

Notes: There are no specific right or wrong answers in this activity. Each site may answer differently based on variables specific to their building. Teams can review sample answers provided by the authors in "Sample: Responses to Scenarios to Calibrate Tier 3 Decisions" on page 290. *Finally, teams should take the information provided in the scenario at face value, knowing teams would have much more information for students at their site.*

Questions to consider as you respond include the following.

- Are there multiple data points to show a need?
- Is the need a universal skill?
- Has the student received high-quality Tier 1 instruction and been supported in Tier 2 instruction?

Scenario	Team Response	Rationale for Response
Scenario A: The site reviews data from a recent universal screener for mathematics. Data are examined for a student named Jerome, who performed at the 13th percentile. Looking at past assessments, Jerome's assessment scores have dropped from the 21st percentile to the 17th percentile and now the 13th percentile. The most significant area of concern in this assessment is the number and operations domain. The team reviews further information and notes no social skills or attendance concerns. The team receives classroom assessment data and notes concerns regarding number and operations.	☐ Proceed with consideration for Tier 3 intervention. ☐ Explore other opportunities for student support.	
Scenario B: The site is reviewing attendance data and notices that a student named Kendall has missed four out of the last fifteen school days. The absences are spread out over three weeks with no noted excuses or family contacts for these absences. The team looks at historical data and notices no attendance concerns over the last three years. However, there have been sixteen absences this school year with an increasing frequency. The team contacts the family, who shares that they are trying to get the student to school, but the student is often resistant. The family is open to suggestions and support. Tier 2 interventions are planned, but the family communication suggests more significant mental health concerns.	☐ Proceed with consideration for Tier 3 intervention. ☐ Explore other opportunities for student support.	

Scenario	Team Response	Rationale for Response
Scenario C: The site reviews data from a recent universal screener for reading. Data are examined for a student named Logan, who performed at the 17th percentile. Looking at past assessments, Logan's scores include the 51st percentile, 53rd percentile, and 50th percentile. These assessments do not show a consistent area or domain of low performance. The team receives classroom assessment data and does not notice consistent concerns. The team reviews further information and notes there are no academic skills, social skills, or attendance concerns.	☐ Proceed with consideration for Tier 3 intervention. ☐ Explore other opportunities for student support.	
Scenario D: After analyzing student data received from state assessments, the team further explores data in mathematics for a student named Shiv. Shiv performed at the 16th percentile on the most recent state assessment. In addition, she has performed below the 20th percentile on the last three state assessments. The team reviews other data points and notices that Shiv performs at the 45th–55th percentile on a local assessment and meets as many grade-level standards as average peers. The team knows that state assessments are done using a schoolwide schedule, and the local assessment is done in normal class time like a regular unit assessment.	☐ Proceed with consideration for Tier 3 intervention. ☐ Explore other opportunities for student support.	
Scenario E: After looking at recent universal screening data, the intervention team notices that Franklin has consistently performed two or more grade levels below expectations across all reading domains, and his performance continues to drop compared to his peers. When looking at team notes from the previous year's analysis, the team discovered that Franklin was not placed in an academic intervention—even though site data consideration guidelines across assessments warranted it—because the team believed there were social behaviors impacting learning. The team also noticed that Franklin was not supported in a social skill intervention.	☐ Proceed with consideration for Tier 3 intervention. ☐ Explore other opportunities for student support.	

Scenario F: A teacher refers a student named Rae for review, noting behavioral concerns that are becoming more frequent. The teacher shares that the family has been supporting Rae's behavior and that there have been informal interventions in the classroom. Rae has been receiving Tier 2 social skill interventions organized by the school for a semester. However, her discipline referral rate is increasing, her academic performance is decreasing, and she is becoming a danger to peers due to increased acts of physical aggression.	☐ Proceed with consideration for Tier 3 intervention. ☐ Explore other opportunities for student support.	
Scenario G: After looking at progress-monitoring data from a Tier 3 mathematics intervention and the most recent local assessment, the intervention team notices that a student named Javon has made significant progress, is now performing at the 35th percentile, and is on grade level or one grade level below in all domains. The school data show that students consistently performing at or below the 25th percentile are currently served in a Tier 3 intervention. That means Javon should be moved out of his Tier 3 intervention. The interventionist, however, is not sure Javon will continue to make progress without the intervention.	☐ Proceed with consideration for Tier 3 intervention. ☐ Explore other opportunities for student support.	

Sample: Responses to Scenarios to Calibrate Tier 3 Decisions

Taking Action *reference: Essential Action 7.3—Prioritize Resources Based on the Greatest Student Needs, p. 276*

Reminder: There are no specific right or wrong answers in this activity. Each site may answer differently based on building-specific variables. Teams can review sample answers provided by the authors in the following table. *Finally, teams should take the information provided in the scenario at face value, knowing teams would have much more information for students at their site.*

Scenario	Possible Response	Rationale for Response
Scenario A	Proceed with consideration for Tier 3.	Multiple data points show Jerome needs support in a universal skill. The site can further explore possible Tier 3 interventions.
Scenario B	Proceed with consideration for Tier 3.	There is a shared concern about Kendall between the school and the family, with more significant concerns shared by the family. In addition, the increased frequency of absences may warrant a more intensive approach. The site can further explore possible Tier 3 interventions.
Scenario C	Explore other opportunities for student support.	A single data point initiated a conversation about the support Logan needs. Other relevant data points do not demonstrate the same concerns. Therefore, the site can explore the barriers Logan is experiencing on this specific assessment rather than apply a Tier 3 intervention.
Scenario D	Explore other opportunities for student support.	Concerns about Shiv's performance only come from the state assessment, not other assessments. Therefore, the site can explore the barriers Shiv is experiencing on this specific assessment rather than apply a Tier 3 intervention.
Scenario E	Proceed with consideration for Tier 3.	While there might be much debate about this scenario, it is essential to note that Franklin's performance is a growing concern, and there have not been significant actions to support this. The site can consider Franklin for a Tier 3 academic intervention and develop social skill development plans if there is still a need.
Scenario F	Proceed with consideration for Tier 3.	Based on the information known, Rae is showing a need for intensive support. Tier 1 and Tier 2 support can continue and be refined while Tier 3 support is considered and added.
Scenario G	Explore other opportunities for student support.	Schools must prioritize resources for supporting student needs. With that in mind, the school can exit Javon from the Tier 3 intervention and develop a transition plan to provide less support and monitoring for him.

Tool: Planning for and Prioritizing Tier 3 Interventions

Taking Action *reference: Essential Action 7.3—Prioritize Resources Based on the Greatest Student Needs, p. 276*

Instructions: Guiding coalitions and intervention teams should work together to respond to the prompts in the following five steps. These prompts detail the interventionists available to support students struggling with the universal skills of learning and prioritize actions when identified student needs outweigh the available intervention resources.

Step 1: Make Goals and Priorities Clear

The intervention team starts the prioritization process by screening data, reviewing school goals, and creating an inventory of students who need support. The team uses this information to make decisions when there may not be sufficient resources to meet all identified needs.

What are the school's established goals?	
What are the most significant areas of need based on student data? **Sample:** *Fifth-grade mathematics is more of a concern than other grade levels.*	

Step 2: Take an Inventory of Staff Available for Intensive Interventions

The intervention team takes an inventory of all available staff who can deliver intensive interventions. This inventory includes indicating each staff member's area of expertise, specific training or familiarity with interventions, and availability for delivering interventions. This step is typically completed once per school year and then modified following changes in availability or expertise.

Staff Name	Area of Expertise Reading, writing, number sense, English language, social and academic behaviors, or health and home	Specific Training or Intervention Familiarity	Time Available
Sample: Mrs. A	**Sample:** Reading; writing	**Sample:** Reading specialist	**Sample:** 8:30–11:00 a.m.; 11:30–2:30 p.m.

Step 3: Match Staff Availability to Student Availability

The intervention team takes inventory of all available staff who can deliver intensive interventions and matches their availability to student availability. This step takes the general inventory of available staff and creates a menu of interventionists—an availability dashboard—for each grade level or class in the school. The time students are available shall not conflict with their Tier 1 instruction or Tier 2 interventions in grade-level essentials.

Grade or Class	Time Available	Staff Available	Staff Area of Expertise
Sample: Third grade	**Sample:** 10:00–10:30 a.m., daily	**Samples:**	
		Mrs. A	Reading; writing
		Mr. J	Number sense
		Mrs. O	Social and academic behaviors
		Mr. M	English language

Step 4: Match Interventions

The intervention team, having established who is available to serve each grade or class without disrupting essential learning instruction and intervention, creates a list of interventions the school needs to deliver. The team uses the availability dashboard to appropriately match staff available and students in need. The prioritization protocol (step 5) supports decision making when no staff members are available.

Grade or Class	Intervention Needed (Include group size.)	Do We Have Available Staff?	Who and When?
Sample: Third grade	**Sample:** Reading Comprehension: four students	☑ Yes ☐ No	**Sample:** Mrs. A, 10:00 a.m., Monday–Friday
		☐ Yes ☐ No	
		☐ Yes ☐ No	
		☐ Yes ☐ No	
		☐ Yes ☐ No	
		☐ Yes ☐ No	
		☐ Yes ☐ No	
		☐ Yes ☐ No	
		☐ Yes ☐ No	
		☐ Yes ☐ No	

Step 5: Create a Prioritization Protocol

The intervention team may need to make tough decisions about how to proceed when identified needs are greater than the support available. In that case, these reflection questions can ensure the team has a productive conversation leading to the best decisions. In addition, the team can look at the root causes of a high demand for interventions.

Questions for Reflection

Are there interventions identified that we cannot offer?

Why are we not able to offer these interventions?

Can schedules be modified for students or staff to match an identified need with a highly trained interventionist?

What interventions most align with our school goals and greatest areas of need (step 1)? Can we prioritize those?

How can we support teachers and students who cannot receive formal intervention at this time?

Suppose we have identified many interventions that we are not able to offer. What can we do to bolster Tier 1 instruction to prevent a need for Tier 2 and 3 interventions later?

Tool: Teacher Referral Form

Taking Action reference: Essential Action 7.4—Create a Systematic and Timely Process to Refer Students to the Site Intervention Team, p. 281

Instructions: The intervention team exists in our school to support students who have needs beyond the expertise of classroom teachers and collaborative teams, including students requiring intensive intervention in the universal skills of learning. If you believe that a student you teach needs intensive interventions, please complete this form and submit it to a member of the intervention team. Someone from the team will get back to you promptly.

Student Name		
Student Grade		
Referring Teacher		
Universal Skill of Concern	☐ Reading ☐ Writing ☐ Number sense ☐ English language ☐ Social and academic behaviors ☐ Health and home ☐ Other	**Specific Concern** *Sample:* Comprehension
Current Observations What data or observations have made you concerned?		
Current Actions What support is currently in place or has been previously tried to support the student?		
Additional Context Do you have any additional information that may help the intervention team?		

Sample: Teacher Referral Form—Academics

Taking Action reference: Essential Action 7.4—Create a Systematic and Timely Process to Refer Students to the Site Intervention Team, p. 281

Instructions: The intervention team exists in our school to support students who have needs beyond the expertise of classroom teachers and collaborative teams, including students requiring intensive intervention in the universal skills of learning. If you believe that a student you teach needs intensive interventions, please complete this form and submit it to a member of the intervention team. Someone from the team will get back to you promptly.

Student Name	Evan J.
Student Grade	Grade 6
Referring Teacher	Mr. Wojtaszek

Universal Skill of Concern	☐ Reading ☐ Writing ☒ Number sense ☐ English language ☐ Social and academic behaviors ☐ Health and home ☐ Other	**Specific Concern** *Sample: Comprehension* Evan cannot demonstrate success in number sense and operations essential for grade-level mathematics standards.

Current Observations What data or observations have made you concerned?	I have noticed number sense needs and a lack of current understanding of operations on classroom mid- and end-of-unit assessments. In addition, our benchmark assessment shows, for the last two assessment periods, that Evan is performing at the second- to third-grade level in the numbers and operations domain of standards. In one-on-one meetings with Evan, I have observed confusion with negative versus positive numbers and current struggles with multiplication and division examples. I will include sample written work.
Current Actions What support is currently in place or has been previously tried to support the student?	I am meeting with Evan for Tier 2 intervention at least three times a week to support achievement and growth. This work focuses on prerequisite skills for grade-level essential standards. In addition, I intentionally observe Evan's work during class to provide timely feedback.
Additional Context Do you have any additional information that may help the intervention team?	Evan is not an attendance or disciplinary concern, so I do not believe other underlying causes need to be addressed. Evan is diligent about their homework and attentive. I have reached out to their family to share my concerns, and they are working to support learning at home based on some suggestions I have provided. Evan wants to do well.

Sample: Teacher Referral Form—Social Behaviors

Taking Action *reference: Essential Action 7.4—Create a Systematic and Timely Process to Refer Students to the Site Intervention Team, p. 281*

Instructions: The intervention team exists in our school to support students who have needs beyond the expertise of classroom teachers and collaborative teams, including students requiring intensive intervention in the universal skills of learning. If you believe that a student you teach needs intensive interventions, please complete this form and submit it to a member of the intervention team. Someone from the team will get back to you promptly.

Student Name	Troy A.
Student Grade	Grade 4
Referring Teacher	Mrs. Morosini

Universal Skill of Concern	☐ Reading ☐ Writing ☐ Number sense ☐ English language ☑ Social and academic behaviors ☐ Health and home ☐ Other	**Specific Concern** *Sample: Comprehension* Troy cannot focus during class and is distracting his peers. He struggles to keep his hands to himself in unstructured time.
Current Observations What data or observations have made you concerned?	Troy becomes off task after about three to four minutes of independent or group work time. He wanders around the classroom and often tries to get peer attention by taking the materials they are working on, tapping them on the shoulder, or messing with their hair. This behavior can escalate to pushing, but this is not often the case. When redirected, Troy can maintain attentiveness for about three to five more minutes before repeating similar behaviors.	
Current Actions What support is currently in place or has been previously tried to support the student?	Troy has had conferences with me, has had parent meetings, and has an explicit reminder sheet on his desk. We have initiated a morning check-in process and a reward system for the student to work toward.	
Additional Context Do you have any additional information that may help the intervention team?	Troy is not an attendance concern or, currently, an academic concern. However, I am worried that academic concerns will arise due to his inability to focus during independent time. I have tried what I know, but I need support in helping Troy build stamina and develop strategies.	

Tool: Teacher Referral Processing Protocol

Taking Action reference: Essential Action 7.4—Create a Systematic and Timely Process to Refer Students to the Site Intervention Team, p. 281

Instructions: Intervention teams should work through each of the following steps after receiving a teacher referral form for a student needing intensive support in the universal skills of learning.

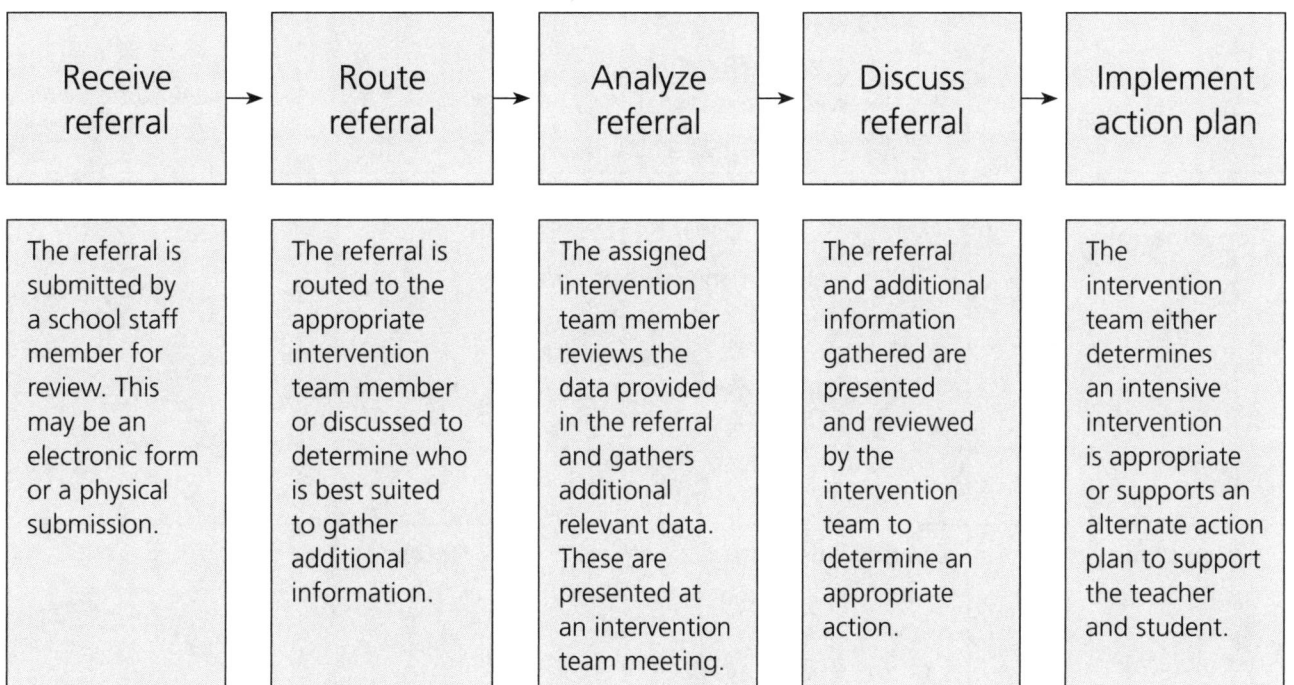

Receive referral	Route referral	Analyze referral	Discuss referral	Implement action plan
The referral is submitted by a school staff member for review. This may be an electronic form or a physical submission.	The referral is routed to the appropriate intervention team member or discussed to determine who is best suited to gather additional information.	The assigned intervention team member reviews the data provided in the referral and gathers additional relevant data. These are presented at an intervention team meeting.	The referral and additional information gathered are presented and reviewed by the intervention team to determine an appropriate action.	The intervention team either determines an intensive intervention is appropriate or supports an alternate action plan to support the teacher and student.

Processing a Teacher Referral to the Intervention Team	
Student Name	
Student Grade	
Referring Teacher	
Universal Skill of Concern	☐ Reading ☐ Writing ☐ Number sense ☐ English language ☐ Social and academic behaviors ☐ Health and home ☐ Other

Specific Concern
Sample: Comprehension

page 1 of 2

Additional Information	What steps will the intervention team or a member of the intervention team take to gain more information? ☐ Meet with the referring staff. ☐ Review academic data. ☐ Review behavioral or other student records. ☐ Observe the student. ☐ Interview the student. ☐ Other: _____	**Notes:**
Intervention Team Conversation	**Guiding questions:** • What were the results of the referral analysis and additional data gathering? • Based on this information, should the student be receiving an intensive intervention? • If so, can the team prioritize this student for an intervention?	**Notes:**
Action Plan Note: The team should ensure that communication goes to the referring teacher promptly.	**Guiding questions:** • As a result of the referral, what will occur? • If the student has been prioritized for an intervention, what is the intervention? When will it occur? What is the goal? • If the student has not been prioritized for an intervention, what plans can be implemented to support the teacher and student?	**Notes:**

Notes:

The Big Book of Tools for RTI at Work © 2025 Solution Tree Press • SolutionTree.com
Visit **go.SolutionTree.com/RTIatWork/BBTRTI** and enter the unique access code found on the book's inside front cover to access this reproducible.

Tool: Action Plan to Support a Referred Student

Taking Action *reference: Essential Action 7.4—Create a Systematic and Timely Process to Refer Students to the Site Intervention Team, p. 281*

Instructions: After the intervention team considers a referred student for intensive interventions, a team representative should complete this action plan and deliver it in person to the referring staff member. A conversation should be part of the delivery versus simply delivering the form. Doing so provides the referring teacher with context for the intervention team's decision and ensures the team can address any additional concerns the referring teacher may have. Staff with expertise in the struggling student's area of need, and who can support the classroom teacher or teachers in implementing the recommended actions, should monitor each plan.

Student Name	
Student Grade	
Referring Teacher	

Universal Skill of Concern	☐ Reading ☐ Writing ☐ Number sense ☐ English language ☐ Social and academic behaviors ☐ Health and home ☐ Other	**Specific Concern** *Sample: Comprehension*
Intervention Team Recommendations	The intervention team reviewed student information because of a referral for support. The team is unable to provide an intensive intervention at this point. However, the team has developed a recommended action plan to provide support.	**Rationale:**
Action Plan Each recommendation by the team shall also include a staff member who can support implementation of the recommendation.	**Recommendation 1:**	Supporting staff member: Details:
	Recommendation 2:	Supporting staff member: Details:

page 1 of 2

Action Plan (cont.)	Recommendation 3:	Supporting staff member: Details:
Follow-Up Plan	The intervention team will review this referral and student data to continue support.	Staff member: Date:

Sample: Action Plan to Support a Referred Student

Taking Action reference: Essential Action 7.4—Create a Systematic and Timely Process to Refer Students to the Site Intervention Team, p. 281

Student Name	Jesus R.	
Student Grade	Grade 3	
Referring Teacher	Ms. Neubeck	
Universal Skill of Concern	☑ Reading ☐ Writing ☐ Number sense ☐ English language ☐ Social and academic behaviors ☐ Health and home ☐ Other	**Specific Concern** *Sample: Comprehension* Decoding
Intervention Team Recommendations	The intervention team reviewed student information because of a referral for support. The team is unable to provide an intensive intervention at this point. However, the team has developed a recommended action plan to provide support.	**Rationale:** The intervention team understands the concerns about Jesus and agrees that he needs support. As we analyze our available resources, students in need, and intensive interventions, we cannot provide intensive support at this time. We believe targeted Tier 2 support lessons and spaced practice will support the student.
Action Plan Each recommendation by the team shall also include a staff member who can support implementation of the recommendation.	**Recommendation 1:** During designated Tier 2 instructional time, the reading teacher will provide explicit instruction on immediate prerequisite reading skills, specifically focusing on foundational skills. This instruction will occur twice per week.	Supporting staff member: Reading teacher Details: The reading teacher will provide instruction twice weekly to the student and others in the class needing immediate prerequisite skill support for the current unit of study. This instruction will start within five school days.
	Recommendation 2: The reading teacher will collaborate with the classroom teacher to develop relevant foundational skill learning opportunities for use during independent time that support the prerequisite skills the student needs.	Supporting staff member: Reading teacher Details: The reading teacher will collaborate with the classroom teacher and provide sample independent or group work within five school days.

Action Plan (cont.)	**Recommendation 3:** Provide opportunities to practice reading at home using relevant text for the student's goals. The responsibility for learning does not rely on practice outside of school. However, this is a connection that can accelerate learning.	Supporting staff member: Counselor Details: The counselor will connect with the classroom teacher and the family to ensure they understand simple strategies they can use to support their student's development. This connection will occur within three school days.
Follow-Up Plan	The intervention team will review this referral and student data to continue support.	Staff member: Principal Date: Three weeks

Tool Overview: Intervention Evaluation and Alignment Chart

Taking Action reference: Essential Action 7.5—Assess Intervention and Reinforcement Effectiveness, p. 284

In *Taking Action: A Handbook for RTI at Work, Second Edition*, Mattos and colleagues (2025) suggest that effective interventions have the following six attributes.

1. **Targeted:** Effective interventions identify a specific standard, learning target, or behavior. Furthermore, all students assigned to an intervention share the same identified need. When interventions are not focused on a specific standard, learning target, or behavior—or when students assigned to the same intervention have wide-ranging needs—it is impossible for the support provided to be focused enough to produce results.

2. **Systematic:** A process exists at the school level to identify the exact needs of students assigned to interventions. No matter how effective a school's interventions may be, it cannot help more students learn at higher levels unless students are assigned to the right interventions.

3. **Research based:** If we provide students with additional time and support for learning, we must ensure that the instructional practices we use during interventions are highly likely to work. To do otherwise wastes both our instructional time and efforts. As such, schools implement instructional practices during interventions that are either supported by research or have a proven track record of success in their building.

4. **Administered by a trained professional:** For an intervention to work, it must be delivered by professionals with the right expertise. Stated differently, instructional practices administered by untrained or unskilled practitioners are unlikely to ensure that the additional time and support provided to students pay dividends.

5. **Timely:** Tier 2 interventions provide students timely support in mastering grade-level essential standards. That means schools constantly monitor their learners, and students are assigned to interventions as soon as needs are identified. The goal is to prevent students from falling too far behind to receive any real benefit from our interventions.

6. **Directive:** Students must attend interventions once their needs are identified. Why? Because the students struggling the most in our classrooms are often the least likely to seek opportunities for extra help. We can't provide additional time and support to learners who choose not to attend the interventions we are offering.

Use "Tool: Intervention Evaluation and Alignment Chart" (page 306) and "Protocol: Intervention Evaluation and Alignment Chart" (page 307) to evaluate the Tier 2 interventions you currently offer.

Reference

Mattos, M., Buffum, A., Malone, J., Cruz, L. F., Dimich, N., & Schuhl, S. (2025). *Taking action: A handbook for RTI at Work* (2nd ed.). Bloomington, IN: Solution Tree Press.

Tool: Intervention Evaluation and Alignment Chart

Taking Action *reference: Essential Action 7.5—Assess Intervention and Reinforcement Effectiveness, p. 284*

Instructions: Review "Protocol: Intervention Evaluation and Alignment Chart" on page 307 with your guiding coalition to complete this intervention evaluation and alignment chart.

Our Existing Interventions	Criteria of Effective Interventions	Our Notes
	☐ Targeted ☐ Systematic ☐ Research based ☐ Administered by a trained professional ☐ Timely ☐ Directive	
	☐ Targeted ☐ Systematic ☐ Research based ☐ Administered by a trained professional ☐ Timely ☐ Directive	
	☐ Targeted ☐ Systematic ☐ Research based ☐ Administered by a trained professional ☐ Timely ☐ Directive	
	☐ Targeted ☐ Systematic ☐ Research based ☐ Administered by a trained professional ☐ Timely ☐ Directive	
	☐ Targeted ☐ Systematic ☐ Research based ☐ Administered by a trained professional ☐ Timely ☐ Directive	

Source: Adapted from Mattos, M., Buffum, A., Malone, J., Cruz, L. F., Dimich, N., & Schuhl, S. (2025). Taking action: A handbook for RTI at Work (2nd ed.). Bloomington, IN: Solution Tree Press.

Protocol: Intervention Evaluation and Alignment Chart

Taking Action *reference: Essential Action 7.5—Assess Intervention and Reinforcement Effectiveness, p. 284*

Instructions: Use the following protocol to guide discussions as team members complete "Tool: Intervention Evaluation and Alignment Chart" on page 306.

The leadership or intervention teams can use this activity to evaluate schoolwide interventions, or teacher teams can use it to assess teacher-led interventions. We recommend completing this activity twice per year: (1) before the start of the school year and (2) at the midpoint of each school year.

- List the interventions that you are evaluating in the first column. Record the name of the intervention and a short description. Include one intervention per row.
- The second column lists the criteria for effective interventions. Check off each criterion that your current intervention currently aligns with.
- To evaluate your interventions, ask the following questions.
    - **Targeted:** What exactly is the intervention's purpose? What specific skill, content, or behavior should students learn by the end of the intervention? If you can't specify this, the intervention is not targeted enough. To remedy this problem, make the intervention more focused.
    - **Systematic:** Is there a systematic process to identify every student who needs help in the intervention's targeted area? Once identified, can all students that need the intervention receive it? If the team answers no to either of these questions, what steps can you take to make the intervention more systematic?
    - **Research based:** What research or evidence validates that the intervention is likely to work? If you can't cite any, discontinue the practice and study better methods to reteach the targeted outcome.
    - **Administered by a trained professional:** Who is currently administering the intervention? Are they adequately trained and competent at this task? If not, does the school have better-trained staff, or can the school provide the current staff member with additional training and support to become more effective?
    - **Timely:** How long does identifying and placing students in the intervention take? We suggest it should not take longer than three weeks.
    - **Directive:** Are targeted students required to attend? If not, what steps can you take to ensure students needing help are present for the intervention?
- Record your thoughts on your existing interventions in the third column. Consider the following questions.
    - How well are our current actions achieving our desired outcomes?
    - What strategies can we use to increase our effectiveness?
    - What goals for improvement do we need to commit to?

Source: Adapted from Mattos, M., Buffum, A., Malone, J., Cruz, L. F., Dimich, N., & Schuhl, S. (2025). Taking action: A handbook for RTI at Work (2nd ed.). Bloomington, IN: Solution Tree Press.

Tool: Guiding Coalition Review of Tier 3 Interventions

Taking Action *reference: Essential Action 7.5—Assess Intervention and Reinforcement Effectiveness, p. 284*

Instructions: Over the last quarter, your school has been implementing interventions in the universal skills of learning to the students at Tier 3 of the RTI at Work pyramid. It is time to evaluate the effectiveness of these interventions. Complete this review with your guiding coalition.

School	
Date of Review	
Term or Quarter Being Reviewed	

Step 1: Collect Data on Tier 3 Interventions

Working with your school intervention team, generate a list of all Tier 3 interventions offered during the most recent quarter. Then, document the number of students receiving each intervention and the progress those students are making toward meeting their growth targets.

Name of Tier 3 Intervention We Are Reviewing	Universal Skill of Learning This Intervention Addresses	Number of Students Receiving This Intervention	Number of Students Meeting Growth Targets This Quarter	Percentage of Students Meeting Growth Targets This Quarter
	☐ Reading ☐ Writing ☐ Number sense ☐ English language ☐ Social and academic behaviors ☐ Home and health			
	☐ Reading ☐ Writing ☐ Number sense ☐ English language ☐ Social and academic behaviors ☐ Home and health			
	☐ Reading ☐ Writing ☐ Number sense ☐ English language ☐ Social and academic behaviors ☐ Home and health			

	☐ Reading ☐ Writing ☐ Number sense ☐ English language ☐ Social and academic behaviors ☐ Home and health			

Source: Adapted from Hannigan, J., Hannigan, J. D., Mattos, M., & Buffum, A. (2021). Behavior solutions: Teaching academic and social skills through RTI at Work. *Bloomington, IN: Solution Tree Press.*

Step 2: Review Tier 3 Intervention Data

Review the data collected in step 1 with your school intervention team. Answer the following reflection questions while reviewing the data.

Questions for Reflection

Identify intervention successes. Which interventions offered achieved the highest success rates of students meeting their goals? Why did these interventions have high success rates? How can those practices be replicated in other interventions?

Identify growth areas in interventions. Which interventions offered had lower success rates of students meeting their goals? Why did these interventions have lower success rates? What can we do to increase the effectiveness of these interventions?

Evaluate our portfolio of interventions. What areas of need have not been addressed by interventions offered? What resources, including professional learning, are needed to support current interventions or develop new ones? What action steps will the team take to improve the next cycle of interventions?

Step 3: Consider General Reflection Questions

Use the following questions with your intervention team to determine whether your school has established the foundational practices necessary to ensure that Tier 3 interventions are effective.

Questions for Reflection

Are students being appropriately placed in interventions? Are students needing behavioral interventions put in academic interventions? Are interventions targeted to student needs?

Are our Tier 3 interventions at the appropriate intensity? Are they offered at least five times a week for fifty minutes (recommended)? Are intervention group sizes as small as possible? Do all students in an intervention group have the same needs? Is the staff member with the best training providing the intervention?

Is appropriate progress monitoring in place to inform effectiveness? What evidence are we collecting to monitor this intervention's effectiveness? How frequently are we collecting this evidence? What changes do we need to make to monitor this intervention's effectiveness?

Source: © 2022 by Beaver Dam Unified School District, Beaver Dam, Wisconsin. Adapted with permission.

Resources Designed to
Support Tier 3 Intervention Team Essential Actions

Tool: Intervention Planning Tool for Site Interventionists

Taking Action *reference: Essential Action 8.1—Diagnose, Target, Prioritize, and Monitor Tier 3 Reinforcements, p. 294*

Instructions: After being assigned a group of students to support, an interventionist should use the questions in the following template to develop a targeted plan to move learning forward.

Students	
Date	

Planning Question	Interventionist Response
Universal Skill • What is the universal learning skill these students need support with? (Reading, writing, number sense, English language, social and academic behaviors, health and home) • How is the need for intervention on this skill identified? (Data)	
Specific Skill • What is the specific skill that needs focus? *(Sample: Reading comprehension, reading decoding, mathematics number identification, hands to self, attendance)* • What data will you use to make this diagnostic decision?	
Intervention • What is the specific research-based intervention these students will receive? • What is the intensity of the intervention? *(Sample: Group size, frequency, duration)*	
Goal Setting • What is an attainable growth goal for this academic year to bring these students to—or make significant progress toward—grade level? • What is an attainable growth goal for the first cycle or upcoming cycle of intervention? (Six to nine weeks) • What is the exit goal for students?	
Progress Monitoring • How will progress be regularly monitored toward the goal? (Suggested weekly) • What tool or tools will you use to collect data?	

Tool: Reviewing the Intervention Team Meeting Cycle

Taking Action reference: Essential Action 8.1—Diagnose, Target, Prioritize, and Monitor Tier 3 Reinforcements, p. 294

Instructions: Use the following table to learn more about the four different types of meetings that intervention teams hold. Then, use the reflection questions at the end of this tool to reflect on your intervention team's current work.

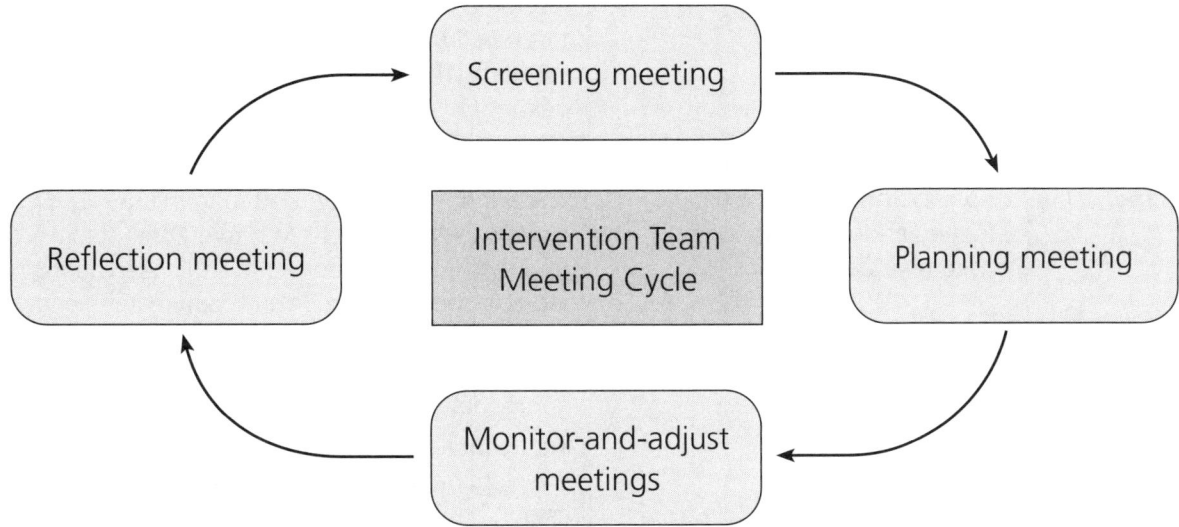

Essential Functions of an Intervention Team		
Use relevant data to identify students needing schoolwide support in social-emotional learning, behaviors, or academics.	Determine specific interventions and establish goals for each student, prioritizing resources based on greatest needs.	Establish and utilize a student referral process, allowing staff to recommend students to the intervention team for consideration and support.
Regularly monitor intervention success at the student level using relevant data.	Make intervention adjustments (entrance, exit, and intensity) based on need during and after intervention cycles.	Assess the effectiveness of interventions offered. Learn from, celebrate the successes of, and adjust interventions based on those assessments.

Intervention Team Planning Questions		
Meeting Topic	**Essential Functions Focus**	**Description**
Screening Meeting	Use relevant data to identify students needing schoolwide support in social-emotional learning, behaviors, or academics.	Before the beginning of the school year and any new intervention cycle, the intervention team conducts a screening meeting to utilize any available data to identify students who need support in universal skills. These data can include

		state assessment data, screening data, classroom assessment data, behavior referrals, attendance data, and other critical information.
		The team uses these data to create a list of students who may need support sorted by universal skill. Team members are assigned to gather more specific information on each student to make a more informed decision about potential interventions. If this meeting is after a previous intervention cycle, students who met their goals are excused from the next round of intervention.
Planning Meeting	Determine specific interventions and establish goals for each student, prioritizing resources based on greatest needs.	At planning meetings, data collected since the screening meeting are used to refine the list of students who need intervention. Often, teams find that further assessments and observations indicate some students don't require intervention. Additional data collected may also provide more specific information to match interventions appropriately.
		The team refines the list of students needing intervention, determines the specific intervention, establishes a student goal, and makes a plan to deliver the intervention. The team is careful to use multiple data points to make informed decisions.
Monitor-and-Adjust Meetings	Regularly monitor intervention success at the student level using relevant data. Make intervention adjustments (entrance, exit, and intensity) based on need during and after intervention cycles.	Monitor-and-adjust meetings refer to a series of meetings in which student progress is checked throughout a cycle of interventions. The team is made aware of the progress-monitoring data of each student in interventions. Successes are celebrated.
		When students are not making anticipated progress, the team discusses what can be done differently to meet student needs and implements those plans accordingly. Often, this is a change in intervention intensity.
		While each meeting of the intervention team cycle is important, monitor-and-adjust meetings are particularly vital. If the team does not pay close attention to progress-monitoring data and use that information for improvement, it is likely that the team will not be pleased with student data after an intervention cycle.
Reflection Meetings	Assess the effectiveness of interventions offered. Learn from, celebrate the successes of, and adjust interventions based on those assessments.	At regular intervals, likely after intervention cycles or at the end of each quarter, the team conducts a reflection meeting to take a holistic look at the interventions offered. Which interventions are most successful? Which interventions are least

| | | successful? How will the team celebrate its success? How will the team address needs? |
| | | In this meeting, the team does not analyze individual student data but instead looks at the overall intervention picture to improve the interventions offered. A result of these meetings could be a plan for professional learning related to interventions, deleting interventions from the team's menu, and exploring new interventions. |

Note: Depending on the frequency of the site's meetings and design for intervention cycles, some of these topics may be combined into one meeting. A team may also consider splitting the cycle between academic and behavioral interventions. Regardless, the team should ensure that each topic is carefully visited in each cycle.

Questions for Reflection

Look back at the meeting agendas for your intervention team. What types of meetings are you regularly scheduling? Are there any types of meetings that you still need to schedule?

What other patterns can you spot in the meeting agendas of your intervention team? How do those patterns affect your school's ability to provide effective Tier 3 interventions to struggling students?

What changes must you make to your school's intervention team meetings? How will those changes help your team function more effectively?

Tool: Intervention Team Meeting Dashboard

Taking Action *reference: Essential Action 8.1—Diagnose, Target, Prioritize, and Monitor Tier 3 Reinforcements, p. 294*

Instructions: Intervention teams can use this tool to monitor Tier 3 interventions. The **Intervention**, **Interventionist**, and **Students** columns are pre-populated by the team based on the interventions being implemented. Before each intervention team meeting, the lead interventionist for a specific intervention enters student progress (not on track to meet goals, on track to meet goals, exceeding goals) in the **Progress** column. In addition, the interventionist can recommend adjustments to a student's intervention plan in the **Recommendation** column. Recommendations could include a change in intervention intensity, recommended exit, the continuation of the current intervention, gathering more diagnostic data to inform the intervention, or a combination. At the intervention team meeting, the team reviews the progress and recommendations student by student. Recommendations are discussed and decisions are listed in the **Meeting Notes** column.

Intervention Team Meeting Dashboard			
Site		Meeting Date	
Meeting Focus		Meeting Facilitator	

Intervention	Interventionist	Students	Progress	Recommendation	Meeting Notes
Sample: Reading comprehension focus group	*Sample:* Mrs. A	*Samples:*			
		Student Name A	Not on track	Change intensity to one on one	
		Student Name B	Exceeding	Recommended exit	
		Student Name C	On track	Continue current intervention	
		Student Name D	On track	Continue current intervention	
		Student Name E	Not on track	Conduct additional assessments	

Intervention	Interventionist	Students	Progress	Recommendation	Meeting Notes

Tool: Teacher and Interventionist Communication Template

Taking Action *reference: Essential Action 8.1—Diagnose, Target, Prioritize, and Monitor Tier 3 Reinforcements, p. 294*

Instructions: We will use this tool to facilitate regular communication between interventionists and classroom teachers. Interventionists should start communication by completing the **Interventionist Update** and **Data Update** columns. After reviewing the report provided by the interventionist, classroom teachers will respond with relevant observations and updates on student progress in the core classroom.

Teacher and Interventionist Communication Template			
Teacher		**Interventionist**	
Student Name		**Student Grade**	
Skill Need		**Intervention**	
Intervention Goal			
Week	**Interventionist Update** Includes the intervention's focus for the week and any notes relevant to the teacher	**Data Update** Includes an update on progress monitoring toward the student's goal	**Teacher Update** Includes teacher observations related to the intervention's focus and updates on skill transfer from the intervention to Tier 1 instruction
Week 1			
Week 2			
Week 3			

Week 4			
Week 5			
Week 6			
Week 7			
Week 8			
Week 9			

Tool: Teacher Report on Student Progress

Taking Action *reference: Essential Action 8.1—Diagnose, Target, Prioritize, and Monitor Tier 3 Reinforcements, p. 294*

Instructions: After students have received four weeks of intensive intervention in a universal skill of learning, classroom teachers should complete this report to provide interventionists with an update about students' ability to transfer new learning to the classroom setting.

Teacher Report on Student Progress	
Teacher	
Interventionist	
Student Name	
Identified Universal Learning Skill Being Addressed	
Intervention	
Questions	**Teacher Response**
What strengths are you noticing in this student?	
Has the student made progress in developing this intervention's targeted skill?	Choose one. ☐ I have yet to notice progress. ☐ I have noticed some progress. ☐ I have noticed significant progress.
Please explain why you chose your answer to the previous question. Reference to classroom data may be helpful.	
What support are you providing in the classroom that may be helpful for the interventionist to know?	
What other information may be helpful for the interventionist to know?	

The Big Book of Tools for RTI at Work © 2025 Solution Tree Press • SolutionTree.com
Visit **go.SolutionTree.com/RTIatWork/BBTRTI** and enter the unique access code found on the book's inside front cover to access this reproducible.

Tool: Considerations to Increase Intervention Effectiveness

Taking Action *reference: Essential Action 8.2—Ensure Proper Instructional Intensity, p. 298*

Instructions: When evaluating an intervention, the lead interventionist records concerns about the intervention and the data that led to those concerns. Each consideration is reviewed in the **Consideration to Increase Effectiveness** column. Then, the intervention's status is recorded in the **Current Status** column. Changes that could be made are recorded in the **Possible Change** column. After reviewing each consideration, the most promising changes can be implemented.

Intervention		Date	

What is the current concern about this intervention?	What data support the current concern?

Consideration to Increase Effectiveness	Current Status	Possible Change
Frequency • Is the group meeting frequently enough for the intervention to have the intended impact? • Can the frequency be increased?	Current Frequency:	☐ We can increase the days per week. ☐ We can increase the number of sessions per day. ☐ Other: **Notes:**

page 1 of 3

Duration • Is the intervention's length sufficient to provide the instruction needed to have the intended impact? • Can the length of time be increased?	**Current Duration:**	☐ We can increase the days per week. ☐ We can increase the number of sessions per day. ☐ Other: **Notes:**
Group Size • Is the group size small enough for the intervention to have the intended impact? • Can the group size be decreased?	**Current Group Size:**	☐ We can increase the days per week. ☐ We can increase the number of sessions per day. ☐ Other: **Notes:**
Targeting • Is the intervention correctly targeting the specific needs of the students being served? • Can the intervention be modified to be more targeted, or should a different intervention be used?	**Current Intervention:**	☐ We can increase the days per week. ☐ We can increase the number of sessions per day. ☐ Other: **Notes:**

Training • Is the person delivering the intervention adequately equipped to do so? • Can support for the interventionist be provided, or is there someone more appropriate to deliver the intervention?	**Current Interventionist and Training:**	☐ We can increase the days per week. ☐ We can increase the number of sessions per day. ☐ Other: **Notes:**
Based on the expertise and available evidence, which of the possible changes to the intervention does the team believe will have the most significant impact on student learning?		
When and how can the changes be implemented?		

Tool: Communicating Intervention Plans to Parents

Taking Action *reference:* Essential Action 8.3—Determine Whether
Special Education Is Needed and Justifiable, p. 303

To the parent or guardian of: _____

As you know, the promise we make to the parents of our community is that we will ensure all students learn at the highest levels. To meet the challenge of that promise, we have created a system of interventions to provide each student with the unique combination of additional time and support necessary to aid their learning without missing out on new instruction in grade-level essentials. Your child is currently receiving interventions in our building. You can learn more about those interventions by reviewing the following information.

Targeted Intervention Plan For:			
Type of Intervention (Circle all that apply.)	**Targeted Area of Support** (Check all that apply.)	**Frequency**	**Additional Details** Who is providing the intervention? How has the student responded? What is being covered?
Support With Grade-Level Essential Standards	☐ Science ☐ Social studies ☐ Mathematics ☐ Language arts ☐ Other:	☐ Once a week ☐ Twice a week ☐ Daily ☐ Other:	
Support With Essential Skills and Dispositions	☐ Motivation ☐ Work completion ☐ Self-regulation ☐ Behavior ☐ Other:	☐ Once a week ☐ Twice a week ☐ Daily ☐ Other:	
Support With Universal Skills of Learning	☐ Reading ☐ Writing ☐ Number sense ☐ English language ☐ Social and academic behaviors ☐ Health and home	Daily for _____ minutes.	

Please note that we do not expect you to take any action to address your child's learning needs. We accept responsibility for their success and will work until we find strategies to help them learn. The purpose of this letter is to communicate those efforts to you. However, please let us know if you want to discuss how you can support these intervention efforts at home.

We will update you on your child's progress at the end of the next grading period.

If you have questions, please contact: _____.

Sincerely,

SCHOOL PRINCIPAL

Tool: Intervention Team Reflection Before a Special Education Referral

Taking Action reference: Essential Action 8.3—Determine Whether Special Education Is Needed and Justifiable, p. 303

Instructions: Before initiating a referral for special education services, the intervention team should reflect on the student's experience and ensure that the school's practices have not hindered the student's growth. To conduct this reflection, read each indicator and determine your confidence that your intervention efforts were highly effective.

Student Name		Date	
Area of Concern		Grade	

Reflection Indicator	Analysis
Tier 1 We are confident that the student has received the following. • High-quality instruction on essential grade-level learning • Support available in Tier 1, such as differentiated instruction, to meet grade-level standards We are confident that our school has high-quality Tier 2 instruction in place, and we can point to specific evidence of the effectiveness of our Tier 1 instruction.	☐ Confident ☐ Not confident **Notes:**
Tier 2 We are confident that the student has received the following. • Prompt, high-quality Tier 2 support when they did not show proficiency in essential grade-level learning • Tier 2 support in addition to Tier 2 instruction We are confident that our school has high-quality Tier 2 instruction in place, and we can point to specific evidence of the effectiveness of our Tier 2 interventions.	☐ Confident ☐ Not confident **Notes:**

page 1 of 2

Tier 3	☐ Confident
We are confident that the student has received the following.	☐ Not confident
• Prompt, high-quality Tier 3 support when they demonstrated the need for intensive interventions	**Notes:**
• Tier 3 support in addition to Tier 1 and Tier 2 instruction	
We are confident that our school has high-quality Tier 3 instruction in place, and we can point to specific evidence of the effectiveness of our Tier 3 interventions.	

Data	☐ Confident
We are confident of the following.	☐ Not confident
• We are using multiple data sources to make a recommendation.	**Notes:**
• The data analyzed are as valid as possible.	
• The student's data are significantly different compared to peers in the same conditions.	

If the team has selected *not confident* for any reflection indicators, the team should take additional steps to ensure that a referral for special education services is justifiable.

If the team has selected *confident* for every reflection indicator, the team may decide that a referral for special education services is justifiable. This referral will result in an in-depth evaluation of the student to determine whether they have a disability.

Epilogue

> *If there is one thing for certain at the start of every school year, it is this: educators are going to work hard. The question is not whether we will work hard, but whether we will work hard and succeed or work hard and fail.*
>
> —Mike Mattos, Austin Buffum, Janet Malone,
> Luis F. Cruz, Nicole Dimich, & Sarah Schuhl

In his opening remarks at the RTI at Work Institute in Bellevue, Washington, in August 2022, Mike Mattos—one of the original architects of the RTI at Work process and a coauthor of this companion text—outlined a series of five fundamental assumptions that educators know to be true about the students they serve in their classrooms. Those assumptions are as follows (Mattos, 2022).

1. Not all students learn in the same way.
2. Not all students learn at the same speed.
3. Some students lack the prior skills and knowledge necessary to succeed in school.
4. Some students lack the proper behaviors to succeed in school.
5. Some students have a home life that is counterproductive to academic success.

Those assumptions ring true to anyone who has worked in education for any length of time. Educators *do* have students who come to them every year with academic gaps that interfere with learning or unique challenges that we must address in our teaching. For classroom teachers, those needs can feel overwhelming. How *are* they supposed to teach grade-level essentials to students with significant gaps in prerequisite knowledge and skills? How *can* they ensure that all students learn at the highest levels when some have behaviors that prevent them from fully participating or investing in our instruction? What *should* they do for students who are still struggling to learn after they have taught and retaught their lessons?

The answer is that they can't do it alone. Instead, meeting students' increasingly diverse and unique needs in classrooms is going to require a collective effort. Educators will have to work systematically with one another, targeting their efforts and relying on all their shared know-how. In schools implementing the RTI at Work process, that collective, systematic effort is led by three critical teams: (1) the school guiding coalition, (2) collaborative teacher teams, and (3) the school intervention team (Mattos et al., 2025). Each critical team accepts lead responsibility for a different set of essential actions that—when taken together—comprise an effective *system of interventions.*

To quote our colleague and friend Luis Cruz—an expert on school leadership and culture—the work of guiding coalitions is to "till the soil, creating the conditions necessary for seeds of change to take root" (L. Cruz, personal communication, August 9, 2023). That tilling involves actions ranging from developing a guiding coalition and communicating the moral imperative of intervening for struggling learners to developing a master schedule that allows students to receive additional time and support for learning and coordinating resources to ensure that interventions are delivered effectively and efficiently to all students.

Collaborative teacher teams lead the academic work done at Tier 1 and Tier 2 in the RTI at Work process. Together, they identify a handful of academic outcomes and invest their collaborative energies in finding ways to help all students master those essentials. Recognizing that some practices work better than others, they study instruction together, amplifying strategies that result in higher levels of student learning and abandoning those that don't. They teach prerequisite skills and knowledge, knowing that the best intervention is to *prevent students from struggling.* They also provide supplemental time and support when students struggle to learn, knowing that by the end of the year, *every* student—without qualifiers—must master *every* grade-level essential.

Composed of reading and mathematics interventionists, counselors and school psychologists, nurses and administrators, social workers, and other specialists with deep expertise in specific areas of student need, intervention teams support students with intensive needs in the universal skills of learning. Together, they bring their expertise to bear on challenges that, if not addressed, will prevent students from living successful, fulfilling lives. They coordinate and prioritize support for students, identify interventions that effectively accelerate learning, and monitor and adjust whenever intensive interventions aren't moving students forward fast enough to close their learning gaps before they graduate from school.

All three of these teams are going to work hard next year in your school. That goes without saying. As Mattos and colleagues (2025) remind us in the opening quote of this epilogue, educators are always working hard. Our hope is that the tools and templates offered in this text will help your guiding coalition, collaborative teacher teams, and intervention team *work hard and succeed.* We promise that if you use them to provide explicit structure to your conversations and your actions while implementing the RTI at Work process, you will strengthen your system of interventions and help even more students learn at the highest levels. Now, it's time to take action!

References and Resources

Ainsworth, L. (2013). *Prioritizing the Common Core: Identifying specific standards to emphasize the most*. Englewood, CO: Lead + Learn Press.

AllThingsPLC. (n.d.). *FAQ—PLC*. Accessed at www.allthingsplc.info/faq on March 15, 2024.

Arkansas Division of Elementary and Secondary Education. (n.d.). *Arkansas academic standards*. Accessed at https://dese.ade.arkansas.gov/Offices/learning-services/curriculum-support/arkansas-academic-standards on November 16, 2023.

Bailey, K., & Jakicic, C. (2012). *Common formative assessment: A toolkit for Professional Learning Communities at Work*. Bloomington, IN: Solution Tree Press.

Bailey, K., & Jakicic, C. (2019). *Make it happen: Coaching with the four critical questions of PLCs at Work*. Bloomington, IN: Solution Tree Press.

Bailey, K., & Jakicic, C. (2021). *The collaborative team plan book for PLCs at Work*. Bloomington, IN: Solution Tree Press.

Bailey, K., & Jakicic, C. (2023). *Common formative assessment: A toolkit for Professional Learning Communities at Work* (2nd ed.). Bloomington, IN: Solution Tree Press.

Blount, S., & Leinwand, P. (2019). *Why are we here?* Accessed at www.hbr.org/2019/11/why-are-we-here on March 21, 2023.

Brown, T., & Ferriter, W. M. (2021). *You can learn! Building student ownership, motivation, and efficacy with the PLC at Work process*. Bloomington, IN: Solution Tree Press.

Buffum, A., Mattos, M., & Malone, J. (2018). *Taking action: A handbook for RTI at Work*. Bloomington, IN: Solution Tree Press.

Buffum, A., Mattos, M., & Weber, C. (2012). *Simplifying response to intervention: Four essential guiding principles*. Bloomington, IN: Solution Tree Press.

Buffum, A., Mattos, M., Weber, C., & Hierck, T. (2015). *Uniting academic and behavior interventions: Solving the skill or will dilemma*. Bloomington, IN: Solution Tree Press.

Canady, R. L. (2003, August). *Rethinking your grading practices* [Paper presentation]. Wake County Public Schools Professional Learning Seminar, Raleigh, NC.

Chappuis, J., & Stiggins, R. (2020). *Classroom assessment for student learning: Doing it right—using it well* (3rd ed.). Upper Saddle River, NJ: Pearson Education.

Chappuis, J., Stiggins, R. J., Chappuis, S., & Arter, J. A. (2012). *Classroom assessment for student learning: Doing it right—using it well* (2nd ed.). Boston: Pearson.

Chiprany, D. T., & Page, P. (2025). *Celebrating in a PLC at Work: A leader's guide to building collective efficacy and high-performing collaborative teams*. Bloomington, IN: Solution Tree Press.

colemanmom4 [@colemanmom4]. (2022, June 8). *Curious as to how many educators have investigated why students turn in work late? Are students confident about the content? Do they know how to get started? Are they afraid to ask for help so they delay? Or are they just lazy? Would a student survey help?* [Post]. X. Accessed at https://twitter.com/colemanmom4/status/1534489804343234560 on December 12, 2023.

Conzemius, A. E., & O'Neill, J. (2013). *The handbook for SMART school teams: Revitalizing best practices for collaboration* (2nd ed.). Bloomington, IN: Solution Tree Press.

Dimich, N. (2015). *Design in five: Essential phases to create engaging assessment practice.* Bloomington, IN: Solution Tree Press.

Dimich, N. (2024). *Design in five: Essential phases to create engaging assessment practice* (2nd ed.). Bloomington, IN: Solution Tree Press.

DuFour, R., DuFour, R., Eaker, R., Many, T. W., & Mattos, M. (2016). *Learning by doing: A handbook for Professional Learning Communities at Work* (3rd ed.). Bloomington, IN: Solution Tree Press.

DuFour, R., DuFour, R., Eaker, R., Many, T. W., Mattos, M., & Muhammad, A. (2024). *Learning by doing: A handbook for Professional Learning Communities at Work* (4th ed.). Bloomington, IN: Solution Tree Press.

DuFour, R., DuFour, R., Eaker, R., Mattos, M., & Muhammad, A. (2021). *Revisiting Professional Learning Communities at Work: Proven insights for sustained, substantive school improvement* (2nd ed.). Bloomington, IN: Solution Tree Press.

DuFour, R., & Eaker, R. (1998). *Professional Learning Communities at Work: Best practices for enhancing student achievement.* Bloomington, IN: Solution Tree Press.

Duntemann, J. (2016, March 15). *Odd lots* [Blog post]. Accessed at www.contrapositivediary.com/?p=3665 on February 8, 2024.

Epler, R. (2021, August). *Evaluating your collaborative work* [Professional development session]. Salem Middle School, Wake County Public School System, Raleigh, NC.

Ferriter, W. M. (2020). *The big book of tools for collaborative teams in a PLC at Work.* Bloomington, IN: Solution Tree Press.

Ferriter, W. M., & Cancellieri, P. J. (2017). *Creating a culture of feedback.* Bloomington, IN: Solution Tree Press.

Ferriter, W. M., Graham, P., & Wight, M. (2013). *Making teamwork meaningful: Leading progress-driven collaboration in a PLC at Work.* Bloomington, IN: Solution Tree Press.

Fisher, D., & Frey, N. (2012). Making time for feedback. *Educational Leadership, 70*(1), 42–47.

Frontier Research. (2015, September 18). *Warren Buffett's 5-step process for prioritizing true success (and why most people never do it).* Accessed at www.medium.com/frontier-research/warren-buffetts-5-step-process-for-prioritizing-true-success-and-why-most-people-never-do-it-7127928bf91b on April 23, 2024.

Goodwin, B., & Rouleau, K. (2022). *The new classroom instruction that works: The best research-based strategies for increasing student achievement.* Arlington, VA: ASCD.

Graham, P., & Ferriter, W. M. (2010). *Building a Professional Learning Community at Work: A guide to the first year.* Bloomington, IN: Solution Tree Press.

Grant, A. (2016, November). *Are you a giver or a taker?* [Video file]. TED Conferences. Accessed at www.ted.com/talks/adam_grant_are_you_a_giver_or_a_taker on March 21, 2023.

Gregory, G., Kaufeldt, M., & Mattos, M. (2016). *Best practices at tier 1: Daily differentiation for effective instruction, elementary.* Bloomington, IN: Solution Tree Press.

Guskey, T. R. (2022, October 24). *Can grades be an effective form of feedback?* Accessed at www.kappanonline.org/grades-feedback-guskey on April 17, 2023.

Hall, B. (2022). *Powerful guiding coalitions: How to build and sustain the leadership team in your PLC at Work.* Bloomington, IN: Solution Tree Press.

Hannigan, J., Hannigan, J. D., Mattos, M., & Buffum, A. (2021). *Behavior solutions: Teaching academic and social skills through RTI at Work.* Bloomington, IN: Solution Tree Press.

Hattie, J. (2023, June). *Global research database.* Accessed at www.visiblelearningmetax.com/influences on March 5, 2024.

Hierck, T., Coleman, C., & Weber, C. (2011). *Pyramid of behavior interventions: Seven keys to a positive learning environment.* Bloomington, IN: Solution Tree Press.

Holt, J. (1964). *How children fail.* New York: Pitman.

Kanold, T. D., Toncheff, M., Larson, M. R., Barnes, B., Kanold-McIntyre, J., & Schuhl, S. (2018). *Mathematics coaching and collaboration in a PLC at Work.* Bloomington, IN: Solution Tree Press.

Kerr, D., Hulen, T. A., Heller, J., & Butler, B. K. (2021). *What about us? The PLC at Work process for grades preK–2 teams.* Bloomington, IN: Solution Tree Press.

Kotter, J. P. (1996). *Leading change.* Boston: Harvard Business School Press.

Kotter, J. P. (2012). *Leading change.* Boston: Harvard Business Review Press.

Kramer, S. V. (Ed.). (2021). *Charting the course for leaders: Lessons from priority schools in a PLC at Work.* Bloomington, IN: Solution Tree Press.

Longwell Daniels, B. (2020). *PLC at Work and your small school: Building, deepening, and sustaining a culture of collaboration for singletons.* Bloomington, IN: Solution Tree Press.

Many, T. W., & Horrell, T. (2014). Prioritizing the standards using R.E.A.L. criteria. *TEPSA News, 71*(1), 1–2. Accessed at www.absenterprise.com/wp-content/uploads/2016/06/real-standards.pdf on April 4, 2024.

Marzano, R. J. (2017). *The new art and science of teaching.* Bloomington, IN: Solution Tree Press.

Marzano, R. J., Pickering, D. J., & Pollock, J. E. (2001). *Classroom instruction that works: Research-based strategies for increasing student achievement.* Arlington, VA: ASCD.

Maslow, A. H. (1966). *The psychology of science: A reconnaissance.* New York: Harper & Row.

Mattos, M. (2018, August 7). *Focus: Understanding the role of a guaranteed and viable curriculum in the RTI at Work process* [Conference presentation]. RTI at Work Institute, Bellevue, WA.

Mattos, M. (2022, August 8). *Building the pyramid: How to create a highly effective, multitiered system of supports* [Conference presentation]. RTI at Work Institute, Bellevue, WA.

Mattos, M., Buffum, A., Malone, J., Cruz, L. F., Dimich, N., & Schuhl, S. (2024). *Taking action: A handbook for RTI at Work* (2nd ed.). Bloomington, IN: Solution Tree Press.

Mattos, M., DuFour, R., DuFour, R., Eaker, R., & Many, T. W. (2016). *Concise answers to frequently asked questions about Professional Learning Communities at Work.* Bloomington, IN: Solution Tree Press.

Mendler, A. N. (2021). *Motivating students who don't care: Proven strategies to engage all learners* (2nd ed.). Bloomington, IN: Solution Tree Press.

Minsky, L., & Aron, D. (2021, February 23). *Are you doing the SWOT analysis backwards?* Accessed at www.hbr.org/2021/02/are-you-doing-the-swot-analysis-backwards on March 20, 2023.

Muhammad, A., & Cruz, L. F. (2019). *Time for change: Four essential skills for transformational school and district leaders.* Bloomington, IN: Solution Tree Press.

National Governors Association Center for Best Practices & Council of Chief State School Officers. (2010a). *Common Core State Standards for English language arts and literacy in history/social studies, science, and technical subjects.* Washington, DC: Authors. Accessed at https://learning.ccsso.org/wp-content/uploads/2022/11/ADA-Compliant-ELA-Standards.pdf on December 14, 2023.

National Governors Association Center for Best Practices & Council of Chief State School Officers. (2010b). *Common Core State Standards for mathematics.* Washington, DC: Authors. Accessed at www.corestandards.org/assets/CCSSI_Math%20Standards.pdf on May 22, 2024.

OpenAI. (2023, November 12). *ChatGPT* [Large language model]. Accessed at https://chat.openai.com/share/1b7d60ca-989b-4d40-95f8-45ee8bd6962f on November 12, 2023.

Public Broadcasting Service. (n.d.). *Interview: Gordon B. Hinckley.* Accessed at www.pbs.org/wgbh/americanexperience/features/mormons-hinckley on July 3, 2023.

Rees, P. (Writer & Director). (2004, September 29). Ancient death ray/skunk cleaning/what is bulletproof? (Season 2, Episode 4) [TV series episode]. In A. Savage, J. Hyneman, A. Dallow, P. Rees, M. Donahue, D. Tapster, et al. (Executive Producers), *MythBusters.* Beyond Television Productions.

Reeves, D. B. (2002). *The leader's guide to standards: A blueprint for educational equity and excellence.* San Francisco: Jossey-Bass.

Roberts, M. (2019). *Enriching the learning: Meaningful extensions for proficient students in a PLC at Work.* Bloomington, IN: Solution Tree Press.

Roose, T. (2015, December 6). *Multiplying with the area model error analysis* [Blog post]. Accessed at www.tarheelstateteacher.com/blog/multiplying-with-the-area-model-error-analysis on August 5, 2019.

Schimmer, T. (2016). *Grading from the inside out: Bringing accuracy to student assessment through a standards-based mindset.* Bloomington, IN: Solution Tree Press.

Smith, S. (2019, June 12). *How to be great? Just be good, repeatably* [Blog post]. Accessed at https://blog.stephsmith.io/how-to-be-great on August 9, 2019.

Sonju, B., Kramer, S. V., Mattos, M., & Buffum, A. (2019). *Best practices at tier 2: Supplemental interventions for additional student support, secondary.* Bloomington, IN: Solution Tree Press.

Springer, C. (2021, February 3). *From theory to practice: A jigsaw approach to an elementary master schedule* [Blog post]. Accessed at www.allthingsplc.info/from-theory-to-practice-a-jigsaw-approach-to-an-elementary-master-schedule on April 23, 2024.

Stack, B. M., & Vander Els, J. G. (2018). *Breaking with tradition: The shift to competency-based learning in PLCs at Work.* Bloomington, IN: Solution Tree Press.

Stiggins, R. J., Arter, J. A., Chappuis, J., & Chappuis, S. (2007). *Classroom assessment for student learning: Doing it right—Using it well.* Upper Saddle River, NJ: Pearson Education.

Strickland, C. (2007). *Tools for high-quality differentiated instruction: An ASCD action tool.* Arlington, VA: ASCD.

Tomlinson, C. A. (2017). *How to differentiate instruction in academically diverse classrooms* (3rd ed.). Arlington, VA: ASCD.

Van Horn, S. (2014, November 7). *Working on weekly class SMART goals* [Blog post]. Accessed at www.3rdgradethoughts.com/2014/11/working-on-weekly-class-smart-goals.html on April 18, 2023.

Venables, D. R. (2011). *The practice of authentic PLCs: A guide to effective teacher teams*. Thousand Oaks, CA: Corwin Press.

Webb, N. L. (2002, March 28). *Depth-of-Knowledge levels for four content areas*. Accessed at http://ossucurr.pbworks.com/w/file/fetch/49691156/Norm%20web%20dok%20by%20subject%20area.pdf on December 13, 2023.

Weichel, M., McCann, B., & Williams, T. (2018). *When they already know it: How to extend and personalize student learning in a PLC at Work*. Bloomington, IN: Solution Tree Press.

Wiggins, G. (2012, September 1). *Seven keys to effective feedback*. Accessed at www.ascd.org/el/articles/seven-keys-to-effective-feedback on April 17, 2023.

Willis, J. (2022, June 30). *Guiding students to sustain effort in school*. Accessed at www.edutopia.org/article/guiding-students-sustain-effort-school on August 28, 2022.

Winne, P. H., & Hadwin, A. F. (1998). Studying as self-regulated learning. In D. J. Hacker, J. Dunlosky, & A. C. Graesser (Eds.), *Metacognition in educational theory and practice* (pp. 277–304). Mahwah, NJ: Earlbaum.

World Economic Forum. (2020, October). *The future of jobs report 2020*. Accessed at www3.weforum.org/docs/WEF_Future_of_Jobs_2020.pdf on December 13, 2023.

World Economic Forum. (2023, April 30). *The future of jobs report 2023*. Accessed at www.weforum.org/publications/the-future-of-jobs-report-2023 on March 15, 2024.

Index

A
academic behaviors, 14

B
Bailey, K., 131, 134., 88
Barnes, B., 66
Bartow Country School System (Cartersville, Ga.), 21
Beaver Dam (Wisc.) Unified School District, 258, 262, 310
Behavior Solutions (Hannigan et al.), 59
Best Practices at Tier 2 (Sonju et al.), 136–137
The Big Book of Tools for Collaborative Teams in a PLC at Work (Ferriter), 114–115, 117–118, 210, 213–214, 294
Blount, S., 26
Breaking With Tradition (Stack & Vander Els), 147
Brown, T., 124–126
Buffum, A., 2, 12, 24, 59, 100, 103, 106, 113, 136–138, 141, 144, 150, 163–164, 167–168, 203, 225, 232, 235, 237, 252, 278–279, 305–307
Building a Professional Learning Community at Work (Graham & Ferriter), 210
Butler, B. K., 123

C
"Can Grades Be an Effective Form of Feedback?" (Guskey), 86, 119–120
Cancellieri, P. J., 127–129
Chappuis, J., 87, 124–125
chatbots, 23, 82, 105, 178–179, 199
ChatGPT, 23, 82, 105, 178–179, 199
Checklists
  Concentrating Instruction on Social and Academic Behaviors, 92–93, 155-156
  Differentiation Strategies, 177, 197–198
  Establishing Common Expectations, Targeting Instruction, and Reinforcing Positive Behaviors, 91, 148–150
  Simplifying RTI Culture Survey, 24
Chiprany, D., 21
Classroom Assessment for Student Learning (Chappuis & Stiggins), 124–125
Classroom Instruction That Works (Marzano et al.), 178
Coleman, C., 92–93, 155–156
colemanmom4, 247
collaborative learning, 15–17
collaborative teacher teams. *See* teacher teams
Common Core State Standards for English language arts and literacy in history/social studies, science, and technical subjects, 104–105
Common Formative Assessment (Bailey & Jakicic), 131, 134
comprehending language, 14
comprehending text, 14
Council of Chief of State School Officers, 104–105
Creating a Culture of Feedback (Ferriter & Cancellieri), 127–129
Cruz, L. F., 2, 30, 59, 77, 100, 106, 113, 138, 141, 144, 163–164, 167–168, 203, 225, 232, 235, 237, 252, 278–279, 305–307, 328
culture of collective responsibility, 3, 19–20
  resources, 20–78

D

decoding text, 14
depth of knowledge (DOK) levels (Webb), 215
"Depths of Knowledge Levels for Four Content Areas" (Webb), 215
Design in Five (Dimich), 85
Dimich, N., 3, 59, 85, 100, 106, 113, 138, 141, 144, 163–164, 167–168, 203, 225, 232, 235, 237, 252, 278–279, 305–307
DuFour, Rebecca, 15, 44, 59, 69, 213
DuFour, Richard, 15, 29, 44, 59, 69, 180, 213
Duntemann, J., 7

E

Eaker, R., 15, 44, 59, 213
essential standards, 12–13
establishing a culture of collective responsibility
    resources to support, 20–78
    tools for, 19–20

F

Ferriter, W. M., 114–115, 117–118, 124–126, 127–129, 194, 209–210, 213–214
Fisher, D., 85, 118
Frey, N., 85, 118
"From Theory to Practice" (Springer), 91, 146
The Future of Jobs Report 2020 (World Economic Forum), 154
The Future of Jobs Report 2023 (Word Economic Forum), 154

G

Gemini, 23, 82, 105, 178–179, 199
Goodwin, B., 178
Grading From the Inside Out (Schimmer), 165
Graham, P., 201, 210
Grant, A., 28
guiding coalition, 5, 24, 31, 328
    responsibilities, 12, 17–18
Guskey, T. R., 86, 199–120

H

Hannigan, J. D., 59
Hannigan, J., 59
Hattie, J., 26, 123
Hierck, T., 24, 92–93, 155–156
Holt, J., 25
Hulen, T. A., 123

I

intervention pyramid, 1–4
intervention team, 5, 24, 31, 328
    responsibilities, 12
    resources to support, 257-267, 269-310, 312-316
interventions
    defined, 19

J

Jakicic, C., 88, 131, 134

K

Kanold, T. D., 66
Kanold-McIntyre, J., 66
Kappan Magazine, 86, 119
Kerr, D., 123
Kotter, J. P., 31
Kramer, S. V., 136–137

L

Larson, M. R., 66
Leading Change (Kotter), 31, 35
Learning by Doing (DuFour et al.), 29, 44, 69, 180, 213
Leinwand, P., 26
Lincoln Heights Middle School (Morristown, Tenn.), 66

M

MacArthur Junior High School (Jonesboro, Ark.), 127–129
Making Teamwork Meaningful (Ferriter et al.), 209
Making Time for Feedback (Fisher & Frey), 118
Malone, J., 2, 12, 59, 100–101, 103, 106, 113, 138, 141, 144, 150, 163–164, 167–168, 203, 225, 232, 235, 237, 252, 278–279, 305–307
Many, T. W., 15, 44, 59, 69, 213
Marzano, R. J., 178
Maslow, A. H., 2

Mathematics Coaching and Collaboration in a PLC at Work (Kanold et al.), 66
Mattos, M., 1–9, 12, 15, 20, 24, 44, 59, 69, 80–81, 83–84, 89, 91, 95–96, 100–101, 103, 106, 113, 136–137, 138, 141–142, 144, 150, 163–164, 167–168, 176, 180, 183–184, 187, 203, 213, 225, 232, 235, 237, 252, 256, 259, 261–262, 278–279, 305–307, 327
Mendler, A. N., 93, 158
Motivating Students Who Don't Care (Mendler), 93, 158
MTSS, 11, 15–16, 20
Muhammad, A., 30, 44, 69, 77
"Multiplying with the Area Model Error Analysis," (Roose), 117
multitiered system of supports (MTSS), 2–3

N

National Governors Association Center for Best Practices, 104–105
The New Art and Science of Teaching (Marzano), 178
The New Classroom Instruction That Works (Goodwin & Rouleau), 178
number sense, 14

O

overcoming complications, 14

P

Page, P., 21
Pickering, D. J., 178
Pollock, J. E., 178
The Practice of Authentic PLCs (Venables), 70
Professional Learning Communities at Work process (DuFour & Eaker), 15
    effective guiding coalitions, 21
    foundation, 15–16
    four critical questions, 16–17
protocols
    Developing Schoolwide Criteria for Identifying Students in Need of Tier 2 Behavioral Support, 230–231
    Intervention Evaluation and Alignment Chart, 307
    Universal Screening Planning Guide, 279

Pyramid of Behavior Intervention (Hierck et al.), 92–93, 155–156

R

resources
    to support a culture of collective responsibility, 20–78
    to support intervention team essential actions, 257-267, 269-310, 312-316
    to support schoolwide essential actions, 90–96, 182–188
    to support teacher team essential actions, 80–90, 176–182
response to intervention (RTI)
    exploring Hattie's research on, 25
Roose, T., 117
Rouleau, K., 178
RTI at Work, 2–9, 327–328
    effective guiding coalitions, 21
    Tier 1, 13, 16–17
    Tier 2, 13–14, 16–17
    Tier 3, 14–17
    pyramid, 11–12
    process, 12–15
RTI at Work Institute, 327

S

samples
    Action Plan to Support a Referred Student, 303–304
    Assessment Wrapper for Primary Students, 86, 121–123
    Developing Specific Actions to Address the Needs of Our Peers, 74–75
    Essential Standards Unit Plan, 102–103
    Next-Step Checklist—Sixth-Grade Matter Unit, 129
    Performance Tracking Table—Elementary School Mathematics, 116–117
    Performance Tracking Table—Middle School, 118
    Planning a Cycle of Inquiry for Guiding Coalitions, 50
    Practice Test Tracking Template for Secondary Students, 125
    Predictable-Is-Preventable Plan for Multilingual Students, 172–173

Responses to Scenarios to Calibrate Tier 3 Decisions, 290
Targeting Tier 2 Interventions, 137
Teacher Referral Form—Academics, 297
Teacher Referral Form—Social Behaviors, 298
Tiered Task Card—Middle Grades Mathematics: Slope, 218
Tiered Task Card—Middle Grades Science: Fossils, 217
Universal Screening Review Protocol, 284–285
Schimmer, T., 95, 165
school leadership team. *See* guiding coalition
schoolwide essential actions
    resources to support, 182–188
Schuhl, S., 3, 59, 66, 89, 100, 106, 113, 135, 138, 141, 144, 163–164, 167–168, 203, 225, 235, 237, 252, 278–279, 305–307
Simplifying Response to Intervention (Buffum et al.), 278–279
SMART Goals
    defined, 23
    for team development, 23
social behaviors, 14
Sonju, S., 136–137
Springer, C., 91, 146
Stack, B. M., 147
Stiggins, R., 87, 124–125
Strickland, C., 198
student tools
    Creating a Tiered Task Card to Extend Student Learning, 216
    Learning Profile Survey—Secondary, 186–187, 248–249
    Learning Profile—Primary, 186–187, 250–251
    Next-Step Checklist, 128
    Self-Reflection Template for Students Struggling With Work Completion, 186
    Student Survey on Classroom Feedback, 86
    Student Survey on Missing or Late Work, 186, 246–247
    Tier 2 AI Prompts for High School students, 179
    What Do Successful People Do Differently?, 93, 157–158
surveys
    Midyear Collaborative Team Check-In, 28, 64–66
    Rating Our Readiness for RTI, 24, 52
SWOT analyses, 23
systematic interventions, 19–20
    defined, 19

T

Taking Action (Buffum et al.), 101, 103, 150
Taking Action (Mattos et al.), 3–9, 20, 35, 80–81, 83–84, 89, 91, 95–96, 100, 106, 113, 138, 141–142, 144, 164, 167–168, 176, 180, 183–185, 203, 223, 225, 232, 235, 237, 252, 256, 259, 261–262, 278–279, 305–307
Taking Action references
    Essential Action 2.1—Establishing a Guiding Coalition, 20–24, 31, 34–51
    Essential Action 2.2—Build a Culture of Collective Responsibility, 24–27, 52–61
    Essential Action 2.3—Form Collaborative Teacher Teams, 27–28, 62–69
    Essential Action 2.4—Commit to Team Norms, 30, 70–75
    Essential Action 2.5—Prepare for Staff Resistance, 30–31, 76–78
    Essential Action 3.1—Identify Essential Standards, 80, 99–100
    Essential Action 3.2—Design a Unit Assessment Plan, 81–83, 101–107
    Essential Action 3.3—Create Common Assessments and Begin Instruction, 84–85, 108–118
    Essential Action 3.4—Foster Student Investment, 85–88, 119–129
    Essential Action 3.5—Analyze and Respond to Common Assessment Data, 88–90, 130–139
    Essential Action 4.1—Ensure Access to Essential Grade-Level Curriculum, 90–91, 141–147
    Essential Action 4.2—Identify and Teach Essential Academic and Social Behaviors, 91–93, 148–158

Essential Action 4.3—Create a Balanced Assessment Approach, 94, 159–163
Essential Action 4.4—Co-Create Schoolwide Grading Practices, 95, 164–167
Essential Action 4.5—Provide Preventions to Proactively Support Student Success, 96, 168–173
Essential Action 5.1—Design and Lead Tier 2 Interventions for Essential Academic Standards, 176–179, 190–200
Essential Action 5.2—Identify and Target Immediate Prerequisite Skills, 179–180, 201–207
Essential Action 5.3—Monitor the Progress of Students Receiving Tier 2 Academic Interventions, 180, 208–212
Essential Action 5.4—Extent Student Learning, 181–182, 213–219
Essential Action 6.1—Schedule Time for Tier 2 Interventions and Extensions, 182, 221–227
Essential Action 6.2—Establish a Process to Identify Students Who Require Tier 2 Behavior Interventions, 183–184, 228–237
Essential Action 6.3—Plan and Implement Tier 2 Interventions for Essential Social and Academic Behaviors, 184–187, 238–251
Essential Action 6.4—Coordinate Interventions for Students Needing Academic *and* Behavior Supports, 187, 252–254
Essential Action 7.1—Create a Dynamic, Problem-Solving Site Intervention Team, 257–258, 269–276
Essential Action 7.2—Identify Students Needing Intensive Reinforcements, 259–260, 277–282
Essential Action 7.3—Prioritize Resources Based on the Greatest Student Needs, 260–261, 287–295
Essential Action 7.4—Create a Systematic and Timely Process to Refer Students to the Site Intervention Team, 261–262, 296–304

Essential Action 7.5—Assess Intervention and Reinforcement Effectiveness, 262, 305
Essential Action 8.1—Diagnose, Target, Prioritize, and Monitor Tier 3 Reinforcements, 263–266
Essential Action 8.1—Diagnose, Target, Prioritize, and Monitor Tier 3 Reinforcements, 312–320
Essential Action 8.2—Ensure Proper Instructional Intensity, 266
Essential Action 8.2—Ensure Proper Instructional Intensity, 321–323
Essential Action 8.3—Determine Whether Special Education is Needed and Justified, 266–267
Essential Action 8.3—Determine Whether Special Education Is Needed and Justifiable, 324–326
teacher teams, 5, 24, 31, 328
  resources to support essential actions, 80–90, 176–182
  responsibilities, 12, 16
teaching-assessing-learning cycle, 3
templates
  Developing a Master Schedule for Three Tiers of Instruction, 145
These Are Our Kids slide, 25
Tier 1 interventions, 1, 13, 16–17
  processes that must be coordinated across the entire school, 17
  research to support teacher team essential actions, 80–90
  resources to support schoolwide essential actions, 90–96
  responsibilities of teacher teams, 16
  tools for building, 79–80, 96–97
Tier 2 interventions, 2, 13–14, 16–17
  keys to, 175–176
  processes that must be coordinated across the entire school, 17
  resources to support schoolwide essential actions, 182–188
  resources to support teacher team essential actions, 176–182
  responsibilities of teacher teams, 16
  tools for building, 175–176
Tier 3 interventions, 3, 14–17

characteristics, 14–15
defining characteristics, 255–256
processes that must be coordinated across the entire school, 17
resources to support essential actions, 257–267, 269–310, 312–316
tools for building, 255–257

Time for Change (Muhammad & Cruz), 30, 77

Toncheff, M., 66

tool overviews
Creating a Predictable-Is-Preventable Plan, 96, 169
Creating a Tiered Task Card to Extend Student Learning, 181–182, 215
Creating Next-Step Checklists to Involve Students in the Intervention Process, 87–88, 127
Developing Team Norms, 29–30, 70
Evaluating Your Systematic Response to Student Interventions, 184, 232
Intervention Evaluation and Alignment Chart, 305
Preparing a Prerequisite Pretest, 203

Tools for High-Quality Differentiated Instruction (Strickland), 198

tools
Action Plan to Support a Referred Student, 262, 301–302
Addressing the Three Common Reasons for Resistance to Change, 30, 76–77
Analysis and Planning Template for Guiding Coalitions, 21, 38–44
Analyzing Faculty Survey on the Work of Guiding Coalitions, 22
Analyzing Prerequisite Pretest Results, 179–180, 206–207
Analyzing the Reasons Students Struggle With Work Completion—Data Table, 185–186
Assessment Design Checklist, 84, 111–113
Assessment Purpose Map, 94, 159–160
Assessment Reflection by Type, 94, 162–163
Assessment Stoplight Analysis, 94, 161
Avoiding the Common Pitfalls of Supplemental Intervention Periods, 183
Building a Common Formative Assessment, 84–85, 114
Building Shared Knowledge About Tier 2 Interventions and Extensions, 176, 190–194
Building Your Guiding Coalition, 20, 34–35
Building Your Learning Team's Knowledge About Extensions, 181, 213
Collaboration Time—Planning Guide and Schedule, 29
Commit to Team Norms, 30, 71–72
Common Formative Assessment Pretest, 83–84, 108–110
Communicating Intervention Plans to Parents, 266, 324
Communicating the Purpose of the Intervention Team, 258, 276
Considerations to Increase Intervention Effectiveness, 266
Considerations to Increase Intervention Effectiveness, 321–323
Creating a Predictable-Is-Preventable Plan, 96, 170–171
Creating a *These Are Our Kids* Slide, 25
Deconstructing Essential Standards, 82
Defining Lead Responsibilities for Academic and Behavioral Interventions, 187, 253–254
Desired State for Grading Plan, 95
Developing a Master Schedule for Three Tiers of Intervention, 90–91, 142–145
Developing a Parent Permission Slip for Student Use of ChatGPT in High School Classrooms, 178
Developing a Shared Pacing Guide, 81
Developing a Tier 3 Referral Process Guide, 261
Developing Collective Commitments, 26, 56–57
Developing Exemplars to Make Learning Intentions Explicit, 88
Developing Schoolwide Criteria for Identifying Students in Need of Tier 2 Behavioral Support, 183–184, 228–229
Developing Specific Actions to Address the Needs of Our Peers, 30, 73

Does Our School Alibi?, 25
Does Your School Have an Avoid-at-All-Costs List?, 31
Eliciting Feedback on Our Master Schedule, 91, 146
End-of-Meeting Reflection for Intervention Teams, 257–258, 271–272
Ensuring Access to Essential Grade-Level Curriculum, 90–91, 141
Essential Standards Chart, 81, 100
Essential Standards Student Tracking Chart, 89, 138
Essential Standards Unit Plan, 81, 101
Evaluating Classroom Feedback Practices, 85
Evaluating Our Mission Statement, 26, 54–55
Evaluating Your Plan for Providing Supplemental Interventions, 183, 224–225
Evaluating Your Systemic Response to Student Interventions, 233–235
Examining Your Work With the Team Teaching-Assessment-Learning Cycle, 83, 106–107
Exploring John Hattie's Research on Response to Intervention, 25
Forming Teacher Teams, 27, 62–64
Grading Practices Implementation, 95, 166–167
Grading Reflection and Planning, 95, 164
Guiding Coalition Review of Tier 3 Interventions, 262, 308–310
Have We Created Time for Teacher Collaborative Teams?, 29, 68–69
Helping Students Identify the Connections Between Perseverance and Performance, 93
Identifying Essential Knowledge, Skills, and Dispositions, 92
Identifying Human Resources for Tier 3 Interventions, 260
Identifying Our Interventionists, 257, 269–270
Individual Student Intervention Report, 180–181, 211–212
Intervention Evaluation and Alignment Chart, 262, 306

Intervention Planning Tool for Site Interventionists, 263, 312
Intervention Team Implementation Continuum, 258, 273–275
Intervention Team Meeting Dashboard, 264, 316–317
Intervention Team Reflection Before a Special Education Referral, 266–267, 325–326
Looking at End-of-Unit Assessment Data, 88–89, 132–134
Matching Assessment Strategies With Essential Standards, 84
Monitoring Student Progress After Exiting Interventions, 266
Observational Feedback for Intervention Teams, 258
Performance Tracking Table, 85, 115–118
Planning a Cycle of Inquiry for Guiding Coalitions, 22, 49
Planning for and Prioritizing Tier 3 Interventions, 250–261, 291–295
Planning Interventions for Students With Attendance Issues, 185, 243–245
Practice Test Tracking Template for Secondary Students, 86–87, 124–125
Preparing a Prerequisite Pretest, 179, 204–205
Prerequisite Planning Document, 179, 201–202
Preventions to Proactively Support Student Success, 96, 168
Quarterly Work Behaviors Student Self-Assessment, 186
Questions to Consider When Creating a Schedule for Supplemental Interventions, 182, 221–223
Rating Our Readiness for RTI, 24
Rating the Effectiveness of Interventions on Your Learning Team, 180, 210
Rating Your Readiness for Our New Initiative, 30, 78
Record of Instructional Strategies Used, 90
Re-Engagement Strategies That Work, 177–178
Reflecting on Our Cycle of Instruction, 89, 139

Reflecting on Our Faculty's Readiness for RTI, 24, 53

Reflecting on the Core Work of Collaborative Teams, 28

Reflecting on the Recipe for a Successful Learner, 92, 151–152

Reflecting on the Role Grades Can Play as Feedback, 86, 119–120

Reflecting on Your Master Schedule, 91, 147

Reviewing the Intervention Team Meeting Cycle, 263–264, 313–315

Reviewing the Skills Necessary to Succeed in the Modern Workplace, 92, 153–154

Reviewing Your Plan for Providing Supplemental Interventions for Students Struggling With Social Behaviors, Academic Behaviors, and Health and Home Challenges, 184–185, 238–242

RTI at Work Pro-Solve Intervention Targeting Process: Tier 1 and 2, 187, 252

Scenarios to Calibrate Tier 3 Decisions, 260, 287–289

Scheduling Calendar for Intervention Team Meetings, 264

Site-Based Teams Aligned to the RTI at Work Process, 26–27, 58–59

Six Essential Functions of an Intervention Team, The, 257

Six-Question Guiding Coalition Assessment Inventory, 94

Staff Recommendation Form for Students Needing Behavioral Support, 184, 236–237

Staff Survey on the Efficacy of a Supplemental Intervention Period, 183, 226–227

Standards-Based Mindset Reflection and Planning, 95, 165

The Strengths, Weaknesses, Opportunities, and Threats of Collaboration, 29

The Struggle to Prioritize Planning for Extensions, 181

Student Interview on Entrance to an Intervention, 265

Student Interview to Track Intervention Progress, 265

Supplemental Intervention Practice Reflection Template, 180, 208–209

Surveying Teachers About Universal Screening, 259–260, 286

SWOT Analysis for Guiding Coalitions, 23

Targeting Tear 2 Interventions for an Individual Student, 177, 195–196

Targeting Tier 2 Interventions, 89, 135–136

Teacher and Interventionist Communication Template, 264–265, 265, 318–319

Teacher Referral Form, 261, 296

Teacher Referral Processing Protocol, 261, 299–300

Teacher Report on Student Progress, 265, 320

Teaching Primary Learners About Short-Term Goal Setting, 87, 126

Teaching Secondary Learners to Set SMART Goals, 87

Teaching Students About Self-Regulation, 93

Team Collaboration Time—Planning Guide and Schedule, 67

Team Protocol for Analyzing Assessment Results, 88, 130–131

Team-Based Intervention Plan for Struggling Learners, 176–177, 194

Teams Needed in RTI at Work—A Principal's Reflection, 27, 60–61

Ten Considerations for the Guiding Coalition, 21, 36–37

Ten Considerations for the Guiding Coalition—Behavior Specific, 21

Tier 1 Instructional Strategies to Consider, 83

Tier 2 AI Prompts for Classroom Teachers, 178, 199–200

Tier 2 Intervention Tracking by Individual Teacher, 177

Tracking the Reasons Students Struggle With Work Completion, 185

Understanding Teacher Approaches to Collaboration, 28

Universal Screening Planning Guide, 259, 277–278

Universal Screening Review Protocol, 259, 282–283

Universal Screening Tracking Template, 259, 280–281

Using Academic Data to Target the Work of Guiding Coalitions, 21–22, 46–48

Using AI as a Thought Partner or Content Creator, 83

Using AI Chatbots to Develop Extension Tasks, 182, 219

USING AI Tools to Deconstruct an Essential Standard, 82, 104

Using AI Tools to Develop a Proficiency Scale, 82–83, 105

Using AI Tools to Support Collaborative Team Development, 22–23, 51

Using Faculty Survey Data to Target the Work of Guiding Coalitions, 22, 45

Using REAL to Identify Essential Standards, 80, 99

Vet Your Current Assessment With the Three Design Qualities, 85

Weekly Extension Planning Template, 181, 214

What Should We See in a System of Interventions? 24

What Work Is Your Team *Kind of Doing*?, 27

Who Takes Lead Responsibility for Interventions? 26

Writing a SMART Goal for Team Development, 23

Writing Intervention Goals for Individual Students, 263

U

Uniting Academic and Behavior Interventions (Buffum et al.), 24

universal screening and diagnostic assessments, 12

V

Van Horn, S., 126
Vander Els, J. G., 147
Venables, D. R., 70

W

Webb, N. L., 215
Weber, C., 24, 92–93, 155–156
What About Us? (Kerr et al.), 123
what are they doing all day problem, 79
Why Are We Here?" (Blount & Leinwand), 26, 55
Wight, M., 209
"Working on Weekly Class SMART Goals" (Van Horn), 126
World Economic Forum, 153–154
writing effectively, 14

Y

You Can Learn! (Brown & Ferriter), 124–126

Taking Action, Second Edition
Mike Mattos, Austin Buffum, Janet Malone, Luis F. Cruz, Nicole Dimich, and Sarah Schuhl
The second edition of the bestseller *Taking Action* delves deeper into how educators can leverage the PLC at Work® process to create a highly effective multitiered system of supports. This step-by-step guide defines—tier by tier— the essential actions of the guiding coalition, teacher teams, and intervention team. New recommendations and tools are included to target assessments, engage students, and address resistance.
BKG136

The Big Book of Tools for Collaborative Teams in a PLC at Work®
William M. Ferriter
Build your team's capacity to become agents of positive change. Organized around the four critical questions of PLC at Work®, this comprehensive book of collaborative tools provides an explicit structure for learning teams. Rely on the included resources and best practices to help you establish team norms, navigate common challenges, develop collective teacher efficacy, and more.
BKF898

Learning by Doing, Fourth Edition
Richard DuFour, Rebecca DuFour, Robert Eaker, Thomas W. Many, Mike Mattos, and Anthony Muhammad
Twenty-five years on, the PLC at Work® process continues to produce results across the United States and worldwide. In this fourth edition of the bestseller *Learning by Doing*, the authors use updated research and time-tested knowledge to address current education challenges, from learning gaps exacerbated by the COVID-19 pandemic to the need to drive a highly effective multitiered system of supports.
BKG169

Behavior Academies
Jessica Djabrayan Hannigan and John Hannigan
With student behavioral problems and teacher turnover at all-time highs, educators need behavioral interventions that work. With its practical behavior intervention method, this book replaces problematic behaviors with essential life skills for school and beyond. Educators can implement effective targeted interventions in 25 minutes or less using eight predefined behavior academies and a process to create their own.
BKG114

Behavior Solutions
John Hannigan, Jessica Djabrayan Hannigan, Mike Mattos, and Austin Buffum
When students' behavioral, emotional, and social needs are met, they excel in school and in life. Take strategic action to begin closing the systemic behavior gap with the guidance of *Behavior Solutions*. This user-friendly resource outlines how to utilize the PLC at Work® and RTI at Work™ processes to create a three-tiered system of supports that is collaborative, research-based, and practical.
BKF891

Visit SolutionTree.com or call 800.733.6786 to order.

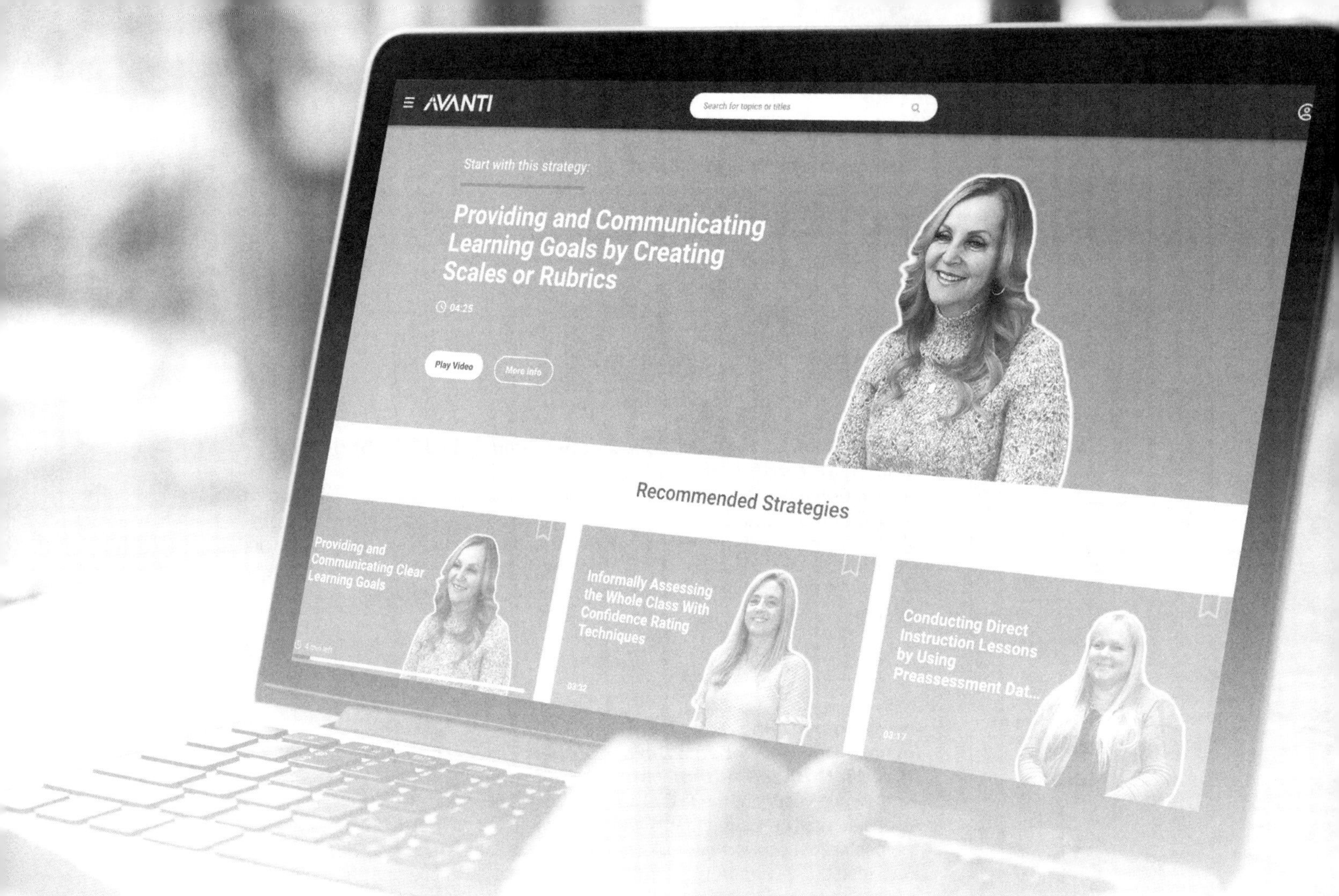

AVANTI

Grow your teacher toolkit by learning from other teachers

Take control of your professional growth and positively impact your students' lives with proven, ready-to-use classroom strategies. With Avanti, you'll get professional learning created by teachers, for teachers.

Learn more
My-Avanti.com/**GrowYourToolkit**